END OF DAYS

THE BOOK OF REVELATION

EXPLAINED

DR. PATRICK C. MARKS

✝ 14:6

Markarian Publishing
Phoenix, AZ

END OF DAYS

The Book of Revelation Explained

Copyright © 2022 by Patrick C. Marks

All Rights Reserved

No portion of this publication may be reproduced, stored in any electronic system, or transmitted in any form or by any means, electronic, mechanical, photocopy, recording, or otherwise, without written permission from the author. Brief quotations may be used in literary reviews.

Cover art by Adam K. Jaynes
Image Credits: Twin Blue Marbles by Reto Stockli, from NASA/NOAA; Chamaeleon Dark Nebulas by Jarmo Ruuth, from apod.nasa.gov. Font: Siberia, allbestfonts.com. Art Credits: Neon blue light flares: Vecteezy.com

Unless otherwise indicated, all Scripture quotations taken from the (NASB®) New American Standard Bible®, Copyright 2020 by The Lockman Foundation. Used by permission. All rights reserved. www.lockman.org

Scripture quotations marked NLT are taken from the Holy Bible, New Living Translation, copyright © 1996, 2004, 2015 by Tyndale House Foundation. Used by permission of Tyndale House Publishers, Inc., Carol Stream, Illinois 60188. All rights reserved.

ISBN-13: 978-0-9832097-7-5

Produced by FourteenSix, Inc.
Printed by Snowfall Press
Published by Markarian Publishing
Printed in the United States of America

Special Thanks:

This book would not have been possible without the support and love of my family, my church family, and friends. Thank you to everyone who encouraged me to get this written. I pray this book is a blessing to everyone who reads it.

TABLE OF CONTENTS

Chapter

1. **Introductions!**
   Revelation 1: 1-3 explained 1
2. **Urgency!**
   Revelation 1: 3-20 explained 15
3. **The test for truth**
   Revelation 2: 1-7 explained 31
4. **This life is not all there is!**
   Revelation 2: 7-28 explained 45
5. **Motivations!**
   Revelation 3 explained 69
6. **What identity will you choose?**
   Revelation 3: 14-22 explained 85
7. **Revelation is about the Jewish people!**
   Revelation's connection to Daniel explained 95
8. **Our only hope is Jesus!**
   Revelation 4:1-4 explained 115
9. **Why your worship matters...**
   Revelation 4: 5-11 explained 129
10. **God has control over your destiny**
    Revelation 5 explained 141
11. **Why there are only 4 horses but 7 seals**
    Revelation 6: 1-2 explained 155
12. **The 2nd seal and Ezekiel's war!**
    Revelation Chapter 6, Part 2 explained 171
13. **The third seal!**
    Revelation Chapter 6, Part 3 explained 185
14. **Why fear the future?**
    Revelation 7: 1-17 explained 195

Chapter

15	**Without excuse!**	
	Revelation Chapter 8 explained	203
16	**Non-negotiable!**	
	Revelation 9 explained	217
17	**God is a warrior-king!**	
	Revelation 10 explained	233
18	**Reach!**	
	Revelation 11 explained	241
19	**Persist!**	
	Revelation 12 explained	261
20	**The beast!**	
	Revelation 13 explained	275
21	**Satisfaction!**	
	Revelation 14 and 15 explained	299
22	**Why God's kindness is so amazing!**	
	Revelation 16 explained	319
23	**The mother of all false religions**	
	Revelation 17 explained	337
24	**Beware materialism**	
	Revelation 18 explained	355
25	**Win the crowns!**	
	Revelation 19 explained	363
26	**No excuse!**	
	Revelation 20 explained	377
27	**Eternal destiny**	
	Revelation 21 explained	397
28	**Now what?**	
	Revelation 22 explained	411

End Notes ... 433

End of Days
The Book of Revelation Explained

Chapter 1: Introductions!
Revelation 1: 1-3 explained...

People fear many things today but learning from the book of Revelation about what God has revealed concerning the end of the world should not be one of those fears. The first word in the book of Revelation is the Greek word ἀποκάλυψις (apokalypsis). In English, an apocalypse is a horrific disaster but in Greek the word apokalypsis means an "unveiling or revealing,"[1] so this book is about Jesus revealing to the world what will happen at the end of the age. It reveals that there are indeed some dreadful things that will happen but, in the end, God will make everything right for His people. He will someday bring about a time of peace and prosperity as it was in the days of the Garden of Eden. Then, after peace on earth, God will bring His people into an eternal state of glory and joy that we cannot now imagine. The book of Revelation does warn the world of some terrible days to come, but for the people of God it is a book of hope!

The Bible is the revealed Word of God, and it clearly explains that God cannot lie, and God cannot fail. The unfailing God of truth also created the heavens and the earth in the beginning. He exists eternally outside of time and because this is true,

God knows as much about the end of time as He does about the beginning.

One way to think about how God sees time compared to how we experience time is to imagine a large hill with a train track at its base and a mine shaft dug into its side. Imagine standing inside this mine shaft looking out at the train track. When a train passes along the track, you will only be able to see one car of the train at a time because from inside the mine shaft your view is limited. Now imagine standing at the top of the hill. From that point of view, you would be able to see the entire train at one time because your point of view is much larger.

Our view of the past is limited to our own experience and memory or limited to eyewitness writings about what other people have seen or heard. This is like being in the mine shaft and trying to remember the train cars. Today we might look at an artifact such as a photograph or video to learn something about the past but no matter the situation, just as if we are inside the mine shaft, our view of the past is always limited. It is the same when we think about the future. From inside the tunnel, we might predict what kind of train car is likely to come next because we have seen a pattern of cars, but the truth is any kind of train car could be next. No matter how often a pattern of train cars repeats itself in our view, the reality is that the future is never guaranteed and always something of a mystery.

Our perception of time itself is like the train cars passing in front of the mine shaft. Each train car is pulled by the one in front of it just like every effect in this world is caused by something else. In fact, everything in the universe is one big train of cause and effect – but without the engine to pull the train, there could be no train passing in front of the mine shaft. In the same way, cause and effect cannot go backwards forever. If it did, then there would never be any uncaused, first cause that could start the chain of cause and effect that we experience in the universe. There must be an ultimate first cause, an engine that pulls the train. The Bible says this eternal, first cause of everything else is God.

Since God is the ultimate first cause of everything, He is something like a person seated at the top of a hill who can see a whole train passing along at the bottom of the hill at one time. It is difficult for us to understand this, but the Bible explains that God knows the past, the present and the future perfectly. From our point of view within time, inside the mine shaft so to speak, the future is uncertain, and all of our decisions are completely free. From God's point of view, the future is completely in God's control and all our decisions are part of what He already knows. This does not mean we are pre-programmed robots because inside this timeline we are free; it is just that God has a much higher view. For this reason, God can reveal the future to us and that is what the book of Revelation and other Biblical prophecies are all about.

The best way to be prepared for a future that only God can know is to go through the book of Revelation, chapter by chapter and verse by verse, to find out what God has revealed. To make sense of it, we need to bounce back to other Scriptures in the Bible. In fact, the only way to properly understand the book of Revelation is to see it as one part of the whole Bible, not something separate.

Of course, Revelation is about the future but not every future event is going to affect every person. It is for this reason that Revelation also illustrates or pictures important principles about God and how believers should live in the present that apply to everyone at every time.

Revelation 1:1 - 2 (NASB)
The Revelation of Jesus Christ, which God gave Him to show to His bond-servants, the things which must soon take place; and He sent and communicated it by His angel to His bond-servant John, ² who testified to the word of God and to the testimony of Jesus Christ, even to all that he saw.

There is no historical reason anyone should doubt this book was written by the apostle John. [2] The writings of early church fathers from the first and second century A.D. agree that John was the writer. Since John was the last surviving eyewitness of the life and teachings of Jesus, his credibility as the writer carries considerable weight. Multiple witnesses among the earliest leaders of the church say that John wrote Revelation when he was confined to the prison island of Patmos in the Aegean Sea during the reign of Emperor Domitian. Domitian died in A.D. 96 and after his death, John was released. While the evidence is limited, it seems likely that John made his way to Turkey and settled in the city of Ephesus where he died at a ripe old age. [3]

John the apostle had great credibility with the earliest church leaders. He had been a close friend of Jesus. He was the only one of the twelve disciples who directly witnessed the crucifixion. He was an eyewitness to the resurrection, and he wrote down what he had seen and heard from Jesus in the New Testament gospel named after him. Yet even with all his connection to Jesus, John remained humble. For example, in the Gospel of John, he does not directly identify himself by name but calls himself "the disciple whom Jesus loved." Throughout the book of Revelation, he honestly owns up to making several big mistakes. John's honesty shines through his writing.

John makes it clear, right from the start of Revelation, that this is a revelation of Jesus Christ. It is not a revelation of John. Revelation is not John's coded message about the politics of his time. It is not his speculation about what might happen in the future either. Revelation is specifically the unveiling of future events given by Jesus Himself. Today's media and conspiracy websites love to pick and choose Scripture passages from Revelation to make sensational predictions. This has allowed it to be misused, abused, and avoided over the years. But John testifies that it is a revelation from Jesus who is God in the flesh.

John says in verse two that this book is "the testimony of Jesus Christ, even to all that he saw" but the word "even" is not in the Greek text. This means that the book of Revelation is not just about the vision John saw, but about the entire testimony of Jesus. In other words, Revelation is the unveiling or revealing of how the entire testimony of the Bible concludes.

God has revealed Himself to human beings since the creation, but He specifically revealed Himself through the Jewish people. The Jews are God's

people. It was through their national history that God unveiled the Bible and through the family of David, their greatest king, that Jesus was born. Revelation proclaims that God has not abandoned His people.
    To truly understand the book of Revelation, it is important to first remember than John was a Jewish man. The book of Revelation is specifically about how all the promises made to the Jews about the promised Savior of the Jewish people, the Messiah, will come to pass. The first Christians were Jews and while the message of Jesus as Savior spread to non-Jewish "Gentiles," God did not replace the Jewish people with Gentile Christians. Romans chapter eleven makes this very clear. Romans 11:25 says,

> **Romans 11:25 - 27 (NASB)**
> For I do not want you, brothers and sisters, to be uninformed of this mystery—so that you will not be wise in your own estimation—that a partial hardening has happened to Israel until the fullness of the Gentiles has come in; [26] and so all Israel will be saved; just as it is written: "The Deliverer will come from Zion, He will remove ungodliness from Jacob." [27] "This is My covenant with them, when I take away their sins."

    Revelation is a Jewish book! Too many writers have interpreted Revelation as having nothing to do with the nation of Israel or the Jewish people. While some of the events in Revelation do concern Gentile Christians today, this book is really about the fulfillment of the Old Testament promises made to the Jewish people. This means the key to understanding Revelation is to see how it links back to the Old Testament. In history there have been at least four popular ways people have interpreted Revelation. Only one of these methods, the Contextual-Futurist method, really takes the Old Testament into account and that is the method I will use in this book. There are 404 verses in the book of Revelation and at least 265 of these verses have portions of, or refer to, at least 555 verses in the Old Testament. [4] Over 70% of Revelation is taken from the Old Testament [5] so it truly is the whole testimony of Jesus summing up all sixty-six books of the Bible.

Revelation has always been controversial. As early as the second century A.D., one of the common ways people thought about Revelation was the Idealist or Allegorical view. In this view, Revelation is not an authoritative outline of future events revealed by God. The Allegorical view is that Revelation is only a symbolic illustration of good triumphing over evil. The word "allegory" means "a representation of an abstract or spiritual meaning through concrete or material forms; figurative treatment of one subject under the guise of another." [6] So, an allegory is a concept, idea, or story with a symbolic meaning. Since an allegory is symbolic, it is arbitrary by nature. An allegorical writing can mean almost anything, and the meaning is essentially random. For example, one allegorical writer may decide that the picture of the sky full of stars represents large groups of people over centuries of meaningless, dark existence. Another allegorical writer may decide that the sky full of stars represents the glory of God as it says in Psalm 19:1. If Revelation is only an allegory, then it will mean different things to different people and no one meaning will have any more authority or validity than any other. If this is the case, then the book of Revelation really has no meaning at all.

The Allegorical view: Revelation is purely symbolic of good triumphing over evil.

The Allegorical view fails, however, because in the first two verses, John makes it clear that this book is an unveiling by Jesus. The book is based on His authority. The meaning of Revelation is explained right from the start in verse two. It is the wrapping up or completion of the testimony of Jesus as a whole, so Revelation makes sense out of the promises made to the Jewish people from the past.

A second popular way to understand Revelation is called the Historicist view. Since the first three chapters of Revelation concern Christian churches that existed at the time the book was written, Historicists think the rest of Revelation is a symbolic illustration of church history. Some Historicists think the symbols line up with church history in historical order. Others think the symbols in Revelation only represent particularly important events in church history and the events are not necessarily in historical or sequential order. Still other Historicists think the entire book is just a vivid, symbolic, or poetic explanation of persecution in history.

The problem with the Historicist view is that Historicists do not agree at all on which symbol fits which time in history. Some identify certain verses with early church persecution or the black plague in the Middle Ages, but others identify the same sections differently. No single Historicist view has a strong anchor in the rest of Scripture or in history because each scholar has his or her own subjective view. There are as many different Historicist views as there are Historicists.

The Historicist view of Revelation: It is symbolic of the church age.

Thirdly, there is the Preterist view. There are "full" Preterists and "partial" Preterists in this group. Full-Preterists think Revelation is symbolic of events that took place in the first century A.D. Scholars who take this view generally believe Revelation must have been written before the destruction of the Jewish temple in Jerusalem in 70 A.D. They think most of the symbolism has to do with the historical destruction of the Jewish temple and the persecution of Jews and Christians that took place in those days. Even the verses in Revelation about the second coming of Jesus are interpreted as "A coming of Jesus in judgement" just as His first coming in Bethlehem was "a coming of Jesus in the flesh." Some Full-Preterists believe the entire church age over the last two thousand years is the beginning of the kingdom of God on earth. Some believe the world will continue to become more and more "Christian" until God and His people overtake the world system. Some full and partial Preterists, but not all, believe that Gentile (non-Jewish) Christians have replaced the Jews as the people of God. Some of them think God has rejected the Jews as His people and all the promises to the Jews in the Old Testament now apply to the church.

Full Preterism: The Revelation events already happened in A.D. 70.

Partial-Preterists agree with Full-Preterists that much of Revelation is about the destruction of the temple and the persecution of believers in the first century A.D., but they believe the second coming of Jesus at the end of the age is yet to come. Most Partial and Full-Preterists believe Revelation was written prior to A.D. 70, but the evidence in history is strong that Revelation was written in the 90's, at least 20 years after the destruction of the temple. There is, in fact, no compelling evidence that Revelation was written prior to A.D. 95. [7]

A second problem with Preterism is that there are literal, specific land promises made by God to the Jewish people found in the Old Testament that have never been fulfilled. [8] Romans chapter eleven makes it clear these promises to the Jewish people cannot be spiritualized into promises fulfilled by the New Testament church either. Romans chapter eleven explains that while people become part of the family of God by faith rather than by birth, there are still two distinct programs in God's plan for future history: one program is for national Israel and one program is for the Church. This can be seen clearly in a close examination of Romans 11:11-16 which reads,

Romans 11:11 - 16 (NASB)
I say then, they did not stumble so as to fall, did they? Far from it! But by their

wrongdoing salvation has come to the Gentiles, to make them jealous. [12] Now if their wrongdoing proves to be riches for the world, and their failure, riches for the Gentiles, how much more will their fulfillment be! [13] But I am speaking to you who are Gentiles. Therefore, insofar as I am an apostle of Gentiles, I magnify my ministry [14] if somehow I may move my own people to jealousy and save some of them. [15] For if their rejection proves to be the reconciliation of the world, what will their acceptance be but life from the dead? [16] If the first piece of dough is holy, the lump is also; and if the root is holy, the branches are as well.

Romans 11:11 and verse 15 explain that the Jewish people have not fallen beyond recovery. God has allowed a veiling of their understanding so that the Gentiles can be saved and also to provoke the Jewish people to jealousy. Jewish blindness that Jesus is their Messiah is only temporary. The apostle Paul, inspired by the Holy Spirit, also asks a rhetorical question in Romans 11:15 to make this point:

Romans 11:15 (NASB)
...for if their rejection proves to be the reconciliation of the world, what will their acceptance be but life from the dead?

The implication is, that the Jewish people as a nation will all eventually come to faith in Christ. This future fact is prophesied in the book of

Revelation and other Scriptures. Romans chapter eleven and Revelation rule out the idea that non-Jewish Christians replace Israel and take over the Old Testament promises made to the Jewish people. The promises God made to the Jewish people and nation are literal events yet to be fulfilled.

Not all Preterists think Gentile Christians replace the Jewish people. There are many passages in the Old Testament that link clearly with passages in Revelation, so it is difficult to convincingly interpret these passages to be about Gentile Christianity rather than the Jewish people and nation. In short, the promises, called "covenants," that God made with the Jewish descendants of Abraham have not yet been fulfilled and must therefore be fulfilled in the future or else Old Testament prophecy must be false.

Finally, there is the Contextual-Futurist point of view. Contextual-Futurists think that Revelation is a combination of symbolic or visionary illustrations that link with literal, physical events on the earth. The symbols provide a rich, emotionally compelling color to the literal events because these events are profound. In most cases in the book there is a vision, dream, or heavenly view of something followed by a physical, literal event but seeing where the symbol ends, and the literal begins can take a little effort to discern. In many cases the visionary part of the prophecy is a direct reference to something in the Old Testament and in other cases the explanation of the symbol is written right into the text. This pattern of symbol linked to literal is so obvious and consistent throughout the book that I have decided to call it the "Revelation Refrain."

Contextual-Futurists look at the meaning of the symbolic part of the Revelation Refrain primarily in the Old Testament. Contextual-Futurists believe the best way to interpret Scripture is by using other Scriptures, but they also recognize that the Bible is a fully human book. This means the Biblical writers sometimes used human figures of speech that would have made sense in the first century and within Jewish culture. It is important to recognize figures of speech as non-literal. Also, Biblical human writers sometimes use round numbers, and poetic illustrations. In Revelation, round numbers and poetry need to be understood from a first-century Jewish point of view. The Contextual-Futurist way of interpreting Revelation avoids a harsh, unthinking, or wooden literalism and also avoids an arbitrary or subjective interpretation.

Contextual-Futurists see the symbols in Revelation from a very practical point of view. They believe that symbols are tools that give intensity and power to words. Symbols can be analyzed and connected to other passages of Scripture which means they are essentially timeless so that Revelation can have an impact in every century – including in modern times. Symbols can also be a strong bridge between cultures so that Revelation is useful in every human culture as well. For example, a fire breathing dragon is understood in any culture and the sight of such a creature can be emotionally compelling even to modern audiences.

Finally, Contextual-Futurists think that symbols require the people of God to dig deeper. Symbols illustrate the character and feeling of a coming future event while at the same time inspiring the reader to find underlying principles from the Scriptures.

Revelation was meant to be much more than an outline of the future. Since it uses symbols and metaphors linked to literal events, Christians can also discern practical principles about the nature of God, the nature of human beings and how we should live in the present. No one knows exactly how many of the literal events in Revelation anyone will live to see, but the principles related to living for God in the present have been a blessing to thousands of believers at every point in the last two thousand years – and can continue to be a blessing to modern readers. This is the reason it is written in Revelation 1:3,

Revelation 1:3 (NASB)
Blessed is he who reads and those who hear the words of the prophecy and heed the things which are written in it; for the time is near.

End of Days
The Book of Revelation Explained

Chapter 2: Urgency!
Revelation 1: 3-20 explained...

The book of Revelation unveils how the Old Testament promises made to the Jewish people will be fulfilled in the future. It also reveals the future events leading to the return of Jesus, the Jewish Messiah. This is especially important to remember because the best way to understand Revelation is to look at it through the lens of a first century Jewish believer in Jesus and connect it with the Jewish prophecies about the Jewish Messiah. The Old Testament prophecies say that Messiah Jesus will one day return to this planet to rule as King over the whole earth. His second coming is not just about taking believers to heaven, but also about fulfilling the promises God made to the Jewish people.

Some Christians today wonder why anyone should study the book of Revelation. After all, if Revelation is about the future of the Jewish nation, how does that concern Christians dealing with everyday problems in the present? And if it is true that Christians will be taken out of the world in an amazing supernatural event called "the Rapture" long before any of the things described in Revelation take place, why should Christians study

Revelation at all? The answers to these questions are found in Revelation 1:3 which reads,

> **Revelation 1:3 (NASB)**
> Blessed is he who reads and those who hear the words of the prophecy and heed the things which are written in it; for the time is near.

The word "heed" is τηρέω (tay-reh'-o) [9] which means "to obey or treasure." So, the principles about how God relates to people, illustrated in Revelation, are principles that everyone can obey and treasure, even if the actual future events are not things you may live to experience.

One of those principles is the principle of "readiness." Jesus warned that His final coming will be like a thief in the night – unexpected, sudden and without warning. Today, many people have lost the sense of urgency about the second coming of Jesus. Some people rationalize that since Jesus has not returned in the last 2,000 years, it seems less and less likely that He will return. Some Christians spiritualize the idea of the second coming of Jesus because there have been so many false predictions about His return, but Revelation 1:3 warns us not to fall into this trap. In fact, in Revelation 1:3 Jesus specifically says, "the time [of His return] is near." The word "near" in the original Greek is ἐγγύς (en-gü's) [10] and this means "imminent, ready to come to pass." The sense of this word in Greek is not the same sense as an English phrase such as "lunchtime is near" or "the pen is near the notepaper on my desk." Instead, it means that when these prophecies begin to come to pass, there will be no delay because the sequence of events will rapidly unfold.

A good illustration of ἐγγύς (near) may be the world-wide Covid-19 pandemic that unfolded in the spring of 2020. Between January and March 2020, life proceeded as always but on March 13, 2020, the President of the United States declared a national emergency. Within days, authorities called upon the American people to shut down most "non-essential" businesses, churches, social and sporting events. In only a few weeks' time every restaurant in America changed to drive-through only. By late spring of 2020, most Christian churches in the Western world became "online only" and because people panicked, every grocery story looked like a hurricane had blown through it. For those who experienced the Covid-19 pandemic, the change was sudden, worldwide, and rapidly unfolded to affect every person on earth. In the same way, the events in Revelation will unfold quickly and every person around the world will feel the effects.

People misunderstand if they think the events in Revelation are not "near" because they have not happened since the first century. The truth is the prophecies in Revelation have been unfolding since the book was written. This is so because the book is addressed to seven physical churches that existed when Revelation was written. The very first prophecies about those churches were fulfilled starting in the first century A.D. at the time John wrote the text of Revelation. Revelation 1:4 reads,

Revelation 1:4 (NASB)
John to the seven churches that are in Asia: Grace to you and peace, from Him

who is and who was and who is to come, and from the seven Spirits who are before His throne...

While these seven churches in Asia actually existed in the first century, John uses a particular Greek wording to show that he means more than just the seven physical churches. In Greek, this wording suggests "the whole essence of something." [11] In other words, John was writing to the seven churches but also to all Christians as one collective "church." Revelation is therefore written to all churches everywhere so that what Jesus reveals in this book is what He is saying to every church throughout history. In fact, John adds that this revelation message also comes from "the seven spirits who are before God's throne." Again, the Greek wording means "the essence or whole of God's spirit" so this message is straight from the heart of God.

Some critics of the Bible think the Bible is inconsistent because some passages say there is only one God, but other Scriptures, such as these verses in Revelation, suggest God is more than one. A little careful study, however, shows there is no real inconsistency in these teachings.

It is true that the Bible says there is only one God and also says that God is a trinity of persons. This is mysterious but it is not irrational or inconsistent. For example, a triangle is only one thing, but it has three distinct points. A triangle is a trinity that makes up a unity. Each of the points of a triangle are distinct. The three points are not separate points or else the triangle would not be a triangle. A triangle is only a triangle because it is a shape with three distinct, but not separate, points. In a similar way, the Bible says that God is a trinity of persons but only one Being. Here in Revelation chapter one, the Bible also uses a Biblical, symbolic, figure of speech when it says, "the seven Spirits of God" because whenever the Bible uses the number seven symbolically it means "perfection" or "completion." For example, in Zechariah 4:1-6, the prophet sees seven lampstands in a vision and the angel speaking to Zechariah explains that the seven lampstands represent the Spirit of God in a singular, whole, and complete sense. So, Revelation 1:4 means that God in His "singular, whole and complete" essence is revealing this book.

God is one Being in a Trinity of Persons similar to a triangle which is one shape with three distinct points.

Revelation 1:5-8 goes on to give us a deeper description of Jesus and a preview of His final return. Revelation 1:5-8 reads,

> **Revelation 1:5 - 8 (NASB)**
> ...from Jesus Christ, the faithful witness, the firstborn of the dead, and the ruler of the kings of the earth. To Him who loves us and released us from our sins by His blood [6] and He has made us to be a kingdom, priests to His God and Father to Him be the glory and the dominion forever and ever. Amen. [7] Behold, He is coming with the clouds, and every eye will see Him, even those who pierced Him; and all the tribes of the earth will mourn over Him. So it is to be. Amen. [8] "I am the Alpha and the

Omega," says the Lord God, "who is and who was and who is to come, the Almighty."

Jesus reveals this book to John and, according to these verses, He is the "firstborn of the dead." In ancient Jewish culture, the firstborn was the person in the family with the highest rank. This person was not always the first child born in the household. For example, in the Old Testament, Jacob had twelve sons. The first in birth order was Reuben but the "firstborn" was Judah. Judah was actually fourth in birth order, but he held the rank of "firstborn" so when the Bible describes Jesus as "firstborn" it does not mean "first created" or "first to be physically born." It means that Jesus has the highest rank.

Revelation 1:7 says the second coming of Jesus will be a world-wide experience and every person on earth will have an intense, emotional reaction to His return. This verse rules out any interpretation that the second coming of Jesus will be a secret return or merely a personal spiritual experience. The reference in verse seven to "those who pierced him" is not specifically about the Roman guards who pierced His side at the crucifixion nor is it about the Jews in the first century. It is a poetic way of referring to the Jewish people as a whole group because over the centuries after Jesus rose from the dead, a majority of Jewish people have rejected Jesus as their Messiah. In the last days, all Jewish people will turn to Jesus as their King and everyone who mocked or ignored the promises of God that Jesus will return in glory will be stunned into amazement on the day of His return.

The second coming of Jesus will be a worldwide event no one will be able to deny.

>   **Revelation 1:9 – 11 (NASB)**
>   I, John, your brother and fellow partaker in the tribulation and kingdom and perseverance which are in Jesus, was on the island called Patmos because of the word of God and the testimony of Jesus. [10] I was in the Spirit on the Lord's day, and I heard behind me a loud voice like the sound of a trumpet, [11] saying, "Write in a book what you see, and send it to the seven churches: to Ephesus and to Smyrna and to Pergamum and to Thyatira and to Sardis and to Philadelphia and to Laodicea."

In the first century A.D., when Revelation was written, the Island called Patmos was a Roman prison island located just off the coast of Turkey in the Aegean Sea. John was not only the last of the eyewitnesses of Jesus, but at the time of his exile to Patmos, he was an old man in his nineties. Most of the other eyewitnesses of Jesus had been killed defending their testimony that Jesus lived, died, and rose again from the dead. John had already suffered greatly for his leadership of the first Christians and his testimony about the life of Jesus. Ancient tradition says that John had been boiled in oil because of his testimony, yet he survived, only to be sent as an old man to labor in the Patmos mines.

Yet even with all the suffering John had endured, verse ten says he was "in the Spirit on the Lord's day." Today we might think this means he had a vision on a Sunday, the Lord's Day, but the original language uses the word "Lord" as an adjective. This means it would be more like saying, "I was having a Lordy day." In other words, John was so filled with the joy and assurance of his faith in Jesus that even in his old age, even exiled to hard labor on a prison island, he was nearly floating along in the Spirit of His Lord and Savior Jesus Christ. John was so focused on Jesus that it filled up his whole day. In this attitude, John had the vision of Revelation, and it was intense, like the voice of a trumpet.

Revelation 1:12 says,

> **Revelation 1:12 – 17 (NASB)**
> Then I turned to see the voice that was speaking with me. And having turned I saw seven golden lampstands; [13] and in the middle of the lampstands I saw one like a son of man, clothed in a robe reaching to the feet, and girded across His chest with a golden sash. [14] His head and His hair were white like white wool, like snow; and His eyes were like a flame of fire. [15] His feet were like burnished bronze, when it has been made to glow in a furnace, and His voice was like the sound of many waters. [16] In His right hand He held seven stars, and out of His mouth came a sharp two-edged sword; and His face was like the sun shining in its strength. [17] When I saw Him, I fell at His feet like a dead man.

These few verses are the only physical description of Jesus in the Bible. There is no description of Jesus' physical appearance in His biographies, which are called the "Gospels," a word meaning "good news." The reason for this is probably because in the Old Testament, the prophecies about the coming Messiah point out his humble appearance. Isaiah 53:2 says that the Messiah "...has no stately form or majesty that we would look at Him, nor an appearance that we would take pleasure in Him."

Of course, John had seen Jesus in the flesh, but here in Revelation chapter one, John sees Him in His glorified state and the result is that he fell on the ground like a dead man. Seeing God in all His perfection and power and glory is more than anyone can endure so Jesus had a humble physical appearance as a man to protect people from the purity and perfection of God as He appears in the spiritual.

Another reason Jesus appeared in a humble, average, physical state has to do with preserving human freewill. The Bible teaches that God in His essence is overwhelming just as John experienced in Revelation chapter one. Real love, however, must be a free choice or else it could not be real love. If a person is exposed to God in His glorified state, the experience would be so intense that free choice on the part of a finite human being, seeing God in His glory, would be impossible. God has carefully balanced the universe so there is just enough evidence that only a fool would say there is no God but not so much evidence that freewill could not exist.

In the end of days, God will end the freewill of human beings and reveal Himself in His true glory. When Jesus is revealed in His perfection and holiness and power, this experience will be so overwhelming it will literally consume anyone's ability to make any choices at all. Philippians 2:9 says,

> **Philippians 2:9 – 11 (NASB)**
> For this reason also God highly exalted Him, and bestowed on Him the name which is above every name, [10] so that at the name of Jesus every knee will bow, of those who are in heaven and on earth and under the earth, [11] and that every tongue will confess that Jesus Christ is Lord, to the glory of God the Father.

Jesus is the King of Glory. In fact, the description of Jesus in Revelation 1:12-17 is the same as Daniel 7:9 and 13. The prophet Daniel lived long before Jesus, but he prophesied about His coming. Daniel did not know the exact details of the coming of Messiah Jesus, but he did know that the Messiah would come twice – first in humility and the second time in glory. Daniel 7:9 and 13 reads,

> **Daniel 7:9, 13 - 14 (NASB)**
> I kept looking until thrones were set up, And the Ancient of Days took His seat; His garment was white as snow, and the hair of His head like pure wool. His throne was ablaze with flames, its wheels were a burning fire... [13] I kept looking in the night visions, and behold, with the clouds of heaven One like a son of man was coming, and He came up to the Ancient of Days and was presented before Him. And to Him was

given dominion, honor, and a kingdom, so that all the peoples, nations, and populations of all languages might serve Him. His dominion is an everlasting dominion which will not pass away; and His kingdom is one which will not be destroyed.

Jesus is God in the Flesh – the King of Glory.

Revelation 1:17b - 18 (NASB)
And He placed His right hand on me, saying, "Do not be afraid; I am the first and the last, [18] and the living One; and I was dead, and behold, I am alive forevermore, and I have the keys of death and of Hades.

The phrase "I am the first and the last" in verse seventeen is a figure of speech that God also used in Exodus 3:14 as He spoke to Moses from the burning bush. By using this figure of speech, first century Jewish people would have recognized that Jesus is claiming to be the same Being who spoke to Moses. "I am the first and the last" means that God is self-existent. God does not owe His existence to anything or anyone. It means that Jesus and God are the same Being.

Only the true God can know the future because everything and everyone other than God owes existence to someone or something else. Everything that begins to exist is an "effect" and every effect must have an adequate cause, but the chain of cause and effect cannot go back forever. If the chain of cause and effect did go backwards forever, then there would never be a First Cause and in that case the chain of cause and effect would be grounded or started in nothing. That makes no sense because nothing cannot do or cause anything. There must, therefore, be an Uncaused Cause of everything else. There must be a Being who exists eternally because if ever there had been a time in the universe when there was truly nothing, then nothing would exist now – because nothing cannot do anything!

The Bible says that God is the one who simply exists. He is what He is, always has been what He is and always will be. Jesus is the eternal grounding of the entire chain of cause and effect in the universe. The universe is not God or a part of God because God is eternal, and the universe is something that began to exist. Modern scientists have theorized repeatedly about the compelling evidence that the universe began in a sudden start, but no one can explain how absolutely nothing can cause absolutely everything. Jesus says He is the first and the last, the eternal Being with the power to create life and master death.

The existence of the Biblical God explains how the universe came from nothing.

Since God is "the first and the last," He is absolutely in control of everything, including the future. Revelation 1:19 reads,

> **Revelation 1:19 (NASB)**
> Therefore write the things which you have seen, and the things which are, and the things which will take place after these things.

The word "therefore" is a connection word. It means that since Jesus is the eternal God who controls life, death and the future, John can write what He reveals about the future with confidence. In fact, this verse shows the full outline of what Jesus is going to reveal in the rest of the book. John was told to write three things: What he had seen so far, what he would see about the situation happening in the churches of his own time, and what he would see about the future.

In the book of Revelation, chapter one records what John had seen concerning the glory and authority of Jesus as He is in His glorified state. It is about the glory and authority and eternal essence of Jesus. Since Jesus is the eternal God, His revelation about the future is not a prediction, a guess, or just an analogy showing the triumph of good over evil. This is an unveiling of the future given by the God of power and glory who is totally in control of the universe and absolutely certain about what the future holds.

In Revelation chapter two, John writes about the things which were happening in the Christian churches in his time. He does this in seven short letters to seven select churches from the first century. These letters represent the ongoing present, so the problems and character of each first century church can also be found in local churches in our present time. Historicists point out how church history seems to show the character of each of the seven first-century churches matches the character of the kind of church that dominated Christianity during seven distinct time periods over the last two thousand years. The Historicist description of church history may be somewhat arbitrary, but what is clear is that the character of the first-century churches has shown up in church history and those character traits exist in some churches to the present day.

Finally, John was to write about "the things which will take place after these things." Chapters four through twenty-two lay out the future history of the world at the end of the church age. These future events are what happens immediately before, during and after the Great Tribulation. These chapters also include a very brief snapshot of the 1,000-year reign of Jesus on the earth called "the Millennium," and a tiny glimpse of eternity beyond the end of the Millennium.

Revelation 1:20 (NASB)
As for the mystery of the seven stars which you saw in My right hand, and the seven golden lampstands: the seven stars are the angels of the seven churches, and the seven lampstands are the seven churches.

This is the first example of what I call "the Revelation Refrain." The "Revelation Refrain" is a pattern in the book of Revelation connecting a vision of something symbolic or heavenly to something literal or physical. In this case, the seven stars are the angels of the seven churches and the seven lampstands are the seven churches. The meaning of these symbols is explained in the text itself. In Scripture, "stars" are used symbolically to mean angels or messengers from God. The word "angel" in Greek is ἄγγελος (ä'n-ge-los) which means "a messenger, envoy, one who is sent, an angel, or a messenger from God." [12] This means a star or stars used symbolically in Scripture can mean not only the spiritual beings we call angels, but also human messengers such as prophets or pastors. Knowing which is which depends on the context of the Scripture. In this case, the word "angel" is linked to the word "church" in Greek which is ἐκκλησία (ek-klā-sē'-ä). Ecclesia means "a gathering of citizens called out from their homes into some public place or assembly for a common purpose" [13] so the related word "angel" in this context must mean the pastor of the church. Obviously, we mean something more than just a public gathering when we think about "Church," but based on the Greek meaning of the word, a church should be a gathering of believers, called out of their everyday lives for the greater purpose of being about God's business.

End of Days:
The Book of Revelation Explained

Chapter 3: The Test for Truth!
Revelation 2: 1-7 explained...

Revelation probably uses the Revelation Refrain so that the pattern in the symbols may give the reader a deeper sense of the emotion and power of the information. The context determines what is symbolic and what is literal. This requires some effort to discern, but the book is meant to be understood by anyone who takes the time to read its message. For example, in Revelation chapter one John sees "in the spirit," so the vision of Jesus walking among the seven lampstands holding seven stars in His hand is symbolic. Jesus explains the symbols right in the text. The stars are symbolic of seven angels that link to seven physical churches.

Some Bible scholars think these seven churches are not only the physical churches from the first century, but they also represent seven distinct periods of church history. The problem with this idea is that Jesus does not specifically say this is the case. Different scholars also come to different conclusions about where one church time-period begins and another one ends. There are periods in church history where the dominant form of the church in the western world did seem to line up with a description of one of these churches, but it is better not to be too rigid in this thinking.

Regardless of whether the seven churches are exactly any one time period in church history or not, two things stand out in Revelation chapters two and three. First, these chapters give the impression there could be a long period of time between the life and times of Jesus here on earth and when He will return. That implication was significant for first century Christian readers of Revelation since early Christians believed that Jesus was returning immediately. Understanding there could be a lengthy period before His return was important in the first century so that believers would not lose hope under persecution. John wrote in his eyewitness gospel biography of the life of Jesus that Jesus never actually promised He would return within the lifetime of the eyewitnesses, even though many people seemed to think so in the first century. John 21:21 says,

> **John 21:21 - 22 (NASB)**
> So, Peter, upon seeing him, said to Jesus, "Lord, and what about this man?" Jesus said to him, "If I want him to remain until I come, what is that to you? You follow Me!" Therefore this account went out among the brothers, that that disciple would not die; yet Jesus did not say to him that he would not die, but only, "If I want him to remain until I come, what is that to you?"

The second thing that stands out in the description of the seven churches are the positive and negative characteristics that can dominate a church. These characteristics can also apply in the personal life of an individual Christian, so reading through these chapters can warn a believer about their present spiritual condition.

Seven churches may be seven distinct times during the church age.

Whether the seven churches are seven distinct times or not, the church age is "the set-up" for the final Great Tribulation. Jesus also described the church age in Matthew chapter twenty-four when speaking to His disciples at the Mount of Olives. This event is sometimes called "the Olivet discourse." In Matthew 24:4, Jesus said,

> **Matthew 24:4 - 8 (NASB)**
> And Jesus answered and said to them, "See to it that no one misleads you. For many will come in My name, saying, 'I am the Christ,' and they will mislead many people. And you will be hearing of wars and rumors of wars. See that you are not alarmed, for those things must take place, but that is not yet the end. For nation will rise against nation, and kingdom against kingdom, and there will be famines and earthquakes in various places. But all these things are merely the beginning of birth pains.

Jesus is saying that the labor and delivery process a woman goes through to give birth is symbolic of the time of His return. This means the world will experience a time of preparation before the Great Tribulation period because in the process of being pregnant, a woman's body goes through a set-up process preparing her for labor. This set-up includes practice contractions called "Braxton-Hicks" as well as other physical changes. Braxton-Hicks contractions are sometimes called "false labor." They can be intense enough that a woman having her first baby may think she is in labor, but Braxton Hicks contractions do not last long and relax fairly quickly. Real labor begins when contractions are longer, stronger, do not simply fade away and come upon the mother in a more regular timing. In addition, although not always, the bag of waters may break at the start of labor. In the same way, Jesus warned there would be "wars and rumors of wars" but just as a woman should not be alarmed by Braxton Hicks contractions, the many wars and rumors of wars that have happened in the last 2,000 years are not real labor.

The end of the church age will be a process similar to a woman's birth pains from first contractions to delivery.

There is a clue in Matthew chapter twenty-four that may be something like the breaking of the bag of waters and the start of real labor. Dr. Arnold Fruchtenbaum believes that Isaiah 19: 1- 4, Second Chronicles 15:1-7 and other Jewish sources show that Jesus is using a specific Jewish figure of speech in Matthew twenty-four to explain when the real labor pains will begin. Dr. Fruchtenbaum writes,

> To understand what the idiom "nation against nation, and kingdom against kingdom" means, it is necessary to return to

the Jewish origin of these statements...This expression is a Hebrew idiom for a world war. Jesus' statement here is that when a world war occurs, rather than merely a local war, that world war would signal that the end of the age had begun...The rabbis clearly taught that a worldwide conflict would signal the coming of the Messiah. Jesus corrected this idea slightly, for He said that when the world war occurs, while it does not signal the coming of the Messiah, it will signal that the end of the age has begun." [14]

The first time in human history when the entire globe was truly at war at the same time was in 1914 with the start of World War I. Since European powers had spent centuries building colonies worldwide, when World War I started, the fighting literally spread around the planet as each colony also went to war. Some people think World War II was just a continuation of World War I since the same countries stirred up the conflict again in 1939, but there was a break in world-wide war between 1918 and 1939. In the years between World War I and World War II there was also the Great Depression, an economic disaster that for the first time, also affected the entire earth. Since Jesus used this specific Hebrew figure of speech about World War, it is not unreasonable to conclude that the first true "birth pain" was World War I from 1914 – 1918. A number of other world-wide birth pains have followed since World War I. These include the world-wide Spanish flu epidemic from roughly 1918 - 1920, the Great Depression starting in 1929, World War II from 1939 – 1945, the great famines in the Ukraine and China in the 1950's, the rise of world-wide Islamic terrorism and, most recently in 2020, the Covid-19 world-wide pandemic. Each of these events was world-wide or had world-wide effects, each increased in intensity, then subsided, and each can be seen as part of the set-up for the final seven years of judgement Jesus describes in Revelation.

Since the destruction of the nation of Israel in 70 A.D., Biblical prophets including Jesus said to expect the nation of Israel to be regathered as a nation. This regathering of Israel was also prophesied in Isaiah 66:8 and it came to pass on May 14, 1948. The Bible also implies in Daniel 9:27 that there will be a third Jewish temple which means that Jerusalem must come back under Jewish control. This prophecy was fulfilled on June 7, 1967, during the Six Day War.

Based on a Hebrew figure of speech, the beginning of the end of the church age will begin when, for the first time in human history, the whole planet would be at war at one time.

After these prophecies are fulfilled, the book of Revelation and other prophetic books tell us to expect some key events. Each key event is prophesied in Revelation and other Scriptures and will be explained in later chapters of this book, but this is a summary for now:

- In the near future, there will be an attempt to form a one-world government, but this attempt will collapse quickly.

- After the one-world government collapse, the world will reorganize into ten political jurisdictions. The Bible describes these as "ten kingdoms," but these will also collapse quickly.
- During or after these catastrophic political events, one political leader will rise in increasing power. The Bible calls this man the "Antichrist" among other names.
- At some point in the Antichrist's rise to power, he will cause a time of false peace and security. People will foolishly place their trust in his leadership.
- At some point, the Antichrist will confirm a group of peace treaties with the nation of Israel. This event, according to Daniel 9:27, begins the final seven years of history - a time-period called the Great Tribulation.
- Halfway through this final seven-year time period, the Antichrist will openly declare his claim to be God. He will then demand the world worship him and require everyone to accept a mark of loyalty to him in the right hand or the forehead in order to do any kind of business.
- At the end of the seven years, the Antichrist's capital city will be destroyed, and he will gather his forces together to try to destroy Jerusalem and the remnant of the Jewish people hiding in the wilderness.

Jesus, however, will return to save His people.

- After the defeat of the Antichrist and the physical return of Jesus to the earth, Jesus will take power as King of the earth and reign for 1,000 years. The 1,000-year reign of Jesus is called either the Millennium or the Kingdom of God.

At some point before the final seven years of earth history begins, believers in Jesus will be instantly translated into resurrection bodies in an event theologians call the "Rapture." What the book of Revelation describes as future-history in chapters four through nineteen are events that will happen after the Rapture. Scripture tells us the Rapture can happen at any time and Matthew chapter twenty-four explains there will be many plagues, earthquakes, wars, and false religions before the final seven years begin. All these events are warnings that the Great Tribulation is coming soon.

The return of the Jews to Israel as a nation again is fulfillment of a prophecy that sets the stage for the coming Great Tribulation.

Revelation 2:1 (NASB)
To the angel of the church in Ephesus write: The One who holds the seven stars in His right hand, the One who walks among the seven golden lampstands, says this…

The city of Ephesus was about three miles inland from the Turkish coastline. In the first century it was famous for a huge temple to the Roman goddess Artemis, also known as the goddess Diana. This temple was considered one of the wonders of the world at the time. It had 127 pillars in its colonnade, each about sixty feet tall, and while it was an impressive structure, Ephesus was also well-known for its thriving sex industry. Temple prostitution was commonly practiced, and brothels and sex shops of every kind infested the city. The apostle Paul worked in Ephesus for two years alongside his friend and young protégé Timothy. Ancient church tradition says that John lived out his final years in Ephesus. The book of Acts and other historical documents show that Christian influence in Ephesus led to many people converting to Christianity and abandoning paganism – including giving up the worship of Diana. These conversions led to a downturn in cult businesses, and this affected the local economy as more and more people quit buying cult books or idols. The economic threat from these conversions to Christianity led to riots and persecution of Christians. The book of Revelation tells us that Jesus was very much aware of the difficult environment these Christians faced. In Revelation 2:2-3, He said,

> **Revelation 2:2 - 3 (NASB)**
> 'I know your deeds and your labor and perseverance, and that you cannot tolerate evil people, and you have put those who call themselves apostles to the test, and they are not, and you found them to be false; [3] and you have perseverance and have endured on

account of My name, and have not become weary.

Believers in the Ephesian church were unashamed to test what people in town were saying and teaching. They were unashamed to investigate whether a popular teacher's doctrine was rational or contradicted the teachings of the true apostles of Jesus and the teachings of the Old Testament. Clearly, they understood that truth will never contradict the revealed Word of God. This Ephesian understanding of truth and a willingness to expose what is false is an attitude rapidly being lost today.

It has become increasingly popular today to believe that whatever a person wants, or desires is more important than what is healthy or good or true. In fact, it is common to read on social media that anyone who points out the flaws in another person's belief system is hateful. In fact, some contemporary denominations and popular teachers claim that it is "unchristian" to offend anyone by pointing out false teaching while at the same time they openly criticize the literal teachings of the Bible itself.

Jesus, however, was pleased that the Ephesian Christians engaged in testing truth claims. He commended the Ephesians for exposing what was false and persevering with the truth. The Lord obviously wants His people in every time period to stand up for the truth.

Believers should not grow weary in testing and proclaiming what is true and what is error.

While we should stand up for the truth today, we

also need to guard against a legalistic, arrogant, or unloving attitude. Jesus said in Revelation 2:4,

> **Revelation 2:4 (NASB)**
> But I have this against you, that you have left your first love.

Jesus is saying that right actions do not cancel out the wrong attitudes. Jesus wants us to test what people teach, but Jesus will also test the testers for the right attitude of love when they do their testing! The Ephesians did not lose their first love as if they had dropped something between the couch cushions and could not find it again. No, they left their first love. This may not have been a conscious act, but the point is that the things that led up to leaving their first love were intentional.

For the Ephesian Christians, knowing what was right and wrong was not their problem. Instead, they had become so busy being correct that they did not take care to deliver the truth to others in love. They had the right package, but they were delivering it wrong.

This is not an uncommon problem today either. There are believers who know why the Bible can be trusted historically, prophetically, and doctrinally, but instead of showing these facts with gentleness and respect, they deliver those facts with a verbal bazooka. Christians can be as right as rain about what the Bible teaches, and yet vaporize everyone with that "rightness." Without the love of Jesus, being right is useless which is why First Peter 3:15 says,

First Peter 3:15 (NASB)
...always being ready to make a defense to everyone who asks you to give an account for the hope that is in you, but with gentleness and respect.

Christians should be unashamed to stand up for the truth but always with gentleness and respect.

The words "first love" in Greek are πρῶτος ἀγάπη (protos agape). Protos means "first in time" or "first in rank or order" [15] but Jesus is not just talking about the excitement the Ephesians may have felt when they first turned to Jesus. This is because the Greek word ἀγάπη (agape) means "a desire to seek the highest and best interests of another person in a sacrificial way." [16] "Agape" love can be connected to feelings, but it is not primarily an emotion at all. It is an active choice, so Jesus is saying that the Ephesians had neglected to seek the highest and best interest of Jesus Christ and other people in a sacrificial way. They had not made agape love their highest priority or first in rank in their life. Jesus warns them in Revelation 2:5,

Revelation 2:5 (NASB)
Therefore, remember from where you have fallen, and repent and do the deeds you did at first; or else I am coming to you and will remove your lampstand out of its place - unless you repent.

The word "repent" means to "willfully turn around." The Ephesian Christians needed to make a choice from the heart to make seeking the highest and best interests of Jesus and other people their highest priority. Jesus also uses the word μνημονεύω (mnēmoneuō), meaning "to bring to mind or remember." [17] This is a bit deeper than just bringing up a memory. It refers to "a focused action of thinking" or "a thought-out decision" and all these words in Greek are in the continual sense.

Christians should pursue a lifestyle of self-reflection, continually turning back to prioritizing Jesus and His way of life in their everyday lives.

> **Revelation 2:6 - 7 (NASB)**
> But you have this, that you hate the deeds of the Nicolaitans, which I also hate. [7] The one who has an ear, let him hear what the Spirit says to the churches. To the one who overcomes, I will grant to eat from the tree of life, which is in the Paradise of God.'

Obviously the Nicolaitans promoted some sort of false teaching and actions that the Lord hated. They are mentioned elsewhere in Revelation so we will cover who they may have been later. The point here is that the message to the Ephesians was not just to the Ephesians because Jesus challenges anyone who has an ear to hear what the Spirit is saying to the Ephesians. The Lord's call to the Ephesians extends to every believer down to the present day. God wants all believers to test truth claims and expose lies but always remember to prioritize seeking the highest and the best interest of Jesus and others in everything we say and do.

End of Days:
The Book of Revelation Explained

Chapter 4: This life is not all there is!
Revelation 2: 7-28 explained...

Human history is a recurring drama. Over and over again human cultures are eventually destroyed by human nature itself. Human pride against God, greed and lust for power, and indulgence in immoralities erode cultures until the most powerful empires in history are inevitably brought down. This pattern, repeated so often, will happen again and Revelation is about the rise and fall of the final world empire.

When Revelation was written, the Roman empire was experiencing a time of prosperity. The Romans had crushed all opposition. The threat of pirates and bandits was at an all-time low.[18] The Empire had built more than ten thousand miles of cobblestone roads, many of them lit up at night by streetlights, so that trade flowed relatively freely throughout the civilized world. In 90 A.D. there was a widespread peace and free citizens of the empire were reasonably happy.

Within the Roman peace, however, there were occasional downturns. Local wars or rebellions had to be put down by the authorities. In some locations, poor crop yields led to local famines and plagues occasionally broke out creating panic and fear from time to time. There was an overall peace in the Empire, but it was a fragile peace and Rome knew it. To keep order, Roman authorities had to flex some military and political muscle, so Roman law was absolute, and it was harshly enforced. For example, there was a form of religious freedom in the Empire. There were dozens, even hundreds of gods that people could worship in nearly every Roman city, but over time social and political pressure led to Emperor worship. After one too many religiously-inspired rebellion, there was extreme social, political and legal pressure to burn incense to the emperor as proof that the citizen's highest loyalty, religiously and politically, was to the Emperor! Not to do so was seen as an act of treason.

Christians, for the most part, had no problem pledging loyalty to Rome politically. The apostle Paul, for example, was an honest citizen of the empire. He made it clear in his letters that being a Christian was about the kingdom of God, not about politics. In Paul's view, so long as the authorities did not require a believer to do something that contradicted God's commands, Christians should be good citizens. Paul wrote in Romans 13:1,

> **Romans 13:1 - 7 (NASB)**
> Every person is to be subject to the governing authorities. For there is no authority except from God, and those which exist are established by God. ² Therefore whoever resists authority has opposed the ordinance of God; and they who have opposed will receive condemnation upon themselves. ³ For rulers are not a cause of

fear for good behavior, but for evil. Do you want to have no fear of authority? Do what is good and you will have praise from the same; [4] for it is a servant of God to you for good. But if you do what is evil, be afraid; for it does not bear the sword for nothing; for it is a servant of God, an avenger who brings wrath on the one who practices evil. [5]Therefore it is necessary to be in subjection, not only because of wrath, but also for the sake of conscience. [6] For because of this you also pay taxes, for rulers are servants of God, devoting themselves to this very thing. [7] Pay to all what is due them: tax to whom tax is due; custom to whom custom; respect to whom respect; honor to whom honor.

Political loyalty is not a problem for Christians up until politicians demand that we violate our higher loyalty to God and His ways.

In Revelation chapter two, the church at Smyrna was faced with the tension between loyalty to God and loyalty to society, a situation Christians can easily relate to today. The church at Smyrna and Christians today face constant social criticism about the Bible's teachings concerning morality and the fact that only the Biblical God is real. The pressure on churches to essentially swear allegiance to our culture's views is intense and growing day by day.

For example, in 2013, the Supreme Court of the State of New Mexico made a legal decision in a case against a photography company that would not shoot photos of a gay wedding. The court ruled against Elane Photography saying that the photography company was "compelled by law to compromise the very religious beliefs that inspire their lives" and that disobeying their religious beliefs was "the price of citizenship." [19] This was the same question faced by the church at Smyrna and it is still being asked of Christians today.

When the price of citizenship is higher than loyalty to Jesus, will loyalty to Jesus trump loyalty to the state? Jesus said in Revelation 2:8-9,

> **Revelation 2:8 - 9 (NASB)**
> And to the angel of the church in Smyrna write: The first and the last, who was dead, and has come to life, says this: [9] I know your tribulation and your poverty (but you are rich), and the blasphemy by those who say they are Jews and are not, but are a synagogue of Satan.

God was fully aware of the dilemma the people at Smyrna faced and He knows that Christians today may face the same thing. Jesus knows there may be economic fallout and persecution if we remain loyal to Him. But in the Lord's view, whatever persecution we may face to remain loyal to Him actually makes us fabulously wealthy – even if we cannot see that wealth in the moment.

Loyalty to Jesus should be greater than any loyalty to the culture, society, family or personal desires.

The people in Smyrna were familiar with the concept of wealth. The ruins of the city of Smyrna are in Izmir, Turkey today. In ancient times it was considered one of the most beautiful cities in the world. It had a deep-water harbor which brought in trade from all over the Mediterranean. Wealth from imports and exports flowed through the city and nearly everyone had a piece of the pie. The central street in the city was called "the Golden Street" and not just because business was booming. There was also the gorgeous sparkling temple to Cybil at one end of the golden street, and the imposing temple to Zeus at the other. Everywhere people looked there was wealth and opportunity – except among the Christians. Since Christians would not burn incense to the emperor as a god, they were forced into poverty even when almost everyone else was making money.

Revelation 2:8 was written specifically to "the angel of the church in Smyrna." As we have seen, the word "angel" means "a messenger from God" and it can refer to a human messenger such as a prophet or pastor. In this case, ancient history records that the first century pastor of the church in Smyrna was a man named Polycarp.

Ancient tradition says that Polycarp was a student of John, and John is the writer of the book of Revelation. Polycarp lived into his nineties and as persecution against Christians in Smyrna increased, the public demanded the execution of Polycarp because he was the leader of the church. Some people were reluctant to call for Polycarp's death because he was old and well-known for being kind and gentle. Nevertheless, there were Jewish and pagan religious people at the time who resented him because many of them had been willing to compromise their loyalty to God by making the annual sacrifice to the emperor. Polycarp had spoken out against them, so his teaching, and his leadership pricked the conscience of people who were only outwardly religious. These people were jealous, and embarrassed, and they wanted blood. They were also very influential, so a warrant was issued for Polycarp's arrest.

The authorities searched for Polycarp, but his followers had hidden him on a farm outside the city. While he was there, Polycarp had a dream in which he saw his pillow burst into flames and a voice tell him, "Be the man, Polycarp." When soldiers finally tracked him down, he was mentally and spiritually prepared to die for his faith. Tradition says that Polycarp welcomed the soldiers who came to arrest him and voluntarily went with them back to Smyrna. On the day of his execution, the governor pleaded with him to simply declare the emperor was Lord and be spared but Polycarp just said, "Eighty and six years have I served Christ. How dare I now revile my King who saved Me?"

Polycarp was burned alive, but he never cried out in pain. A soldier quickened his death by stabbing him, but his death became an inspiration for others to stand firm in their faith. Perhaps it was the letter to the church at Smyrna in Revelation that inspired Polycarp because it says in Revelation 2:10-11,

> **Revelation 2:10 - 11 (NASB)**
> Do not fear what you are about to suffer. Behold, the devil is about to cast some of you into prison, so that you will be tested, and you will have tribulation for ten days. Be faithful until death, and I will give you the crown of life. [11] He who has an ear, let him

hear what the Spirit says to the churches. He who overcomes will not be hurt by the second death.'

The Lord knows we are emotional creatures. He knows we struggle with fear and anxiety so the Lord told the people of Smyrna not to fear suffering because any suffering they must endure is only temporary and He has promised them eternal life. The words in Greek in this verse are in an emphatic sense meaning it could be translated, "Stop fearing. These tribulations are only temporary." The tribulations the people of Smyrna faced were inspired by Satanic forces. On occasion, there may be supernatural, demonic forces behind the trials that we face, but God allows challenges in our lives because it is a test of our faith. Jesus said the same thing in John 16:33. He said,

John 16:33 (NASB)
These things I have spoken to you so that in Me you may have peace. In the world you have tribulation but take courage; I have overcome the world.

Today, we will face the same challenges as believers did in ancient Smyrna. Christians who choose to follow Jesus risk losing friends, risk being trolled on social media and as the time of the Great Tribulation draws near, there will be increasing persecution. Christians will increasingly need to choose loyalty to Jesus over fear, even fear of death. If believers are willing to be faithful until death, there is the reward of the Crown of Life.

The Second Death Jesus mentions is eternal separation from God in the Lake of Fire. In that place there will be a continual dying, a continual regret and this horror will continue forever to anyone who chooses loyalty to the culture over loyalty to Jesus!

There is a risk of suffering to anyone who chooses loyalty to Jesus, but that suffering will only ever be temporary.

There is an absolute spiritual law explained in the Bible – it is called the Law of Sowing and Reaping. It is a simple law and there are no exceptions to it. This law says that whatever you plant - that is what will grow! If you plant apple seeds you should only expect to see apple trees grow and if you plant apple seeds, you should not expect apricot trees to grow. This law is true in the natural world but also in the Spiritual. Whatever you plant spiritually is what will grow in your life. If you plant God's truth, then God's wisdom and direction will dominate your thinking. If you plant seeds of the philosophies and mindsets of the world into your heart, then your thinking will become compromised and poisoned. In Revelation chapter two, the law of sowing and reaping is illustrated in the church at Pergamum. Revelation 2:12 says,

Revelation 2:12 - 13 (NASB)
And to the angel of the church in Pergamum write: [13] 'I know where you dwell, where Satan's throne is; and you hold fast My name, and did not deny My faith even in the days of Antipas, My witness, My faithful

one, who was killed among you, where Satan dwells.

Pergamum was a beautiful city in northwestern Turkey, about twenty-five kilometers inland from the Aegean Sea. It was famous for having a medical university and one of the largest libraries in the ancient world where it is said there were 200,000 scrolls. [20] Pergamum was a center of learning, but it was also a center for pagan religions. The city was infested with temples and strange cults. [21] It was famous for mixing every kind of idea. In Pergamum, there was a steady social diet of "whatever works for you." There was a hodge-podge of philosophies and religions, the occult and intellectual study - all mixed together. In the first century, non-Christians in Pergamum were offended by the Christian belief that Jesus was the only way to truth since they believed all of the "truths" in their town were equally valid.

On the surface, the people of Pergamum appeared tolerant of every kind of religion or philosophy. They were, however, grossly intolerant of Christianity because Christians insisted that Jesus was "the Way, the Truth and the Life" as it says in John 14:6. From a Christian perspective, Jesus is not "one way" among many or "one truth" equally true with other ideas or "one lifestyle" just as acceptable as any other lifestyle. Pagan intolerance of Christians led to persecution. In fact, Jesus names Antipas as someone who died because of his loyalty to Jesus and there were others as well.

Of course, mixing and matching beliefs is a familiar issue today. A recent study found that about 25% of professing Christians also say they believe in reincarnation, but reincarnation is a Hindu belief. The same study found that around 45-51% of professing believers think that many different religions can give a person eternal life, but Jesus said in John 14:6 "I am the way, the truth and the life." [22] Just as in Pergamum, with all this mixing and matching it is not surprising there is an increasing hostility toward Christians who insist that Jesus is the only way to eternal life.

Pergamum was also famous for unrestrained sexual activity mixed into occult worship. Many of the religions in Pergamum used various forms of sex as part of religious ritual. It was a common belief that any kind of sexual activity was acceptable, and this belief clashed with the Christian teaching that sexual intimacy should only happen between a man and a woman in a marriage covenant.

Despite the cultural pressure, the people of the church at Pergamum had held onto the name of Jesus. They were known as Christians, followers of Jesus, and they had held onto their tradition of faith even when persecution in the city had become so severe it resulted in the death of Antipas. As it is in our churches today, for some people attending the church in Pergamum, being a Christian was just a religious label, not a commitment of the heart. This is why Jesus said in verse 14,

> **Revelation 2:14 (NASB)**
> But I have a few things against you, because you have some there who hold the teaching of Balaam, who kept teaching Balak to put a stumbling block before the sons of Israel, to eat things sacrificed to idols and to commit sexual immorality.

The teachings of Balaam are found in the Old Testament book of Numbers. Balaam was a sorcerer hired to curse Israel by the pagan king Balak. The people of Israel are the people of God and no matter how hard Balaam tried; he simply could not pronounce a curse on Israel because God restrained him. Once Balaam realized God was holding him back, he advised Balak to try a different tactic to hurt Israel. In Numbers 31:15, it says that Balaam advised Balak to use sexual seduction to bring Israel down. Balaam told the king to get some of the local, pagan women to seduce the Israelite men. Numbers 31:15 says,

> **Numbers 31:15 - 16 (NASB)**
> And Moses said to them, "Have you spared all the women? Behold, they caused the sons of Israel, through the counsel of Balaam, to be unfaithful to the Lord in the matter of Peor, so that the plague took place among the congregation of the Lord.

In Numbers chapter twenty-five, king Balak convinced the women of Peor to invite Israelite men to a wild party which was actually a worship feast to their gods. This feast included ritual sexual infidelity as an act of worship to the false gods. The men fell for the trap because sexual temptation drew them in, and they ended up worshipping false gods.

There is a similar thing happening today. The modern argument is that sex between consenting adults should not be a problem because everybody is doing it anyway. But just because many people do something does not make it acceptable to God. God has made it plain that sexual intimacy is only for a man and his wife. The belief that extra-marital sexual activity is okay is what drew the Christians at Pergamum to mix Christianity with other cultic beliefs just as Balak's girls used sex to draw the men of Israel into the worship of other gods. Today, loose attitudes among professing Christians toward extra-marital sex is just Balaam's old trick once again.

Revelation 2:14 says "you have there some who hold the teaching of Balaam." The word "hold" in Greek, is κρατέω (krä-te'-ō) which means "to hold fast, possess, or be powerful in." [23] In other words, this letter was written to people in the church who said aloud that they were Christians, but instead, they "held fast" or "were strong in" the compromised teachings of Balaam. They were not sold out to following Jesus in their personal lives, particularly in the area of sexual activity.

In our sex-saturated culture today, nothing much has changed from the attitude that was popular in ancient Pergamum. There are plenty of people who profess to be Christians but mix a loose view of sexual morality and other false teachings into their "Christian identity." For example, David Ayers reports in his research on a 2018 General Social Survey (GSS) that found only 37% of fundamentalist adults said that sex outside marriage was "always wrong," and 41% said it was "not wrong at all." Among professing believers, 86% of females and 82% of males in the study reported having at least one opposite-sex partner since age 18, while 57% of females and 65% of males admitted to having three or more sexual partners. [24]

Christians will continue to wrestle with sexual temptation, particularly because pornography and loose attitudes toward sex are at the center of our culture. Jesus is not condemning Christians for falling into temptation or struggling to live according to His standards. He is condemning those who say that its perfectly acceptable as a Christian to be sexually active outside of marriage.

The Godly standard for sexual activity is it should only happen between a man and his wife in marriage and Christians should uphold this standard.

So-called leaders in Pergamum were also aggressive and authoritarian as well. Revelation 2:15 says,

> **Revelation 2:15 (NASB)**
> So you too, have some who in the same way hold to the teaching of the Nicolaitans.

There is some dispute about exactly who the Nicolaitans were, but the context of these verses is linked with sexual immorality. The word "Nicolaitan" comes from two Greek words: "to rule, subdue or destroy" and "the people" meaning quite literally "destruction of people." [25] They were spiritual leaders who exerted strong influence over the people. They were not servant leaders. They used their influence to manipulate people into accepting as normal what the Bible says is immoral and they created a sharp distinction between the people and clergy-leaders. Jesus taught that leaders in His church should not be oppressive authority figures over others. However, the Nicolaitans advanced the idea that the clergy had special knowledge only they could understand. Eventually, the rift between the clergy and common people in the congregation grew so large that clergy were often seen superstitiously as if they had special, mystical powers. There have been many examples over the centuries of clergy taking advantage of people, enriching themselves and even enslaving people who fear their supposed special connection with God. Jesus hates this teaching! He said in verse sixteen,

> **Revelation 2:16 (NASB)**
> Therefore repent; or else I am coming to you quickly, and I will wage war against them with the sword of My mouth.

The word "repent" is μετανοέω (me-tä-no-e'-ō) in Greek and it means "to change the mind." [26] Jesus did not say that everyone in Pergamum should feel guilty and ashamed, because repentance is not about trying to earn a way back into God's good graces. Repentance is recognizing what is wrong and changing direction. It is simple and powerful, but it takes faith to believe. This is the reason Jesus adds in verse seventeen,

> **Revelation 2:17 (NASB)**
> The one who has an ear, let him hear what the Spirit says to the churches. To the one who overcomes, I will give some of the hidden manna, and I will give him a white stone, and a new name written on the stone

which no one knows except the one who receives it.'

The person who overcomes the temptations to try to justify being sexually active outside of marriage and resists the temptation to rule over others in the church, will receive a great reward. Jesus knew it would be difficult to overcome those temptations for the people at Pergamum, just as He knows it will be a challenge today which is the reason the word "repent" is in a continuous sense. He is saying that repentance should be a constant, continuous changing of the mind from what the world says is acceptable to what God says is right.

Jesus says that if a repentant lifestyle becomes the believer's mindset, then in the end He will give the believer a white stone. In a first century court of law, a "not guilty" decision by the judge was sometimes made public when the judge gave the accused a white stone. Also, in ancient times, when a person had a major life change, his or her name was sometimes changed to commemorate the change. For example, Abram believed God's promise, so God changed his name to Abraham. Jacob had an intense encounter with God, so God changed Jacob's name to Israel. In the same way, Jesus promises that if Christians will live a repentant lifestyle, then on the last day He will give the repentant believer a white stone that says, "Not guilty." He will also give each believer a new name.

Christianity is a body of people who live a daily repentant lifestyle.

Each of the letters to the seven churches end with some variation of "let he who has an ear hear what the Spirit says to the churches." This means that what the Holy Spirit reveals to the church as a whole group is also relevant to the individual Christian. Each warning is intended for all Christians at all times. For example, after Pergamum, Jesus sends the next letter to the church at Thyatira. They were guilty of mixing the common beliefs of the local culture with the true teachings of Jesus and they illustrate why a standard for correct spiritual or moral teaching is so vital for both churches and individual Christians. Revelation 2:18 says,

> **Revelation 2:18 - 19 (NASB)**
> And to the angel of the church in Thyatira write: The Son of God, who has eyes like a flame of fire, and His feet are like burnished bronze, says this: [19] 'I know your deeds, and your love and faith and service and perseverance, and that your deeds of late are greater than at first.

The people in Thyatira could not hide the true character of their hearts from Jesus just because they were known for doing many good deeds. In the Bible, whenever flames, fire or burnished bronze are used symbolically, it generally pictures judgement or purification. Jesus was not going to ignore what was going on in Thyatira.

Jesus will confront compromised character in one way or another.

Thyatira was the smallest of the seven churches; yet it is the longest letter! The city itself was not large but it was famous for the dying of expensive purple, scarlet and red cloth. These specific colors were expensive because the dye used to produce these shades came from the tiny ocean dwelling *Murex brandaris* snail. [27] Each snail only provided one small drop of dye after being hand-harvested and shelled. One pound of this purple dye was worth three years' salary at the time. In Acts 16:14 we can read about Lydia who was a businesswoman from Thyatira who did business in purple cloth. This fabric and color was so valuable that only the very wealthy, the nobility or royalty could afford it.

Since Thyatira had a booming purple cloth business, other businesses flourished as well so the city was organized into trade guilds. A trade guild would be something like a modern-day labor union, such as the teacher's union or the electrician's union. Today's unions are typically intended to protect the interests of members, so a teacher's union is designed to help teachers negotiate salary, benefits and working conditions with employers. In ancient Thyatira, trade guilds organized members so that prices and competition were somewhat regulated, but just as some labor unions today can be corrupt, so were ancient trade guilds. Payoffs, bribes and unreasonable membership rules were the norm since each guild had its own rules and leadership. One of the common rules was that each guild would meet on a regular basis at the temple of the patron god of that trade. To be a member of the guild, each guild required dedication sacrifices and celebration feasts to the patron god.

The pressure to be part of these guilds was enormous. If a person was not a member, it was nearly impossible to do business in that trade. It was also a great temptation to be part of the guilds because many of the celebration feasts in the temples included the use of temple prostitutes. Between the pressure and the temptation there were professing Christians from various trades who tried to mix being a member of a guild and being a member of the church. Certain leaders in the church taught that this practice was not an issue, but Jesus says in verse nineteen,

> **Revelation 2:19 (NASB)**
> 'I know your deeds, and your love and faith and service and perseverance, and that your deeds of late are greater than at first. [20] But I have this against you, that you tolerate the woman Jezebel, who calls herself a prophetess, and she teaches and leads My bond-servants astray, so that they commit acts of immorality and eat things sacrificed to idols.

Jezebel may have been the name of an influential woman in the church at Thyatira. It could also be a symbolic reference to leaders who taught the same things as the Jezebel of the Old Testament, because calling someone a "Jezebel" in those days would be like calling someone a "Hitler" or a "Judas" today. In First Kings chapter sixteen, the Bible says that Jezebel was famous for bringing the occult worship of Baal, along with temple prostitution, into Israel. She was known to have been a ruthless occult leader who used her power to have her enemies murdered and she used sexual enticement to get her way. Since the trade guilds of Thyatira participated in the sexual occult worship of false gods, calling church leaders "Jezebels" was appropriate because they taught that trade-guild sexual-religious practices were perfectly acceptable for Christians in Thyatira.

Jesus uses the word "woman" in a singular tense, so it is likely that Thyatira had a single influential woman in the congregation who claimed to be a prophetess and since the church tolerated her teaching, she had some significant influence.

In general, there is nothing wrong with a prophet or prophetess, even in New Testament times. For example, there were legitimate prophetesses in the New Testament such as Anna in Luke 2:36 and the four daughters of Philip in Acts 21:9. The test of an authentic prophet or prophetess is that the message they give must always line up with Scripture. Truth is that thing which corresponds or matches the facts and, since God's revealed word is truth, a true teaching must match what has been revealed in Scripture. First Thessalonians 5:19 says,

> **First Thessalonians 5:19 - 22 (NASB)**
> Do not quench the Spirit, [20] do not utterly reject prophecies, [21] but examine everything; hold firmly to that which is good, [22] abstain from every form of evil.

Truth is that thing which corresponds to what is real, and God's Word is truth so a true teaching from God will always match with what the Bible teaches.

First Thessalonians 5:19-22, Deuteronomy 18:22, and other Scriptures show that the true prophetic voice of God is never contradictory. Any teaching that contradicts the teachings of the Bible is false, which is the reason Jezebel in Thyatira can only "call herself" a prophetess because Jesus is calling her out as a false prophetess.

Jezebel had a position of some perceived spiritual authority in the church, and she taught that being part of the pagan sacrificial system in the city was acceptable. She led men to join in these immoral practices and she participated in them herself. Based on what we know about the trade guilds, she probably reasoned that since idols were not real and people need to do business in order to make a living, it followed that there was nothing wrong with sacrificing to the patron gods of the guilds or participating in the temple prostitution rituals.

It seems likely that Jezebel used some variation of "everybody's doing it and you need to fit in" and dressed it up with some spiritual words but First Thessalonians 5:19-22 says we need to reject and expose any spiritual teaching that contradicts God's word. Jesus exposed her false teaching, but He still gave Jezebel a chance to repent. Revelation 2:21 says,

Revelation 2:21 - 23 (NASB)
I gave her time to repent, and she does not want to repent of her sexual immorality. [22] Behold, I will throw her on a bed of sickness, and those who commit adultery with her into great tribulation, unless they repent of her deeds. [23] And I will kill her children with

plague, and all the churches will know that I am He who searches the minds and hearts; and I will give to each one of you according to your deeds.

God will expose false teaching, but He still gives false teachers or those deceived by their teaching a chance to repent.

The word "immorality" in Greek is πορνεία (por-nā'-ä) [28] which means any sort of illicit sexual behavior such as adultery, fornication, homosexuality, and so on. These deeds all have spiritual and physical consequences; therefore, Jezebel and her followers were warned about sickness, tribulation, disease, and death. Today, some people argue that the ancients simply did not understand safe sexual practice and since we do understand these health issues today, this sort of warning is outdated. But if safe sex solved the sexually transmitted disease problem, it should not be a problem today – but it is!

The Bible teaches that sex was created by God, and He intended it to happen only between a man and his wife within the safety of a lifelong, committed marriage. Any sort of sex outside of heterosexual marriage is condemned by God, so spiritual leaders who teach that sex outside of marriage is acceptable, contradict God's Word. God's Word and common experience show that participating in immoral sexual deeds will devastate relationships and individual self-esteem leaving a person empty, emotionally shattered, and psychologically compromised.

God created sex so He has the right to make the rules about it.

> **Revelation 2:24 (NASB)**
> But I say to you, the rest who are in Thyatira, who do not hold this teaching, who have not known the deep things of Satan, as they call them...

Jezebel and her followers said their teachings about sex were "deep spiritual truth." Jesus called it Satanic! Any supposedly deep spiritual teaching that promotes immorality is false and demonic and the spirit of Jezebel's teaching is still with us in modern times. There are leaders today saying that since God is love, then any sort of "love" in a consensual relationship is acceptable to God. They say this is the deeper meaning of "love" and Christians today ought to reject old fashioned notions about sex because that puts a limit on "love." This modern twist is not a "deep spirituality;" it is just deep things of Satan all over again.

Jesus does not condemn people for fighting against sexual temptation and He does not reject people for failing in this area if they repent because He has given His own blood to wash away sin. Where Jesus has an issue is with false teachers who try to make sexual sin "no big deal." He says in Revelation 2:24,

> **Revelation 2:24 - 29 (NASB)**
> I place no other burden on you. [25] Nevertheless what you have, hold firmly until I come. [26] The one who overcomes, and

the one who keeps My deeds until the end, I will give him authority over the nations; ²⁷ and he shall rule them with a rod of iron, as the vessels of the potter are shattered, as I also have received authority from My Father; ²⁸ and I will give him the morning star. ²⁹ The one who has an ear, let him hear what the Spirit says to the churches.'

Jesus says that fighting off sexual temptation is burden enough since everyone struggles with temptation. There is no need to add shame or guilt because Jesus offers forgiveness to anyone who repents. The Lord wants us to hold fast to the truth of His mercy and forgiveness until He calls for us.

End of Days:
The Book of Revelation Explained

Chapter 5: Motivations!
Revelation 3 explained...

Jesus calls Christians to live in the world yet not be part of the world's culture. Everyday activities such as keeping a job, paying bills, and interacting with people are necessary, but how believers go about doing those things makes all the difference as far as God is concerned. In Revelation chapter three, the church at Sardis illustrates the difference between doing good things and doing things with the right heart.

In the first century, the citizens of Sardis had a general attitude of confidence. They were known to be pleasure-loving and focused on their own self-interests. Like other Roman cities in the first century, pagan temples filled with ritual drug use and temple prostitution infested the city. The general attitude of complacency came from the fact that the city was easily defended because of its position at the top of a high plateau. [29] The plateau is bordered on three sides by imposing, 1,500-foot-high cliffs, so the residents of Sardis felt secure.

1,200 years before the first century, Sardis had been the capital city of the kingdom of Lydia. Five major trade highways converged at Sardis pouring wealth and trade through its single entrance. Some scholars believe the legendary story of Midas and his magical golden touch came from Sardis since the city was known for accurately weighted gold coins. But the wealth, confidence and pride of Sardis led to its downfall.

Sardis was defeated twice in its history even though the city should have been easily defended. The ancient historian Herodotus recorded the first defeat of Sardis by the Persians in 549 B.C. He said that during the siege of the city a Persian scout watched a defending soldier on the Sardis city wall accidentally drop his helmet. Later in the day, around sunset, the Persian scout watched the defending solider creep down the cliff face to get his helmet using a secret goat path. Later that night the Persians used the goat path to send soldiers, single file, all the way to the top of the cliff and since the city believed no one could breach the cliffs, the Sardis defenders were asleep when the Persians arrived. The Persians simply walked in, opened the gates, and captured the city. Sardis was literally robbed of its freedom "like a thief in the night."

Christians must guard against the dangers of complacency.

Unfortunately for the people of Sardis, complacency became a city-wide attitude, and the city was taken a second time in 214-215 B.C. in the exact same way. They should have learned the lesson from their history but just like today, most people do not learn from the mistakes of the past. When Antiochus Epiphanes attacked in 214 B.C. there was no watch on the Sardis city walls at all. Revelation 3:1 reads,

Revelation 3:1 (NASB)
To the angel of the church in Sardis write: He who has the seven Spirits of God and the seven stars, says this: 'I know your deeds, that you have a name that you are alive, and yet you are dead.

The word "church" in Greek is ἐκκλησία (Ecclesia) and it means "The called-out ones." [30] This word can be applied to any group of people who are set apart from everyday life for some purpose so in Greek you could call a classic car convention "The Ecclesia of classic cars." A Christian Ecclesia (or church) is a group of people called out of everyday life to encourage and support one another to follow Jesus. Unfortunately, the word "church," in everyday usage, has now changed. Most people think of church as a religious institution or organization, but the original meaning of the word refers directly to the people. A church, therefore, should not be just a marketing organization for religious thought or a spiritually oriented business. Too often modern churches get so caught up in programs and presentations and this important point can be forgotten. That is exactly what happened in Sardis. They had a good reputation as an active and busy congregation, but Jesus said that just because they had a good reputation, that did not mean they were truly alive from His point of view. In fact, Jesus said they were really dead.

The word "dead" is νεκρός (ne-kro's) in Greek. [31] It means "lifeless" and it comes from the Greek word for corpse or dead body. Biologically, when a person dies, his or her body immediately begins to decay because all human beings have bacteria already at work inside the body. While humans are alive, bacteria either works to help digest food or it is being regulated by the immune system, but once death occurs, these bacteria begin to decompose the body from within.

There is a great deal of activity going on in a corpse, but no matter how many billions of bacteria are active and busy, the body is still dead. All the activity happening in a dead body is just the dead body feeding on itself. In the same way, the Christians in Sardis were very active, but their attitudes were self-focused, and the result was death, rot, and putrefaction.

The Biblical description of dead, self-focused religious actions is not limited to Sardis. Jesus said something similar to the Pharisees before they crucified Him. They also were very active and very religious. They excelled in wearing the right religious clothes so that everyone would be impressed. They used the right words and followed the right religious activities in public, but all their apparently good actions were really self-focused. Jesus said they were careful to give to the poor, but they were motivated to give because they wanted public praise for helping the poor. They prayed in public using beautiful, poetic, grand words but only so everyone would be impressed. They studied the Scriptures and even memorized entire books of the Bible, but their motivation was to make themselves look good or to gain wealth and power for themselves. This is why Jesus said to them in Matthew 23:27,

> **Matthew 23:27 (NLT)**
> What sorrow awaits you teachers of religious law and you Pharisees. Hypocrites! For you are like whitewashed tombs - beautiful on the outside but filled on the inside with dead people's bones and all sorts of impurity.

The Pharisees, like many people in the church at Sardis and as many professing Christians today, were not willing to risk their public reputations to be in real relationship with broken people. They would only "help" from a distance, making a big public announcement about their financial giving but never helping people in a personal, sacrificial way. Their actions were focused in on their own comfort and reputation and, since that was the case, their "busy-ness" was just like bacteria feeding on a corpse – active but dead. Jesus said in Revelation 3: 2-3,

> **Revelation 3:2 - 3 (NASB)**
> Be constantly alert, and strengthen the things that remain, which were about to die; for I have not found your deeds completed in the sight of My God. ³ So remember what you have received and heard; and keep it, and repent. Then if you are not alert, I will come like a thief, and you will not know at what hour I will come to you.

The people in Sardis were not in trouble with Jesus because they tolerated false teaching or immorality. Their problem was incomplete deeds, so Jesus tells them to remember what they had received and heard, but He is not talking about just remembering the central Christian message that Jesus died for the sins of the world because He uses the Greek word πῶς (po's) in this sentence. [32] Po's in this sentence and with this grammatical structure means "how or in what way," rather than "what" as in "what content" so a richer translation of this sentence could be, "Remember or take thought about the way or manner that you receive and hear this message I am giving you." In short, this is a personal, individual warning and they need to take it seriously. He told them that their works were incomplete and dead, but they can repent (turn around) from those dead deeds.

Jesus told them to wake up, be on guard, vigilant and watchful, something the ancient inhabitants of Sardis were known not to do. That complacent attitude had cost them their freedom as a city twice in their history so Christians in Sardis who knew this history should "receive, hear and keep" the message carefully.

In the same way, Christians should do good deeds but how those deeds are done makes all the difference. The Pharisees gave to the poor – but only to look good to others and feel good about themselves so their giving was incomplete. Christians today should take this warning to the people at Sardis to heart when thinking about participation in outreaches, mission trips, ministry volunteerism in the church or even participation in small groups or Bible studies. Jesus is saying Christians should be vigilant, on guard, and watchful that none of these things are done to feed the ego.

Christians are warned to watch out for self-absorbed motivations in doing good deeds.

The people of Sardis and the Pharisees were also known for complacency. They did some good deeds, but they were also so concerned about their reputation, personal safety, and comfort that they avoided doing good deeds that might be risky or unpleasant. Spiritual complacency grows when a Christian prioritizes personal comfort and safety over God's lead, but God sometimes calls people to abandon comfort and safety to advance His kingdom. Church history is filled with examples of men and women who started difficult ministries or went to the mission field and other risky adventures, all without any thought of being praised or admired or compensated. It requires consistent prayer and reflection to be vigilant against self-focused motivations and complacency. Revelation 3:4 says,

> **Revelation 3:4 - 6 (NASB)**
> But you have a few people in Sardis who have not soiled their garments; and they will walk with Me in white, for they are worthy. [5] The one who overcomes will be clothed the same way, in white garments; and I will not erase his name from the book of life, and I will confess his name before My Father and before His angels. [6] The one who has an ear, let him hear what the Spirit says to the churches.'

There were a few people in the congregation at Sardis who had not given in to complacency and self-focused deeds. They had trusted Jesus to wash away their sins and they were determined not to soil themselves by being self-absorbed. That determination was what allowed them to follow Jesus in a pure way. This sort of purity, symbolized by white garments, is not achieved just by doing good deeds. Instead, by being constantly watchful for the right heart to overcome complacency and self-focused motivations, their deeds can be pure and valuable in the Kingdom of God. Jesus promises that if we overcome self-focused motivations, it proves that our citizenship in heaven is genuine because our name will not be blotted out of the book of life. The people of Sardis would have understood this promise because in ancient Greece, city-states maintained a book of citizenship. Once a citizen was born into the state, his or her name was recorded just as the Bible says every human being who is conceived is written into the Book of Life. In ancient times, if a citizen was convicted and condemned for certain crimes, their name would be blotted out of the citizenship register. In the same way, if a person's sins are not washed away, once that person dies, his or her sins will condemn them, and their name will be blotted out of the Book of Life.

Christians must be continually watchful against any self-focused motivation in doing things for the kingdom of God.

Many Christians believe they are too small or insignificant to make much difference in the Kingdom of God. Most people are not going to lead armies or go off to the mission field and lead tens of thousands of people to Jesus. It's easy to think that not being Billy Graham or one of the apostles means we have very little to offer the Lord, but nothing could be further from the truth. God's willingness and ability to do amazing things with people that society thinks are unskilled or even useless is a truth we need to embrace today just as they needed to believe this in the church at Philadelphia.

The city of Philadelphia was founded on the edge of Roman and Greek civilization. Beyond the city's boundaries were tribes of people the Romans considered uncivilized barbarians. The tribes beyond the borders were wildly different than Greek-influenced cultures in the Roman Empire. The barbarian tribes, for the most part, did not live in settled cities or villages, their languages were unattractive to Roman ears, and their choice of food, clothing, and customs were different. They were also known to occasionally dash into a Roman village on a sudden raid only to disappear into the wild lands beyond the borders.

The city of Philadelphia was founded by Attalus in the second century B.C. specifically to try and spread Greek civilization to the barbarian tribes. Over the centuries, Philadelphia may or may not have tempted uncivilized tribes to try and follow Greek and Roman civilized life, but the city did become the guardian of the main trade route from Europe to eastern markets. It was the gateway on the edge of the empire allowing trade and wealth to pour in from barbarian lands. Jesus spoke to the church at Philadelphia in Revelation 3:7 where He said,

Revelation 3:7 (NASB)
And to the angel of the church in Philadelphia write: He who is holy, who is

true, who has the key of David, who opens and no one will shut, and who shuts and no one opens, says this:

The key to understanding Revelation is seeing how deeply rooted it is in the Old Testament. The opening of this refers to Isaiah 22:22 which reads,

Isaiah 22:22 (NASB)
Then I will set the key of the house of David on his shoulder, When he opens no one will shut, When he shuts no one will open.

When Isaiah chapter 22:22 was written, a high official named Shebna had the "key of David" in his control. Shebna had a government position as the chief-steward of the royal house of David. His job was something like the American Secretary of State today. As chief steward, Shebna represented the government of Judah to the rest of the world, so it was a position of honor and authority. Unfortunately, Shebna was corrupt and obsessive about his own self-interest rather than the interest of the country. Since Shebna's personal comfort was more important to him than having integrity in his job, Isaiah explained in chapter twenty-two that God was removing him from his office and replacing him with a man named Eliakim. According to Isaiah, Eliakim's heart was all about God and doing things right in God's sight, so Eliakim deserved the office of chief-steward.

In Isaiah's time, the chief-steward carried a large master-key to the palace, attached by a colorful cord to his shoulder, as a symbol of his authority. This key meant he had the right to open or shut access to the king. The chief-steward was able to open up opportunity and government support or resources to anyone he wanted to in the name of the king.

Revelation 3:7 says Jesus has the same kind of authority that Eliakim had in the days of Isaiah. Jesus has ultimate authority to open or shut opportunity and resources from God just as the chief-steward did for the house of David. Revelation 1:8 says Jesus also has the keys of Hades and death itself so, He can also open and shut life and death itself.

Jesus has ultimate authority to grant access to God and to eternal life.

Revelation 3:8 (NASB)
'I know your deeds. Behold, I have put before you an open door which no one can shut, because you have a little power, and have kept My word, and have not denied My name.

The word "little" in Greek is μικρός (me-kro's) which means "small" or "little" but not in the sense of an amount. [33] Instead, this word is about rank or significance. The people in Philadelphia thought they were insignificant in the grand scheme of the Kingdom of God because they only had, in their view, a "little power" but in the Lord's view they had kept His Word and had not denied His name. That was enough for Jesus to open a door of opportunity to the resources and blessings of God that no one could shut, and Jesus had the authority to do that for them despite how they thought about themselves.

A person does not need to be "important" in the eyes of others to be used by God for something eternally valuable.

As Christians, we often think we are too weak to be used by God for anything significant, but God looks at the heart. Jesus looks for a heart willing to keep His Word because He does not need us to be perfect people before He is willing to strengthen us and use our lives to advance His kingdom. A "little" strength, combined with a willing heart, is all that God needs to help believers succeed. Second Corinthians 12:9-10 puts it this way,

> **Second Corinthians 12:9 - 10 (NLT)**
> ..."My grace is all you need. My power works best in weakness." So now I am glad to boast about my weaknesses, so that the power of Christ can work through me. [10] That's why I take pleasure in my weaknesses, and in the insults, hardships, persecutions, and troubles that I suffer for Christ. For when I am weak, then I am strong.

Paul is not saying we now have a license to sin because we are Christians. No - grace is undeserved favor, forgiveness, and help so when we are weak and give into temptation, we can confess that sin to the Lord and turn away from it (1 John 1:9). Since we follow this lifestyle of repentant faith in Him, Jesus forgives us. Our faith in His forgiveness gives us new hope to carry on living for Jesus another day so our failure and weakness in life does not dominate our lives. In this way, our weakness drives us to cling to Him more and more so sin that normally would lead to eternal death is short-circuited.

> **Revelation 3:9 (NASB)**
> Behold, I will cause those of the synagogue of Satan, who say that they are Jews and are not, but lie - I will make them come and bow down at your feet and make them know that I have loved you.

Scholars are not certain what it means that there were people falsely claiming to be Jewish in the congregation at Philadelphia. It could mean they were claiming to be Jewish because they thought this would give them a greater status in the church than non-Jewish Christians. Another possibility is that there were people claiming to be Jews living in the area who were critics of the church, but they were not truly living as Jews. But it seems most likely there were people in that congregation who followed some variety of "replacement" teaching.

In the first century, and even today, there are people who think that non-Jewish Christians "replace" ethnic Jewish people as the "new" people of God, but any variation on this sort of replacement teaching is not Biblically sound. The Jewish people will always be God's chosen people. Christians are added into the chosen people of God, but non-Jewish Christians will never replace the Jews. God has a plan for the Jewish people as an ethnic group, and they will all eventually turn to Jesus as Messiah.

In fact, the apostle Paul warns Christians not to think of themselves as superior even to unbelieving Jews. He said that Gentile Christians are like wild olive branches being grafted in or surgically added into a cultivated olive tree. Romans 11:17 says,

> **Romans 11:17 - 21 (NASB)**
> But if some of the branches were broken off, and you, being a wild olive, were grafted in among them and became partaker with them of the rich root of the olive tree, [18] do not be arrogant toward the branches; but if you are arrogant, remember that it is not you who supports the root, but the root supports you. [19] You will say then, "Branches were broken off so that I might be grafted in." [20] Quite right, they were broken off for their unbelief, but you stand by your faith. Do not be conceited, but fear; [21] for if God did not spare the natural branches, He will not spare you, either.

Gentile Christians do not replace Jewish people. God has a plan for ethnic Jews and the nation of Israel, and the book of Revelation explains how that plan will unfold.

People falsely claiming to be the people of God has not gone away. Some people today claim to be Christians but explain away or ignore Biblical teaching, especially the Bible's teaching about morality and lifestyles. They are also dishonest about why the Bible is reliable and trustworthy because they look for ways to cast doubt on Biblical authors and historical events such as Noah's Flood, creation in six days and so on. Just as it was in the days of the church at Philadelphia, they claim to be Christians, but accept as acceptable what God says is morally wrong, but Jesus promised the people in Philadelphia that one day these sorts of people will acknowledge that the "literalists" were right. This promise remains in effect for us today. Revelation 3:10 says,

> **Revelation 3:10 - 11 (NASB)**
> Because you have kept the word of My perseverance, I also will keep you from the hour of testing, that hour which is about to come upon the whole world, to test those who dwell on the earth. [11] I am coming quickly;

Since this "hour of testing" that will come upon the whole world has not happened yet, this promise remains in effect for us today. Jesus promises that if we remain loyal to Him and hold fast to the teachings of His Word, we will not go through the Great Tribulation. If we remain unashamed of the message of Jesus and do not try and twist it to make it more acceptable to people today, then we will be taken out of the world before it begins. Since the Rapture of the church can happen at any moment, Revelation 3:11 says,

> **Revelation 3:11b - 13 (NASB)**
> ...hold firmly to what you have, so that no one will take your crown. [12] The one who overcomes, I will make him a pillar in the temple of My God, and he will not go out from it anymore; and I will write on him the name of My God, and the name of the city

of My God, the new Jerusalem, which comes down out of heaven from My God, and My new name. [13] The one who has an ear, let him hear what the Spirit says to the churches.'

"Hold firmly" in Greek is κρατέω (krä-te'-o) which means "to be strong, mighty, or to prevail." [34] Just like believers in the church at Philadelphia, Christians today need to take the opportunity to study the Word seriously, be aggressive in outreach to unbelievers and continue to follow Jesus as our lifestyle, day-in and day-out. It is easy to get burnt-out as a believer and there is constant temptation to think it must be "me time" now after years of serving and striving to live for the Lord. Many Christians easily feel discouraged when positive results from our prayers do not happen right away and it is tempting to think there is little point in continuing to try and live the Christian life when we make mistakes, but Jesus wants us to hold fast to what we have, even if it seems like so little.

The people in Philadelphia obviously felt worn down but Jesus wanted them to hold fast, and He is saying the same thing to us today. We need to overcome our fears of failure because He promises to wash our sins away. We need to leave our inadequacies behind and hold fast to what we believe because we only need a little strength and a lot of Jesus to overcome. If we do overcome, Jesus promises to give us a monument to celebrate our faith, a pillar with our names written on it and that is the key to this part of Revelation.

End of Days:
The Book of Revelation Explained

Chapter 6: What identity will you choose?
Revelation 3: 14-22 explained...

There will always be unanswered questions about the Bible, about the nature of God and why things happen to us in this life, but there is also more than enough evidence for anyone to trust that Jesus is the living God. He stands at the door of everyone's life inviting every person to abandon an empty existence and receive the abundant, fulfilling life people are looking for. Revelation 3:14 says,

> **Revelation 3:14 - 15 (NASB)**
> To the angel of the church in Laodicea write: The Amen, the faithful and true Witness, the Beginning of the creation of God, says this: [15] 'I know your deeds, that you are neither cold nor hot; I wish that you were cold or hot.

The city of Laodicea was in southwestern Turkey. It was famous in ancient times for the manufacture of magnificent wool overcoats made from a breed of locally farmed sheep that had natural, coal-black wool that did not need to be dyed. The city was also well-known for a popular eye medicine sold throughout the Roman Empire.

From these industries, among others, the city was well-known and so much wealth flowed through its streets that the city built, owned, and operated its own mint for casting gold and silver coins. The city's wealth saturated the people's thinking with an attitude of self-sufficiency and indifference that was so widespread that city authorities were expected to bribe any group that threatened the city rather than defend it militarily.

Laodicea's name is directly related to the Greek word Laodikea, which means "rule of the people." Church history shows that the Laodicean believers were more focused on what was popular rather than teaching Biblical truth. This problem is the theme of the whole letter.

The city of Laodicea also had a public water utility problem. There were two sources of fresh water piped into the city. One source was a hot spring, the other a cold spring and since both used pipes rather than aqueducts to move the water into town, the result was a public water supply that was tepid or lukewarm. Jesus said that, like the city water supply, believers in Laodicea were not really hot and not really cold when it came to a commitment to Him. They said they were believers, but they did not follow His command authentically in their day-to-day lives.

<u>Lukewarm "Christians" profess to be believers, but do not live out their faith authentically.</u>

Jesus also said He is "the Beginning of the creation of God," using the Greek word ἀρχή (är-kha') which means "the origin of." [35] In other words, Jesus is not "the first thing created" but He is "the origin of" everything in creation. He is "the Beginner," that is "the Starter" or "Designer" or "Maker" of everything that has ever existed in the history of the universe. Since He is the "Beginning of the creation of God" then whatever He says is absolute truth.

Jesus is also the "Amen, the faithful and true witness." Amen means "that's the truth" or "so be it," so, Jesus only speaks truth, and He speaks it faithfully. [36] He made these points at the start because His assessment of their deeds in Laodicea was the truth regardless of what they thought of themselves. The Laodiceans did some good deeds, they thought they had a nice church and were a benefit to the local community, but they apparently shared the local attitude of self-righteousness and "go along to get along" also. They were successful in their community, but Jesus said they were not fully committed to Him, so their "success" did not matter. In Revelation 3:16, Jesus says,

Revelation 3:16 (NASB)
So because you are lukewarm, and neither hot nor cold, I will spit you out of My mouth.

The people in Laodicea had no clarity about what they stood for. They had just enough knowledge of Jesus to call themselves Christian, but they held onto too much of what the world offered to be full followers of Jesus. This is true today also. Some people know enough about what Jesus taught to restrain themselves from fully jumping into the world's way of life, but they are unhappy just dabbling in the world too. Some people are committed in their intellectual belief that God exists, the Bible is trustworthy, and Jesus rose from the dead, but they do not completely sell out to living for Jesus. Being uncommitted makes them unbalanced and since the uncommitted will not admit that their problem is commitment in the first place, they are miserable, not being fully at home in either the world or the church.

Jesus makes it graphically clear what He thinks of such a tepid commitment to following Him. He says He will spit the uncommitted "believer" out and He uses the nasty Greek word ἐμέω (e-me'-o) to describe how He feels. [37] This word means "to vomit or violently expel" which is a scary, unpleasant, and foul experience but Jesus is saying He would rather vomit like that voluntarily than put up with an uncommitted attitude. Jesus says in verse seventeen,

> **Revelation 3:17 (NASB)**
> Because you say, "I am rich, and have become wealthy, and have no need of anything," and you do not know that you are wretched, miserable, poor, blind, and naked...

It made Jesus sick to know how much they proclaimed in public how supposedly well they were doing when secretly they were miserable. They were hiding from the truth and many Christians still do this today. Many people honestly think that if they only have certain physical needs met, that is, if they had "need of nothing," then they would finally feel the happiness and fulfillment they are missing. The problem with this unbiblical thinking is that it is based on believing that the problems in life all come from the outside, so people think "outside" blessings must be the solution. But "outside" blessings, such as a better job or a new romantic relationship, solve nothing if a person has an "inside-the-heart" problem. Everyone who thinks along these lines is perpetually miserable because once the "better" situation comes along, new problems create similar discontent and the shallow, uncommitted heart is forever unsatisfied. These people are always self-focused, ungrateful, and endlessly finding new ways to claim "victimhood." But there is a powerful spiritual truth taught from one end of the Bible to the other, and that is that no exterior achievement or activity will ever give the fulfillment people are looking for.

Only an interior, heart-level, decision to be committed to living for Jesus will ever satisfy.

The Laodicean people were professing Christians, they practiced a form of godliness, appeared successful on the outside and there is no evidence in historical records of any persecution of this church. They likely had good jobs, a nice church, and reasonably good relations with the locals, but underneath it all there was a wretchedness they would not admit. They did not want to voice out loud that there was no satisfaction in their hearts, but they were blind to the true cause. Fortunately, Jesus explained the problem in Revelation 3:18.

Revelation 3:18 (NASB)
I advise you to buy from Me gold refined by fire so that you may become rich, and white garments so that you may clothe yourself, and that the shame of your nakedness will not be revealed; and eye salve to anoint your eyes so that you may see.

The Laodiceans self-focused motivations for their actions lurked underneath the surface. Those motivations were like an impurity mixed into a precious metal such as gold. This is the reason the Lord speaks symbolically about buying pure gold without impurities from Him. But how can anyone truly buy anything from God? Buying something is the process by which a buyer gives something that a seller values, such as money, in exchange for something the seller has that the buyer wants. So, what could anyone give to God that He does not already own?

To understand the answer, it is important to see that this verse about Jesus encouraging the Laodiceans to buy gold from Him is an example of the Revelation Refrain where God uses a symbol to give the listener a deeper sense of what He means. In this case, since buying something requires a sacrifice on the part of the buyer, and God already owns everything, the only thing anyone can sacrifice to God is what God has already given. In our case, God has given human beings free will and the ability to use that free will in this life. Everyone has the ability and the opportunity to freely sacrifice self-comfort and self-direction to submit to Jesus in relationship from the heart. This sort of sacrifice, that is, "buying" from God, is deeper than simple religious observance because we do not naturally want to use our freewill to buy anything other than whatever interests our desires in the moment. To sacrifice our freewill and follow the Lord's lifestyle confronts our natural self-absorbed nature and that sort of confrontation can feel like a fire in the heart. By accepting this "fire," Jesus burns away at self-centeredness until we become rich in humility, self-sacrifice, and Godliness.

When the Bible uses gold symbolically it usually refers to good deeds. Since gold has great value, refined gold without impurities refers to actions that are valuable, costly, tested and found to be pure. It is a costly decision to pursue a full commitment to Jesus in every area of your life and to do this for no other reason than because God is worthy of a total commitment. If your motivation to follow Jesus is because you want a blessing or a benefit from Him, then your motivations are mixed. All Christians are going to occasionally struggle with mixed motivations, but the more you choose to live for Jesus simply because He is worthy of your total devotion, the more these mixed motivations will be burned away. In Matthew 16:25, Jesus said "For whoever wants to save his life will lose it; but whoever loses his life for My sake will find it." He means that by holding onto your self-interest in life, you just lose your life in the end, but if you pursue a full commitment to living for the Lord, which is like "losing" your self-interests or your "life," then you will find the life you are looking for.

White garments in Scripture are usually a symbol of holiness and eye salve or eye medication is symbolic of seeing things clearly. Refined gold, holy living and clearly seeing what is valuable in life are all pictures of someone pursuing a full commitment to Jesus. Today, that sort of commitment may mean sacrificing a friendship that is influencing or pressuring you into participating in worldly things. It may mean taking opportunities that come your way to do things for the Lord that cost your comfort or are a real sacrifice to do. The more you live for Jesus rather than yourself, the more your life gains spiritual gold, and that sort of gold has an eternal reward. First Corinthians 3:11 says,

> **First Corinthians 3:11 - 13 (NLT)**
> For no one can lay any foundation other than the one we already have - Jesus Christ. [12] Anyone who builds on that foundation may use a variety of materials - gold, silver, jewels, wood, hay, or straw. [13] But on the judgement day, fire will reveal what kind of work each builder has done. The fire will show if a person's work has any value.

Jesus wants people to freely commit to Him from the heart. He will allow discipline and challenge to come into even a lukewarm believer's life in order to light a fire toward commitment. He says in Revelation 3:19,

> **Revelation 3:19 - 22 (NASB)**
> I correct and discipline everyone I love. So be diligent and turn from your indifference. [20] "Look! I stand at the door and knock. If you hear my voice and open the door, I will come in, and we will share a meal together as friends. [21] Those who are victorious will

sit with me on my throne, just as I was victorious and sat with my Father on his throne. ²² "Anyone with ears to hear must listen to the Spirit and understand what he is saying to the churches."

The word "love" in Revelation 3:19 is φιλέω (fe-le'-o) in Greek and it means "to be fond of or to like." ³⁸ So, Jesus is speaking to lukewarm people and saying, "Listen! I like you kid, so sell out. I'm standing on the outside of your life – let me in! Sell out! Decide to be all in! Make this decision from your heart and we will be friends. In fact, if you overcome the lukewarm attitude, you will someday be part of my authority over the nations. In the coming kingdom, I will let you be part of my administration but if you won't, I'll vomit you out."

Jesus still calls to everyone to turn around from half-hearted to all-in because if you're all in, God will fill you with life and joy and power and peace of mind!

End of Days:
The Book of Revelation Explained

Chapter 7: Revelation is about the Jewish people!
Revelation's connection to Daniel explained...

Some modern interpretations of Revelation attempt to interpret it through the lens of current events as they relate to America or Europe or modern Christians, but Revelation is all about the Jewish people and the nation of Israel. While the first three chapters of Revelation are about Christians in the first century and the church age since, the book is primarily about how God will fulfill the promises He has made to the Jewish people. This means that to understand Revelation, Christians must recognize Jewish references, symbols and meaning that come from the Old Testament and take care to interpret the Scripture consistently and carefully.

The first rule of Biblical interpretation, sometimes called the "Golden rule," is "When the plain sense of Scripture makes common sense, look for no other sense." A second rule is that whenever symbols are used in Scripture, look to the text itself or to a cross-reference from another passage of Scripture for an explanation.

Prophecy in the Bible is generally not completely literal, nor is everything in prophecy symbolic. It takes careful study to see how symbols link to the physical. It is also valuable to remember that the prophets in ancient times, including John, were given insight into the future in a way similar to how we might look across the top of a distant mountain range on a cloudy day. When looking to a mountain range from a distance, only the peaks may be clearly visible rather than the valleys in between the peaks. In the same way, the prophets saw and wrote down "peak-events." The distances in time or other events between these peaks were not always clear to them.

Revelation 1:19, for example, provides a basic "peak" as an outline for the whole book. Chapter one reveals the power and position of the risen Lord Jesus, and chapters two and three are a description of seven first century church congregations. These seven churches may reveal seven general periods during the church age, but they may also simply reveal problems any church should beware of throughout the church age. Chapters three through twenty-two, however, are about the future. By missing the connection between Revelation and the Old Testament, many Christians have a distorted view of the meaning of Revelation.

Misunderstanding Scripture because it is seen through a modern lens is nothing new. First century Jews did the same thing. They knew the Old Testament prophesied that a savior would come to make things right in the world and bring blessing to the Jewish people. But in the first century, the popular view of those Old Testament prophecies was that this great king, the Messiah, would defeat the Romans because Rome was the political problem in that day. This shows the danger of interpreting Scripture thorough the lens of one's own time and culture because when Jesus came on the scene in the first century, He fulfilled the Old Testament prophecies and He proved who He was through miracles the prophets said He would perform - but the people had interpreted the prophecies of the Messiah through the political and military situation of their time period. Since Jesus did not fulfill those popular anti-Roman expectations, that is one reason He was rejected. Many first century Jews were not open to the fact that prophecies about the Messiah describe Him at two different times. For example, Isaiah 61:1 was a popular prophecy in the first century because of the second half of verse two but there are two parts to the prophecy corresponding with the two different times Messiah will come to earth. First century Jews overlooked this fact.

Jesus Himself quoted Isaiah 61 in Luke 4:22 and said the verse was fulfilled. Isaiah 61:1 reads,

Isaiah 61:1 - 6 (NASB)
The Spirit of the Lord God is upon me, Because the Lord anointed me, To bring good news to the humble; He has sent me to bind up the brokenhearted, To proclaim release to captives, And freedom to prisoners; [2] To proclaim the favorable year of the Lord, And the day of vengeance of our God; To comfort all who mourn, [3] To grant those who mourn in Zion, Giving them a garland instead of ashes, The oil of gladness instead of mourning, The cloak of praise instead of a disheartened spirit. So they will be called oaks of righteousness, The

planting of the Lord, that He may be glorified. ⁴ Then they will rebuild the ancient ruins, They will raise up the former devastations; And they will repair the ruined cities, The desolations of many generations. ⁵ Strangers will stand and pasture your flocks, And foreigners will be your farmers and your vinedressers. ⁶ But you will be called the priests of the Lord; You will be spoken of as ministers of our God. You will eat the wealth of nations, And you will boast in their riches.

Since the Jewish people in the first century were under Roman oppression, the idea that the coming Messiah would bring about vengeance and rebuild their nation was very appealing. Scriptures that spoke of the Jewish people being served by others and eating the wealth of nations was inspiring when the people at that time had little security or resources and felt forced to serve the Roman Empire. Another issue that may have contributed to this interpretation is the fact there was no verse numbering system in the Scripture at that time. Without the verse divisions and numbers as we have them today, and no punctuation such as commas and periods in the original text either, it was easy to misunderstand that there were two distinct parts to what the prophet was saying. Isaiah sixty-one describes two different times in the coming Messiah's career, a point Jesus makes in Luke 4:22 when he only quotes a part of Isaiah 61 saying, "Today this Scripture has been fulfilled in your hearing."

Jesus stopped reading half-way through Isaiah 61:2 because there is an important word in verse two and that is the connect word "and." The word "and" shows the distinction between the first coming of the Messiah and the second coming. Jesus was saying that the first part of this passage was being fulfilled by Him at that moment, but the second part of the verse – the "good part" that talks about the day of vengeance of God and the rebuilding to blessing and glory of the Jewish nation - is something that comes later at His second coming. This is so because many Old Testament Scriptures describe the career of the Messiah in two different parts. It is as if the Messiah is both a suffering servant and a conquering, victorious, military leader but this is not a contradiction because He is to come to the earth twice. His first coming is to offer a spiritual renewal and a spiritual kingdom to the people that will be rejected, there will be a gap in time and at His second coming He will bring a physical renewal and a physical kingdom to His people.

The fact that the Messiah is to come twice was not something that people under Roman oppression in the first century wanted to hear. They wanted the Messiah to destroy Rome, so it was insulting to them to think they might need forgiveness and a change of heart before the Messiah would take over and rule from Jerusalem. Luke 4:28 says,

> **Luke 4:28 - 30 (NASB)**
> And all the people in the synagogue were filled with rage as they heard these things; [29] and they got up and drove Him out of the city, and brought Him to the crest of the hill on which their city had been built, so that they could throw Him down from the cliff.

³⁰ But He passed through their midst and went on His way.

Their rage at having a cherished interpretation of Scripture challenged shows why a spiritual renewal is something people desperately need. Many times, we wish and pray for a solution to a physical problem but do not realize the need for a spiritual, heart-change. God knows that just solving a political or financial or health problem does not change the heart. This is the reason Messiah Jesus came to offer a spiritual kingdom first.

The history of the Jewish people illustrates perfectly why people generally need a spiritual, "heart" solution before a physical solution. After the Jewish people were rescued from Egypt and their physical problem of oppression was solved, they nearly immediately rebelled against God. Over and over, even after miracles at the Red Sea, after pillars of fire in the sky, after water miraculously delivered in the desert and even after bread from heaven appeared every morning on the ground, they still rebelled, they still worshipped other gods, and they still grumbled and complained at nearly every turn in the trail. This was because they had a heart problem, not a physical problem.

Jesus offered a heart renewal, and not the vengeance part of Isaiah 61 first, so He was rejected. God knew the people would have a heart problem and that they would reject the Messiah at His first coming and this is the reason the Old Testament says there will be a gap in time between the first coming and the second. This gap in time is "the church age" and it is prophesied in the Old

Testament as well as the New. Daniel 9:24, for example, says,

> **Daniel 9:24 - 26 (NASB)**
> Seventy weeks have been decreed for your people and your holy city, to finish the wrongdoing, to make an end of sin, to make atonement for guilt, to bring in everlasting righteousness, to seal up vision and prophecy, and to anoint the Most Holy Place. **25** So you are to know and discern that from the issuing of a decree to restore and rebuild Jerusalem until Messiah the Prince there will be seven weeks and sixty-two weeks; it will be built again, with plaza and moat, even in times of distress. **26** Then after the sixty-two weeks the Messiah will be cut off and have nothing, and the people of the prince who is to come will destroy the city and the sanctuary. And its end will come with a flood; even to the end there will be war; desolations are determined.

Based on the context of Daniel 9:24, the "weeks" mentioned are "weeks of years," that is, sets of seven years and this prophecy has been literally fulfilled in history. On March 5, 444 B.C., about a hundred years after Daniel wrote these words, King Artaxerxes Longimanus ruled that Nehemiah should return to Jerusalem to restore and rebuild its walls, just as it says in Daniel chapter nine. This means there should have been 173,880 days from Artaxerxes decree until "Messiah the prince" would come into Jerusalem. We know this because the Jewish people in the fifth century B.C. counted 360 days as one year and sixty-nine weeks of 360-day years is 483 years or 173,880 days. Daniel 9:24 – 26 says that the entire program until the end of the age will be seventy sets of seven years, not sixty-nine, but there will be gap between the sixty-ninth set of seven years and the final seventieth set of seven years. History shows that from Artaxerxes' decree until the day when Jesus the Messiah entered Jerusalem on a donkey with people shouting, "Hosanna to the Son of David; Blessed is the One who comes in the name of the Lord; Hosanna in the highest!" described in Matthew 21:9 there were exactly 173,880 days – just as Daniel prophesied.

Daniel prophesied that the "end will come with a flood" at some point after the Messiah "will be cut off and have nothing." The time when Messiah is "cut off" is the gap between the sixty-ninth set of seven years and the final seventieth set of years. We know from history that just a few days after Jesus rode into Jerusalem to the cheers of the people, he was rejected by the religious leaders. They stirred up the crowd to call for His crucifixion and His death on the cross "cut Him off" from the land of the living just as Daniel prophesied. But Jesus rose again from the dead and after His resurrection, He told His disciples He was going away until a set time when He would come to the earth a second time. The Lord's time in heaven and the church age is the gap. Daniel obviously did not know how long this gap would last but as of today, it has lasted for about 2,000 years. The book of Revelation gives greater detail to what will happen during the seventieth week. Daniel 9:26 says,

Daniel 9:26b - 27 (NASB)
...and the people of the prince who is to come will destroy the city and the sanctuary. And its end will come with a flood; even to the end there will be war; desolations are determined. ²⁷ And he will confirm a covenant with the many for one week, but in the middle of the week he will put a stop to sacrifice and grain offering; and on the wing of abominations will come the one who makes desolate, until a complete destruction, one that is decreed, gushes forth on the one who makes desolate.

The book of Revelation is focused on the Jewish people and nation so it only makes sense as it fits into Old Testament prophecies.

The book of Revelation is, however, primarily a vision or a dream so sometimes the description of events is not necessarily sequential where one event directly follows the last event described. In fact, there are examples of "interludes" between events and "telescope events" in Revelation. Telescope events are descriptions of events in greater detail, and it is sometimes unclear how much time may pass between one event and another. So, since the Rapture could happen at any time, we must be prepared to potentially face trouble in this life just as Christians did in the first century. There are popular Christian preachers today who teach that God only wants to bless Christians. They teach that if we somehow have enough faith, we will not have to deal with difficult times, but this teaching is false. Jesus said in John 16:33,

John 16:33 (NASB)
These things I have spoken to you so that in Me you may have peace. In the world you have tribulation but take courage; I have overcome the world.

The prophet Daniel gave us a preview of the future in Daniel chapter two and chapter seven. This outline lays out the future from Daniel's time until the Messiah returns a second time to set up His kingdom. The book of Revelation is, more or less, an "interlude" or "telescope" prophecy that fits into Daniel.

Daniel chapter two and Daniel chapter seven are different visions, but the meaning of both is the same. Daniel chapter seven simply adds more detail to Daniel chapter two, but both visions say there will be four Gentile (non-Jewish) systems of government that will have direct influence or rule over the nation of Israel before the Messiah returns a second time. Most scholars believe these kingdoms begin with Babylon, then the Medo-Persian empire, the Greek Empire and the Roman empire. Daniel's vision also shows that the fourth government will unfold in several stages. Daniel's vision in chapter two is about King Nebuchadnezzar's dream which God said was about the future. Daniel 2:31 says,

Daniel 2:31 – 38 (NASB)
"You, O king, were looking and behold, there was a single great statue; that statue, which was large and of extraordinary splendor, was standing in front of you, and its appearance was awesome. ³² The head of

that statue was made of fine gold, its breast and its arms of silver, its belly and its thighs of bronze, [33] its legs of iron, its feet partly of iron and partly of clay. [34] You continued looking until a stone was cut out without hands, and it struck the statue on its feet of iron and clay and crushed them. [35] Then the iron, the clay, the bronze, the silver and the gold were crushed all at the same time and became like chaff from the summer threshing floors; and the wind carried them away so that not a trace of them was found. But the stone that struck the statue became a great mountain and filled the whole earth. [36] "This was the dream; now we will tell its interpretation before the king. [37] You, O king, are the king of kings, to whom the God of heaven has given the kingdom, the power, the strength and the glory; [38] and wherever the sons of men dwell, or the beasts of the field, or the birds of the sky, He has given them into your hand and has caused you to rule over them all. You are the head of gold.

Daniel told Nebuchadnezzar that "he" was the head of gold. This means that the kind of political, government system Nebuchadnezzar represented, not just the king himself, is what the dream was about. The Scripture says each new metal in the image or statue from Nebuchadnezzar's dream was a "kingdom" rather than just a "king." This means that each metal in the image represents a different kind of kingdom, that is, a different kind of political, government system. Dr. Fruchtenbaum points out that each of these metals is stronger than the one before, but less valuable, so the systems of government that each Gentile empire represents will, as Dr. Fruchtenbaum says,

> ...decrease the character of authority and rule: Babylon was an absolute monarchy with the monarch above the law; with Media-Persia the monarch was not above the law and he did not have the authority to change his own decrees; the Hellenic kings had no dynastic or royal right to rule, and ruled by force of conquest and personal gifts; the Roman imperialism was a republic which degenerated into mob rule merging with the imperial form of government. [39]

Daniel told Nebuchadnezzar that the gold head represented Babylon. Babylon was a pure monarchy, and the king organized the areas or provinces through leaders appointed directly by the king. These leaders were loyal to the king alone and any expansion of the kingdom was done by the king or his generals through military conquest.

The silver breast and arms represented the kingdom of the Medes and Persians, a kingdom of two connected people groups allied together (the Medes and the Persians) just as there are two arms on the image. Daniel 7:5, however, says that this kingdom was also like a lopsided bear, because while the Medes and Persians were fierce like a bear, they were also lopsided because the Persians dominated the Medes in the alliance. They were also unbalanced because the rule of law was more powerful than the king as we can see from the story of Daniel. When Daniel was condemned to the lion's den by the king's foolish decree, the king himself could not get Daniel out of trouble because he could not override his own decrees once they were put into writing – a truly lopsided situation between the power of the king and the power of Mede-Persian law. This kind of government was spread by conquest and wars led by the king or his generals and governed by dividing up the kingdom into provinces overseen by governors appointed directly by the king.

The belly and thighs of bronze represent the Greek empire, a kingdom divided between east and west just as there are two thighs on the image, but the vision in Daniel 7:6 says this empire is as swift as a leopard with four wings. This is because the Greek empire rose swiftly, in just a few years, under the conquest led by Alexander the Great but at his death the kingdom was divided into four "wings," or four districts, under the rule of Alexander's four generals. The Greek kind of government installed weaker vassal kings from each region and these local leaders often rebelled.

The fourth kingdom is the Roman Empire. The Romans ruled their empire with an iron fist just like the beast in Daniel chapter seven has teeth of iron. The Roman Empire was also divided between east and west just as the statue in Daniel chapter two had two legs of iron. The Romans are known from history for crushing all opposition. The Roman peace (called the Pax Romana) was kept for centuries because Rome smashed any opposition. They had "legs of iron" as it says in Daniel 2:33.

The Roman Empire was imperialist in nature. This means they not only crushed opposition militarily as they expanded their rule, but they also used only Roman citizens as provincial rulers instead of local rulers as the Greeks did before them. In fact, the Romans routinely set up Roman colonies in conquered territory. Roman colonies built towns and villages using a distinct Roman layout, architecture and amenities including public baths, Roman style houses, and other Roman distinctives. Through colonization, the Romans were determined to change the world into Rome.

The Roman empire fell apart from within long ago but the colonial, imperialist Roman mindset lives on in kingdoms, democracies, and communist governments until the present day. In fact, while the Romans had emperors, there was always a "mix" of power between the emperor and a Senate that supposedly represented the people of the Empire, but this mix was brittle and often fractured into civil war. In the same way, democracies, communist governments, and other republic-like systems today try to spread out the balance of power between different branches of government. The result is a brittle system that often fractures because the iron will of a despotic leader does not mix well with the will of the people just like iron and clay do not mix.

Some scholars think this means the final kingdom before the Messiah returns will be a re-establishment of the Roman Empire, just not as strong. There is, however, some more detail in the meaning of the feet of iron mixed with clay in Daniel 7:7, which says,

Daniel 7:7 (NASB)
After this I kept looking in the night visions, and behold, a fourth beast, dreadful and

terrible, and extremely strong; and it had large iron teeth. It devoured and crushed and trampled down the remainder with its feet; and it was different from all the beasts that were before it, and it had ten horns.

The fourth beast in Daniel 7:7 has teeth of iron and ten horns, just as the statue's two legs of iron has ten toes, so these two visions are of the same kingdom. The feet and toes of the image are part iron and part clay which means that some aspect of the iron-like nature of Rome will fail to mix with some other system of government. Daniel 7:17 says,

Daniel 7:17 – 23 (NASB)
'These great beasts, which are four in number, are four kings who will arise from the earth. [18] But the saints of the Highest One will receive the kingdom and possess the kingdom forever, for all ages to come.' [19] "Then I desired to know the exact meaning of the fourth beast, which was different from all the others, exceedingly dreadful, with its teeth of iron and its claws of bronze, and which devoured, crushed and trampled down the remainder with its feet, [20] and the meaning of the ten horns that were on its head, and the other horn came up, and before which three of them fell, namely, that horn which had eyes and a mouth uttering great boasts and which was larger in appearance than its associates. [21] I kept looking, and that horn was waging war with the saints and overpowering them [22] until the Ancient of

Days came and judgement was passed in favor of the saints of the Highest One, and the time arrived when the saints took possession of the kingdom. [23] "Thus he said: 'The fourth beast will be a fourth kingdom on the earth, which will be different from all the other kingdoms and will devour the whole earth and tread it down and crush it.

The fourth empire symbolized by the statue in Daniel chapter two and the beast in Daniel chapter seven is not just Rome; it is the kind of imperialist, colonial government – brittle and unbalanced in power - that Rome represented. In the end times, the governments descended from the Roman system will progress from a state of strength into a brittle, mixed situation. These diverse but brittle government systems will eventually dominate the whole earth but because of the brittle, unstable situation they bring to the earth, they will attempt to organize a one-world government. This one-world attempt will collapse rapidly into ten parts. One leader from one of these ten parts, the Antichrist, will attack and defeat three of the others and after their defeat, the remaining leaders will cave and surrender to him. The Antichrist will move to solidify his power, but he will be destroyed by the return of the Messiah.

The historical Roman system conquered new regions militarily and then set up its own citizens as leaders in a colonial program of expansion. Daniel 7: 23 says this system "will be different from all the other kingdoms" but the word "different" is שְׁנָא (shᵉnâ) in Hebrew and it means "different, to be changed, diverse." [40] In other words, this imperialist system will be expressed in many different, diverse ways throughout the earth as it progresses toward the ten-kingdom stage, and this is exactly what we have seen since the Middle Ages. The idea of spreading a cultural or political way of life by conquering and setting up colonies is exactly the sort of thing we have seen, particularly in the last 500 years. For example, European countries set up colonies worldwide. Asian powers expanded in a similar way, particularly in the early part of the twentieth century. Communist countries also conquered by military might, set up its own citizens as leaders in conquered areas and colonized through programs intended to change the local citizens into communists. Each of these political or cultural examples of imperialism are a mix of the Roman imperialist mindset with their own unique brand of capitalism, communism, or militarism, exactly as Daniel prophesied. Each is diverse or different from the others, but a Roman-like imperialist system, linked with colonization, has literally eaten up the whole earth.

But a mixture of iron and clay does not truly mix. It is a brittle, unstable situation and it was imperialist governments and their colonies that brought the entire earth to war in World War I and II. Just as Rome eventually dissolved into mob rule, so our world today is rapidly becoming more and more unstable. In the past, Rome tried to find stability by instituting laws and ordinances designed to destroy freedom of speech, freedom of assembly, freedom of worship and economic free trade. In the same way, our current mix of imperialism and diverse political systems are falling prey to instability, violent mobs, and economic fallout. The result is that various governments are beginning to restrict free speech, freedom of assembly and freedom of worship just as the ancient Romans did. Daniel 7:24 describes what will happen next:

> **Daniel 7:24 – 28 (NASB)**
> As for the ten horns, out of this kingdom ten kings will arise; and another will arise after them, and he will be different from the previous ones and will subdue three kings. ²⁵ He will speak out against the Most High and wear down the saints of the Highest One, and he will intend to make alterations in times and in law; and they will be given into his hand for a time, times, and half a time. ²⁶ But the court will sit for judgement, and his dominion will be taken away, annihilated, and destroyed forever. ²⁷ Then the sovereignty, the dominion, and the greatness of all the kingdoms under the whole heaven will be given to the people of the saints of the Highest One; His kingdom will be an everlasting kingdom, and all the dominions will serve and obey Him.' ²⁸ "At this point the revelation ended. As for me, Daniel, my thoughts were greatly alarming me and my face grew pale, but I kept the matter to myself."

As the world economic system becomes global in nature and instability continues to grow, more and more leaders will call for world-wide economic, political, and religious control. Eventually governments will attempt a one-world political system, a system that will, as Daniel 7:25 says, "...devour the whole earth and tread it down and crush it." But this world-devouring attempt at global control will rapidly collapse into ten districts. The leader from one of these "kingdoms," the Antichrist, will begin to assert himself until the Great Tribulation begins. In his rise to power, the Antichrist will subdue three governments but the rest of the ten governments will simply surrender to him. Perhaps after the failure of a one-world government, leaders will believe a one-world government is only possible under a single powerful ruler. The Antichrist will be fabulously successful, charismatic, popular, and supported by a religious partner who will give him philosophical and religious credibility. The book of Revelation is about worldwide judgements that will result in the Antichrist's eventual defeat by Jesus Himself. Daniel 2:34 says a "rock, carved out without hands" will smash the feet of iron and clay which means that Jesus the Messiah, the Rock of Israel, will return to destroy the works of the Antichrist and begin a physical kingdom on this earth that will last for 1,000 years. Daniel 2:44 says,

> **Daniel 2:44 (NASB)**
> And in the days of those kings the God of heaven will set up a kingdom which will never be destroyed, and that kingdom will not be left for another people; it will crush and put an end to all these kingdoms, but it will itself endure forever.

Since World War I and the restoration of the nation of Israel in 1948, the birth pains leading up to the world-shattering events in Revelation are happening right before our eyes. These are birth pains, and they cannot be stopped by a vote or a protest.

It is clear that events are lining things up to allow for a global economy, global technology, and global instability. It will not be long until the world attempts to control the planet with one united political system, but it will collapse into ten kingdoms just as Daniel prophesied. This is inevitable because it is God's plan.

<u>Every Christian today should consciously shift from concerns about the things of this world to focus on advancing the Lord's kingdom on earth everywhere and in every way we can.</u>

End of Days:
The Book of Revelation Explained

Chapter 8: Our only hope is Jesus!
Revelation 4: 1-4 explained...

Revelation 4:1 (NASB)
After these things I looked, and behold, a door standing open in heaven, and the first voice which I had heard, lie the sound of a trumpet speaking with me, said, "Come up here, and I will show you what must take place after these things."

The words "after these things" are used twice at the start of Revelation chapter four, once by John who is writing and once by the angel who is revealing this vision to John. These next events obviously happen after what is described in Revelation 1-3, but as noted previously, the book of Revelation has historically been interpreted in four major ways so what exactly does "after these things," based on these four views, mean?

In the Idealist or Allegorical interpretation, Revelation can mean almost anything depending on what meaning is given to the symbols in the book, so "after these things" could mean almost anything. The Allegorical view is arbitrary, based on individual opinion and is, therefore, ungrounded in any solid foundation.

In the Historicist view, Revelation is symbolic of church history and a poetic explanation of the struggle against evil over time but, again, any interpreter can arbitrarily decide what a symbol may mean. In the Preterist view, Revelation is symbolic of events that happened primarily during the destruction of the city of Jerusalem in 70 A.D. Some Preterists are "partial" Preterists believing that most of the events in Revelation happened during the destruction of the Jewish temple but the actual second coming of Jesus and possibly some other events described in the book are still in the future. In the Preterist view, deciding which events are still future depends on the preterist interpreter and they can all be different because not all Preterists agree which symbol relates to which event during the destruction of Jerusalem. Again, this method of interpretation is arbitrary and ungrounded.

All three of these views - the Allegorical, Historicist and Preterist interpretations - have considerable Scriptural problems, can be arbitrary and do not adequately consider the Jewish nature of Revelation or its connection with Old Testament prophecy. It is for these reasons that this book follows the Contextual-futurist interpretation of Revelation.

In the Contextual-futurist view, Revelation is about the fulfillment of promises made to the Jewish people. It is not all symbolic, nor is it all literal. Most of the time the symbols in the book are explained right in the text or link back to the Old Testament. Most of the symbols directly link to something literal that is also described in the context of the symbol itself. Using this method, Revelation chapters one through three describe the types of

Christian congregations that will dominate during the gap in time between Daniel's 69th and 70th weeks of prophetic future-history.

There is, however, another controversial issue surrounding the Contextual-futurist interpretation of Revelation. Since this view sees the events outlined from Revelation chapter four to the end of the book as future events, the question becomes "how many of these events will be experienced by Christians?" There are three schools of thought on this: the pre-tribulation view, the mid-tribulation view, and the post-tribulation view. Each of these schools of thought center on the timing of "the Rapture." The Rapture is the future sudden and unexpected moment when God will miraculously transform believers into resurrection bodies. The word "Rapture" is not found in Scripture, but it comes from the Latin verb "rapio" which means "to catch up" or "to take away" and rapio was used to translate the Greek word "ἁρπάζω" (har-pad'-zo) [41] found in First Thessalonians 4:17 which says,

> **First Thessalonians 4:17 (NASB)**
> Then we who are alive, who remain, will be caught up together with them in the clouds to meet the Lord in the air, and so we will always be with the Lord.

The post-tribulation Rapture view is that Christians will endure everything described in Revelation until the end of the Great Tribulation when Jesus will return, and Christians will be raised into resurrection bodies. The main problem with this view is that the events in Revelation are described as judgements of God against unbelievers but

Scriptures such as First Thessalonians 5:9 and others like it say, "For God has not destined us for wrath, but for obtaining salvation through our Lord Jesus Christ." Also, in all the passages of Scripture that describe the Great Tribulation, the word "church" is never used. First Thessalonians 1:10 says,

> **First Thessalonians 1:10 (NASB)**
> ...wait for His Son from heaven, whom He raised from the dead, that is, Jesus who rescues us from the wrath to come.

The mid-tribulation view is that Christians will be raised at the midpoint of the Great Tribulation three and a half years after it starts when the Antichrist claims he is God and demands worship. The mid-tribulation view, however, implies a specific time for the Rapture and that means the Rapture cannot happen until three and a half years after the Antichrist is revealed and signs the treaty. These are events we wait to see happen in future-history, so how can the Rapture be an event that could happen at any moment, unexpectedly and like a thief coming in the night, if we know it happens at the midpoint of the Great Tribulation? First Thessalonians 5:2 says,

> **First Thessalonians 5:2 (NASB)**
> For you yourselves know full well that the day of the Lord is coming just like a thief in the night.

Over and again, Scripture says the time of the Lord's return is near or "at hand" or even "at the very door." James 5:8 says,

> **James 5:8 – 9 (NASB)**
> You too be patient; strengthen your hearts, for the coming of the Lord is near. [9] Do not complain, brothers and sisters, against one another, so that you may not be judged; behold, the Judge is standing right at the door.

Scripture is consistent that the Rapture can happen at any time before the Great Tribulation begins. Nevertheless, there have been many difficult times in church history and many examples of dreadful persecution, war, and plagues on the human race that believers have had to suffer as well. Just because believers can expect the Rapture before the Great Tribulation does not mean Christians will not have to suffer other tribulations. There are many pieces of the world puzzle that must be in place before the final seven years of the Great Tribulation begin. The Rapture will happen before the Great Tribulation begins and the Great Tribulation, according to Daniel 9:26, will not begin before the Antichrist confirms a peace treaty with Israel. Daniel 9:26 says,

> **Daniel 9:26 – 27 (NASB)**
> Then after the sixty-two weeks the Messiah will be cut off and have nothing, and the people of the prince who is to come will destroy the city and the sanctuary. And its end will come with a flood; even to

the end there will be war; desolations are determined. ²⁷ And he will make a firm covenant with the many for one week, but in the middle of the week he will put a stop to sacrifice and grain offering; ...

This Scripture means we should not let fear overtake us when we see terrible things happening on the evening news. There are false teachers saying the Rapture has already happened and we are already in the Great Tribulation, but this is not true because the Antichrist has not been revealed nor has he signed any treaty with Israel. Other false teachers say that when the Rapture happens it will be a mysterious, secret event and people may not even realize it has happened for days or weeks. This, however, is not what the Bible teaches. First Thessalonians 4:16 says,

> **First Thessalonians 4:16 – 17 (NASB)**
> For the Lord Himself will descend from heaven with a shout, with the voice of the archangel and with the trumpet of God, and the dead in Christ will rise first. ¹⁷ Then we who are alive and remain will be caught up together with them in the clouds to meet the Lord in the air, and so we shall always be with the Lord.

The Rapture will begin with "a shout." This word is κέλευσμα (kel'-yoo-mah) in Greek and it means "a cry of incitement, a shout." [42] The Rapture, therefore, will not be a secret event, but a monumental change in history that begins with an audible cry louder than a trumpet and the whole world will hear it. Everyone will stop and wonder at the sound. It will be a moment no one can deny, the sound will be so commanding that the dead bodies of those who believed in Jesus in life will rise from the dead and be caught up into the air. The word "caught up" is ἁρπάζω (här-pä'-zo) in Greek and it means, "To seize, carry off by force, snatch out or away" so the Rapture will be a miraculous, sudden, forceful transformation of believers!

A common teaching today is that the Rapture will be a mysterious disappearance of millions of believers leaving behind little piles of empty clothing for everyone to see. The thought is that because of its mysterious nature, people will deny the Rapture has happened. No one really knows for certain, but this mysterious disappearance interpretation does not fit with "a shout" or "the voice of the archangel and with the trumpet of God." This idea also does not match with the stories of the three other people in Scripture who were "caught up" into the air: Enoch, Elijah, and Jesus.

In Genesis chapter five, Enoch, the man of God, was translated into heaven directly. There is very little information about this incident except for Genesis 5:24 which reads, "Enoch walked with God; and he was not, for God took him." But second Kings chapter two describes the translation of Elijah and the text provides some interesting details. Verse eleven says,

> **Second Kings 2:11 – 12 (NASB)**
> And as they were walking along and talking, behold, a chariot of fire appeared with horses of fire, and they separated the two of them. Then Elijah went up by a whirlwind to

heaven. [12] And Elisha was watching it and he was crying out, "My father, my father, the chariot of Israel and its horsemen!" And he did not see Elijah again.

Finally, the Bible describes how Jesus was translated into heaven after His resurrection. Acts 1:9 says,

Acts 1:9 – 10 (NASB)
And after He had said these things, He was lifted up while they were watching, and a cloud took Him up, out of their sight. [10] And as they were gazing intently into the sky while He was going, then behold, two men in white clothing stood beside them.

Elisha saw Elijah taken up into heaven and the disciples saw Jesus lifted up as they looked intently up at the sky. We do not know if anyone saw the translation of Enoch, but someone recorded the story and may have been an eyewitness. It could be that the stories of Elijah and Jesus may show a Biblical pattern. First Thessalonians 4:16 says the Rapture will begin with a loud, worldwide trumpet-like shout so just as Elijah and Jesus were seen as they were lifted up, it may be that the Rapture will be witnessed by others as well.

We do not know all the details of the Rapture but the examples we do have in Scripture of people being caught up into heaven in a similar way were witnessed by other people. This sort of event was not done in a dark corner in the past. The idea that the Rapture will be an ear-splitting event where millions of people see millions of other people suddenly caught up into the air, just as Elisha saw Elijah caught up into a fire chariot, is certainly possible. This idea about the Rapture fits the pattern of Elijah and Jesus and fits the description in First Thessalonians 4:16. If the world does see this event, it may explain why the book of Revelation says there will be a great multitude of people left behind who will turn to Jesus. These Tribulation believers will believe in Jesus with a passion so intense they will be willing to be martyred for Him. In the same way, the disciples of Jesus were transformed from scared, bewildered followers hiding in the dark into mighty witnesses of Jesus who were willing to suffer torture and death for their testimony, primarily because they witnessed the resurrection and the ascension.

Revelation chapter three says the Laodicean church was lukewarm. Many scholars think the Laodicean church describes the kind of church that will dominate the time when Jesus returns, and today there are many lukewarm professing Christians. Today, entire denominations deny the trustworthiness and authority of the Bible. It may be that after witnessing the Rapture and realizing they are left behind, people familiar with the teachings in the Bible about the Rapture and the Great Tribulation will suddenly have every reason to go from lukewarm to on fire for Jesus.

The disciples of Jesus were not only willing to suffer and die for their testimony about seeing Jesus rise from the dead, but they were also motivated to preach this message as far and wide as they could. There is a clue in Revelation 7:4 and 9 that may describe a similar outcome from the Rapture. Revelation 7:4 reads,

Revelation 7:4 (NASB)
And I heard the number of those who were sealed, one hundred and forty-four thousand sealed from every tribe of the sons of Israel...

These 144,000 Jewish believers will be witnesses for Jesus and they will probably preach the good news about Jesus worldwide. Today there are only a very small number of Jewish believers in Jesus, but after a worldwide shout so loud it drowns out the thunder of the clouds and millions of people are transformed and caught up into the air, many religious Jews will have all the evidence they need to recognize Jesus as their Messiah. Less than a thousand Jewish people in the first century witnessed the resurrection of Jesus and they nearly turned the world upside down with their preaching, so 144,000 Jewish witnesses in the last days will be able to do something similar. In fact, Revelation says there will be an innumerable number of people who turn to Jesus. Revelation 7:9 and 14 says,

Revelation 7:9, 14 (NASB)
After these things I looked, and behold, a great multitude which no one could count, from every nation and all the tribes, peoples, and languages, standing before the throne and before the Lamb, clothed in white robes, and palm branches were in their hands; [14]..."These are the ones who come out of the great tribulation, and they have washed their robes and made them white in the blood of the Lamb.

The disciples ran and hid for fear of the authorities after Jesus was arrested because they really did not understand who Jesus was, but because of the resurrection, they were changed. In the same way, the 144,000 will realize who Jesus really is after the Rapture and they will become bold preachers, willing to die for Jesus.

There is another reference to people being caught up in a sudden Rapture-like translation from this life into heaven. This reference is not from the past but in the future. In Revelation chapter eleven, the Bible describes two powerful Jewish preachers called "the two witnesses." These men are in addition to the 144,000 but their ministry will be considerably more intense. They will be based in the city of Jerusalem and have miracle powers. Eventually, the Antichrist will overpower the two witnesses and kill them. Their bodies will lay in the street for three days and the world will rejoice over their deaths. They will be raised from the dead by God and their resurrection will be seen by the whole world, probably on television and the internet. Revelation 11:12 says,

> **Revelation 11:12 (NASB)**
> And they heard a loud voice from heaven saying to them, "Come up here." And they ascended to heaven in a cloud, and their enemies saw them.

Once again, this Rapture-like translation into heaven will be seen by others. In the same way, the Rapture of the church will be a powerful, loud, visible experience as a mighty witness to people who have rejected the Lord. First Corinthians 15:51 says,

> **First Corinthians 15:51 – 52 (NLT)**
> But let me reveal to you a wonderful secret. We will not all die, but we will all be transformed! [52] It will happen in a moment, in the blink of an eye, when the last trumpet is blown. For when the trumpet sounds, those who have died will be raised to live forever. And we who are living will also be transformed.

There are professing Christians and denominations who try to explain the Rapture away as symbolic because it seems so fantastic to the modern mind, but the Rapture is what Scripture teaches. Of course, when the Rapture takes place, the world will try to explain it away. Some people may explain it as an alien event and after so many years of incredibly detailed popular films about alien invasions, such an excuse may be believed by many. Others will probably explain it away as a mass hallucination and some may outright deny it by claiming any videos of the event seen on television and the internet are fakes.

It is interesting to note the popularity of films about aliens in the last thirty years or so. Even secular science is popularizing aliens. Credible scientists believe there may be millions of alien worlds waiting to be discovered. The more scientists study the nature of life on earth, the more it becomes clear that life could not have come about on this planet by any random, natural chemistry, so more and more scientists who refuse to consider God as

Creator are suggesting that life may have formed somewhere else in the universe and been seeded on earth by an alien civilization. Could this obsession with aliens, alien life and science fiction be the groundwork for a mindset willing to explain away the Rapture?

God has promised to catch up His faithful believers before the Great Tribulation and this event will shake lukewarm believers who are left behind into an intense devotion to Jesus.

End of Days: The Book of Revelation Explained

Chapter 9: Why your worship matters...
Revelation 4: 5-11 explained...

To worship God means to call out God's worth. It is an act of the heart, an intentional mental and spiritual focus of our attention on our Creator. To worship means to put ourselves in mind of who God is and what is our relationship with Him. The Bible teaches that worship is the entire purpose of human existence in the first place.

Revelation is only one piece of a larger puzzle, so it is vital to see how it fits into the rest of Scripture. Daniel, the prophet, writing in the fifth century B.C., explained there would be sixty-nine sets of seven-year periods between the proclamation that the city of Jerusalem should be rebuilt, and when the Messiah (Jesus), would arrive on earth at His first coming. This prophecy was fulfilled to the day, but Daniel also prophesied there would be a gap between the first and the second coming of the Messiah. This gap is "the church age" and Revelation outlines "Daniel's gap" in chapters one through three, showing that the church age will proceed through seven time-periods. The rest of the book of Revelation outlines what will happen after the church age ends.

The disciples asked Jesus what would be the signs that "Daniel's gap," which we know is the church age, was coming to an end. His answer is recorded in Matthew chapter 24 and Luke chapter 21. Jesus answered this question while standing on the Mount of Olives outside the city of Jerusalem, so His answer is sometimes called the "Olivet Discourse." The Olivet Discourse describes what will happen between Revelation chapters three and four. Jesus also gives a short, detailed summary what the whole book of Revelation describes. Matthew 24:1-3 says,

> **Matthew 24:1 – 3 (NASB)**
> Jesus left the temple area and was going on His way when His disciples came up to point out the temple buildings to Him. [2] But He responded and said to them, "Do you not see all these things? Truly I say to you, not one stone here will be left upon another, which will not be torn down." [3] And as He was sitting on the Mount of Olives, the disciples came to Him privately, saying, "Tell us, when will these things happen, and what will be the sign of Your coming, and of the end of the age?"

The disciples actually asked Jesus three distinct questions even though they likely did not realize it. Jesus had just told them that the temple would be destroyed, and they had been told their entire lives that the temple would remain until the Messiah started His kingdom. While they believed Jesus was Messiah, they did not understand how the temple could be destroyed because they did not understand that His kingdom would be a spiritual reality first before it would become a physical reality. They were shocked that Jesus prophesied the destruction of the temple so, naturally, their first question was "when would the temple be destroyed?"

Their second question was about the signs of His coming because they thought any destruction of the temple must be linked directly with His starting His kingdom in the physical. What they did not understand is that the signs of His second coming would not happen until long after the temple would be destroyed in 70 A.D. This is where the book of Revelation fits into the puzzle. The signs of His second coming are the events that will happen in the second half of the Great Tribulation, and those signs are described in Revelation chapters four through nineteen.

Their third question is about "the end of the age." In the first century A.D., "the end of the age" was a Jewish figure of speech referring to the new age when Messiah will physically rule over the world bringing peace and justice to the earth. The disciples thought the destruction of the temple, the signs of the Messiah's coming rule and the Messiah's physical kingdom, would all happen at the same time. They did not realize they were asking three different questions. The book of Revelation, however, explains that the Messiah's physical rulership over the earth will be a new age that begins after the Great Tribulation and will last for 1,000 years. The Messiah's physical kingdom begins long after the destruction of the temple. While the disciples did not know at the time that they were asking three different questions, Jesus was willing to answer them anyway. Matthew 24:4 says,

Matthew 24:4 – 8 (NASB)
And Jesus answered and said to them, "See to it that no one misleads you. ⁵ For many will come in My name, saying, 'I am the Christ,' and they will mislead many people. ⁶ And you will be hearing of wars and rumors of wars. See that you are not alarmed, for those things must take place, but that is not yet the end. ⁷ For nation will rise against nation, and kingdom against kingdom, and there will be famines and earthquakes in various places. ⁸ But all these things are merely the beginning of birth pains.

Daniel's gap, between the 69th and the 70th weeks, is the church age which has lasted nearly 2,000 years. The disciples had no idea that Daniel's gap would last so long. Jesus used an important figure of speech to leave one clue showing when Daniel's gap would come to an end. Jesus said, "Nation will rise against nation, and kingdom against kingdom" in verse seven. This figure of speech can also be found in Isaiah 19:2, a chapter about a coming civil war in Egypt. Isaiah uses this figure of speech to say that the entire country would be involved in the conflict, not just a localized part of Egypt. Isaiah 19:2 says,

Isaiah 19:2 (NASB)
So I will incite Egyptians against Egyptians; And they will fight, each against his brother and each against his neighbor, city against city and kingdom against kingdom.

Second Chronicles also uses this figure of speech to describe the entire middle east at war. Second Chronicles 15:5 says,

> **Second Chronicles 15:5 (NASB)**
> In those times there was no peace for him who went out or him who came in, because many disturbances afflicted all the inhabitants of the lands. ⁶ Nation was crushed by nation, and city by city, for God troubled them with every kind of distress.

In both Old Testament passages, this figure of speech means that "the whole of a group" is at war. There have been wars all over the world in the last 2,000 years, but it was not until the 20th century that "the whole earth" was truly at war at one time. Dr. Arnold Fruchtenbaum explains why this is significant,

> Jesus had already clearly stated that local wars between a few nations would not indicate that the end had begun. But then He said that when there is "nation against nation, and kingdom against kingdom," this will mean the end of the age has begun…This expression is a Hebrew idiom for a world war. Jesus' statement here is that when a world war occurs, rather than merely a local war, that world war would signal that the end of the age had begun. [43]

For some centuries prior to the start of the twentieth century, many nations began an expansion of their political and economic power by planting colonies in nations around the world. The colony made use of local resources to send goods and supplies back home but the colony also maintained its identity as part of the home country. When war broke out in Europe in 1914, the colonies of each of the combatants all around the earth went to war as well. This meant that for the first time in human history, the entire world was truly at war at one time. According to Jesus, this event signaled the beginning of the birth pains that will eventually give birth to the final seven-year Great Tribulation.

Jesus also said that in addition to the whole world at war, there would be famines and earthquakes in various places. Of course, there have always been famines and earthquakes on earth, but it is interesting to note there have been more recorded earthquakes in the twentieth century than all of human history combined before the twentieth century. In fact, prior to 1914 there were less than 1,000 total earthquakes recorded in history but since 1914 there have been over 900,000! [44] The same thing is true about famines. The most severe famines in known history have all happened in the twentieth century. For example, famine in China and Russia in the 1920's killed more than 30 million people. The great Chinese famine of 1958 killed more than 20 million. [45]

Jesus said the world at war, accompanied by famines and earthquakes, would only be the beginning of birth pains. During the process of human birth, once labor pains begin there is no natural stopping of the process. Once it begins, labor leads to delivery. Based on Dr. Fruchtenbaum's explanation of the "nation will rise against nation" figure of speech, the final process leading to the delivery of the seven-year Great Tribulation (that happens before the Millennial kingdom of the Messiah on earth begins) has started so there is no stopping its progression now. Also, birth pains, once they begin, become more intense and closer together until the birth.

Revelation chapter four describes what will happen in heaven at the beginning of the end of the church age. Revelation 4:5 is an example of the Revelation Refrain showing a heavenly, symbolic vision that links to something literal. There will be literal events that must happen before the Great Tribulation begins. Verse five says,

> **Revelation 4:5 (NASB)**
> Out from the throne come flashes of lightning and sounds and peals of thunder. And there were seven lamps of fire burning before the throne, which are the seven Spirits of God...

The seven lamps are explained in the text itself. These lamps are the seven Spirits of God, but this is not saying that God has seven spirits because the context is a heavenly vision, not a literal or physical reality. In this case, the vision is about the throne of God and whenever the number seven is used symbolically in Scripture it is an illustration of completeness, perfection, or the whole essence of something. In fact, in Zechariah 4:1-6 the prophet sees this same thing but no one in the Old Testament ever thought there were seven gods since the symbolism of the number seven was well known. Zechariah 4:1-6 says,

Zechariah 4:1 – 6 (NASB)

Then the angel who had been speaking with me returned and woke me, like a person who is awakened from his sleep. ² And he said to me, "What do you see?" And I said, "I see, and behold, a lampstand all of gold with its bowl on the top of it, and its seven lamps on it with seven spouts belonging to each of the lamps which are on the top of it; ³ also two olive trees by it, one on the right side of the bowl and the other on its left side." ⁴ Then I said to the angel who was speaking with me, saying, "What are these, my lord?" ⁵ So the angel who was speaking with me answered and said to me, "Do you not know what these are?" And I said, "No, my lord." ⁶ Then he said to me, "This is the word of the Lord to Zerubbabel, saying, 'Not by might nor by power, but by My Spirit,' says the Lord of armies.

The angel then explains to Zechariah that the seven lamps are the Spirit of God – singular! In Exodus chapter twenty-five, Moses also saw this vision because Moses was told to build a single lampstand with a single base. The lampstand represents the perfect Spirit of God, so it had seven arms with seven lamps at the ends of the arms. Exodus 25:31 and 37 says,

Exodus 25:31, 37 (NASB)

"Then you shall make a lampstand of pure gold. The lampstand, its base and its shaft, are to be made of hammered work; its cups, its bulbs, and its flowers shall be of one piece with it. ³⁷ Then you shall make its lamps seven in number; and they shall mount its lamps so as to shed light on the space in front of it.

These Old Testament passages and the visionary nature of what John saw each explain that the symbolic use of the number seven is about the wholeness and the complete essence of God's Spirit. God is one being, but He exists as three distinct persons and His eternal, infinite nature is absolutely perfect. In fact, Isaiah 11:2 uses seven attributes to describe the complete perfection of God, Isaiah 11:2 says,

> **Isaiah 11:2 (NASB)**
> The Spirit of the Lord will rest on Him, the spirit of wisdom and understanding, the spirit of counsel and strength, the spirit of knowledge and the fear of the Lord.

Isaiah is saying that God rests upon, that is, God fully indwells the Messiah, so the Messiah has perfect indwelling of the essence of God, He has perfect wisdom, understanding, counsel, strength, knowledge, and the fear (or reverence) of the Lord. These seven are all found in Jesus the Messiah, so this demonstrates, again, that the number seven used symbolically shows perfection or perfect fulfillment.

The complete essence of God is found in Jesus because Jesus is God in the flesh.

Revelation 4:6 – 8 (NASB)

…and before the throne there was something like a sea of glass, like crystal; and in the center and around the throne, four living creatures full of eyes in front and behind. ⁷ The first creature was like a lion, and the second creature like a calf, and the third creature had a face like that of a man, and the fourth creature was like a flying eagle. ⁸ And the four living creatures, each one of them having six wings, are full of eyes around and within; and day and night they do not cease to say, "Holy, holy, holy is the Lord God, the Almighty, who was and who is and who is to come."

From other Scripture we know there are two types of exalted, powerful, holy angels who exist in the direct presence of God. These are called Cherubim and Seraphim. Both are exceedingly powerful and beautiful. The Seraphim are called שָׂרָף (saw-rawf') which comes from the Hebrew word for "burning." [46] These angels are so bright they appear to be burning as they hover over the throne of God. Cherubim are ker-oob' [47] in Hebrew and they are mysterious creatures that appear to have multiple faces and wings. Both Seraphim and Cherubim are holy beings who exist to worship God. They are beings of great power and personality. In fact, according to Ezekiel chapter twenty-eight, Lucifer – now called Satan - was originally a Cherubim. Isaiah the prophet saw this scene as well. In Isaiah 6:1 he writes,

Isaiah 6:1 – 3 (NASB)
In the year of King Uzziah's death I saw the Lord sitting on a throne, lofty and exalted, with the train of His robe filling the temple. ² Seraphim stood above Him, each having six wings: with two he covered his face, and with two he covered his feet, and with two he flew. ³ And one called out to another and said, "Holy, Holy, Holy, is the Lord of hosts, the whole earth is full of His glory."

The prophecy of Isaiah and Revelation are linked showing us the connection between the Old Testament and the book of Revelation. This is the reason that Revelation can be confusing to people who do not see its connections to the rest of Scripture.

Revelation 4:9-11 (NASB)
And when the living creatures give glory and honor and thanks to Him who sits on the throne, to Him who lives forever and ever, ¹⁰ the twenty-four elders will fall down before Him who sits on the throne, and will worship Him who lives forever and ever, and will cast their crowns before the throne, saying, ¹¹ "Worthy are You, our Lord and our God, to receive glory and honor and power; for You created all things, and because of Your will they existed, and were created."

In Scripture, people who encounter angels are often so overwhelmed they fall on their faces as if dead; yet, with all the beauty and power of Seraphim, Cherubim and other angels, these spiritual beings remain in constant awe of God. Both Revelation and the Old Testament visions of the throne room in heaven describe a place where God is continually worshipped because His essence and perfection are so intense that even the most powerful and beautiful creatures in existence are amazed at Him. It is almost as if the angels dare one another to look up once again at the glory of God and each time they do look up they are overcome, crying out, "Holy, Holy, Holy is the Lord God almighty." The elders around the throne are apparently glorified human beings and they also fall down and throw their crowns before Him. The glory of the holiest of beings and the glory of redeemed human beings is nothing compared to the least part of God's majesty.

The glory and perfection of God in His essence is so overwhelming that even the most powerful beings in the universe are overwhelmed by Him.

End of Days:
The Book of Revelation Explained

Chapter 10: God has control over your destiny!
Revelation 5 explained...

In the beginning, God created the heavens and the earth. He is responsible for designing and upholding the natural systems and laws that keep nature functioning. The book of Revelation does tell us future history, but it is vital to remember that God is the Creator from the beginning. According to the Bible, God is "transcendent" which means He is outside of time, space, and matter. As the transcendent God, He views all of our timeline as one completed whole, which is the reason He is capable of revealing what is, to us, the future. God is both the beginning and the ending. He revealed to Moses the first chapter of the Bible and through the Apostle John He revealed the last chapter in the book of Revelation. In the end, God will deal with the problem of evil once and for all. The book of Revelation shows us how He will make everything right, bring justice to the oppressed and victory to His faithful servants. This means there is nothing for believers to fear from the dreadful things Revelation describes.

The book of Revelation, however, is the written description of a vision, and just like normal dreams, even an inspired vision can seem sort of timeless, as if events are time compressed. In a dream sometimes, the view jumps suddenly from the past to the present and into the future. In a dream, not only timelines but images can also shift quickly from one viewpoint to another. For example, in Revelation chapter one, John sees Jesus with a sword coming out of His mouth and this is clearly symbolic because immediately after seeing this, John hears the Lord speaking in a normal voice. Obviously, it would be exceedingly difficult to speak with a sword in your mouth, but Revelation shows a pattern of symbolic visions linked or followed by something literal or physical – the "Revelation Refrain."

The Revelation Refrain of symbol linked to literal is the nature of prophecy and just as in normal dreams, inspired visions can be time compressed. For example, Revelation chapter four says twice, "after these things," to mean that the vision of heavenly things in chapter four is symbolic of events happening in the spiritual realm during the whole of the church age. No one can be exactly certain when the church age ends because the Rapture of the church can happen at any moment. Daniel tells us in chapter 9:27 that the Great Tribulation only begins when peace treaties are confirmed by the Antichrist with Israel.

There is some difference of opinion about whether the seven churches in Revelation chapter one through three are seven distinct time periods in the church age or simply seven kinds of churches that will exist during the church age. This is especially uncertain because it seems that the last four church "types" overlap each other in dominance and examples of all seven types of churches can be seen today. It is better not to be dogmatic about seven specific time periods and simply recognize that the church age is the gap between Daniels' sixty-ninth and seventieth weeks. We see that Revelation chapters four and five describe the events at the end of the church age leading into the Great Tribulation. Revelation 5:1 says,

> **Revelation 5:1 – 5 (NASB)**
> I saw in the right hand of Him who sat on the throne a book written inside and on the back, sealed up with seven seals. [2] And I saw a strong angel proclaiming with a loud voice, "Who is worthy to open the book and to break its seals?" [3] And no one in heaven or on the earth or under the earth was able to open the book or to look into it. [4] Then I began to weep greatly because no one was found worthy to open the book or to look into it; [5] and one of the elders said to me, "Stop weeping; behold, the Lion that is from the tribe of Judah, the Root of David, has overcome so as to open the book and its seven seals."

There has been much speculation about what is in the sealed book (or scroll). Some Bible scholars think it is a record of the coming judgements later described in Revelation. Others think it is the legal deed to planet earth and some even think it is a divorce decree between God and the people of the earth. All these speculations miss the point because the text clearly says that no one in heaven or on the earth or under the earth is able to open the book or to look into it, so how can any of these ideas be certain? Only the Lord Jesus Himself is worthy to see what the scroll says, so the point is that the future is in God's complete knowledge and control.

Based on these verses, once the seals are opened, then the judgements described later in the book will begin. These judgements will fall upon the Antichrist and His followers, and the Antichrist is the same person described in Daniel chapter seven and second Thessalonians chapter two. Daniel 7:25 describes him this way:

> **Daniel 7:25 – 26 (NASB)**
> And he (the Antichrist of Revelation) will speak against the Most High and wear down the saints of the Highest One, and he will intend to make alterations in times and in law; and they will be handed over to him for a time, times, and half a time. [26] But the court will convene for judgement, and his dominion will be taken away, annihilated, and destroyed forever.

Daniel chapter seven says the Antichrist will begin to take control of the earth by first subduing three of the ten rulers who take charge after the world fails to form a stable one-world government. His arrogance and pride will be unrestrained which is the reason second Thessalonians calls him the "man of lawlessness." Second Thessalonians 2:8 says,

> **Second Thessalonians 2:8 – 10 (NASB)**
> Then that lawless one will be revealed, whom the Lord will eliminate with the

breath of His mouth and bring to an end by the appearance of His coming; [9] that is, the one whose coming is in accord with the activity of Satan, with all power and false signs and wonders, [10] and with all the deception of wickedness for those who perish, because they did not accept the love of the truth so as to be saved.

The seal judgements are warnings, but people will ignore the warnings, and many will choose to follow the Antichrist. Since the Rapture can happen at any time, it is therefore possible the Rapture may not happen until sometime just before or even during the seal judgements. Some Bible scholars think the breaking of the seals is part of the Great Tribulation so the seal judgements must begin after the Rapture, but this is not exactly clear from the text. It could be that the seal "judgements" are really preparations for the wrath of God. In other words, it is a legitimate interpretation of Scripture to suggest that the Rapture may happen at some point all the way up until the breaking of the sixth seal. There is no way to know for certain since the Bible is clear that no one knows the exact timing of the Rapture anyway. First Thessalonians 5:9 says,

First Thessalonians 5:9 (NASB)
For God has not destined us for wrath, but for obtaining salvation through our Lord Jesus Christ.

First Thessalonians 5:9 may refer to the wrath of eternal hell, not to any suffering here on earth including the Great Tribulation. Also, Revelation 6:16 says,

> **Revelation 6:16 (NASB)**
> ...and they said to the mountains and the rocks, "Fall on us and hide us from the sight of Him who sits on the throne, and from the wrath of the Lamb; [17] for the great day of Their wrath has come, and who is able to stand?"

Since the people cry out after the sixth seal is broken that the wrath of God has started, this may mean the first five seal judgements are only preparation for the Great Tribulation. Besides that, the persecutions of Christians and natural disasters that believers have endured through history are not new. There have been other great persecutions of Christians in the past, such as the persecution under Roman Emperor Nero in the first century A.D. There have been world-wide plagues such as the Bubonic plague outbreak in the fourteenth century. And there have been other natural disasters that have affected the whole planet, such as "the year without a summer" in 1816 when volcanic eruptions lowered earth's average temperature [48] so significantly that massive famines resulted leading to horrific numbers of people starving to death worldwide. Christians are not guaranteed blissful times and constant blessing in this life. In fact, Jesus said this clearly in John 16:33:

> **John 16:33b (NASB)**
> In the world you have tribulation, but take courage; I have overcome the world."

Those who teach that Christians should only expect blessing because we are the people of God do a disservice to believers.

> **Revelation 5:5 (NASB)**
> ...one of the elders said to me, "Stop weeping; behold, the Lion that is from the tribe of Judah, the Root of David, has overcome so as to open the book and its seven seals."

Some Bible scholars think the book no one except Jesus can open is like a Roman last will and testament which was typically sealed with leather strips connected by seven wax or clay brackets. Each of the brackets had an impression pressed into the wax as a personal seal by the writer of the will. The seal showed the identity of the writer of the will, and it assured anyone examining the document that the contents of the will had been undisturbed. Only a person with legal authority was allowed to break the seals and reveal the contents of the will. In Revelation chapter five, it is "the Lion that is from the tribe of Judah, the Root of David" who is the only one worthy to break the seals.

The "Lion that is from the tribe of Judah" is a figure of speech from the Old Testament. Genesis 49:9-10 reads,

> **Genesis 49:9 – 10 (NASB)**
> Judah is a lion's cub; From the prey, my son, you have gone up. He crouches, he lies down as a lion, And as a lion, who dares to stir him

up? **¹⁰** The scepter will not depart from Judah, Nor the ruler's staff from between his feet, Until Shiloh comes, And to him shall be the obedience of the peoples.

Shiloh is a reference to the coming Messiah. The "scepter will not depart from Judah" means that the royal right to rule the people will not depart from the tribe of Judah until the Messiah arrives. Jewish Rabbis for centuries interpreted this to mean that the right of the leaders of the Jewish nation to order capital punishment was the sign of the scepter in Israel and this right was not taken away from Jewish leaders until the Romans took control of Israel in the first century A.D.

"The root of David" is a figure of speech from Isaiah 11:1-2 which reads,

Isaiah 11:1 – 2 (NASB)
Then a shoot will spring from the stem of Jesse, and a Branch from his roots will bear fruit. ² The Spirit of the Lord will rest on Him, the spirit of wisdom and understanding, the spirit of counsel and strength, the spirit of knowledge and the fear of the Lord.

Jesse was king David's father and the branch from his roots means the Messiah will be a descendant of David. Jesus perfectly fits these figures of speech and for that reason it is clear that Jesus, and only Jesus, is worthy to open the seals. Revelation 5:6 reads,

Revelation 5:6 – 7 (NASB)
And I saw between the throne (with the four living creatures) and the elders a Lamb standing, as if slain, having seven horns and seven eyes, which are the seven Spirits of God, sent out into all the earth. [7] And He came and took the book out of the right hand of Him who sat on the throne.

Here again is the dream-like Revelation Refrain common in the book of Revelation. One moment John sees a bizarre looking lamb then the narrative jumps to the lamb coming and taking the book out of the right hand of the figure on the throne. Lambs do not normally have seven horns, seven eyes or hands with which to take a scroll, so the vision is obviously symbolic. The text says the seven horns and the seven eyes represent the seven Spirits of God and seven used symbolically in Scripture refers to perfection, completion, and holiness. In Scripture, the Holy Spirit is the lamp, or the light of God's essence and the Lamb of God is the Messiah (Jesus). A horn used symbolically in Scripture represents royal power and eyes used symbolically represent clear understanding or insight. Altogether, the lamb of God possesses the Spirt of God in a complete sense. This Scripture affirms that each person in the Trinity is fully God, yet distinct in another way.

The Lamb of God, Jesus, is worthy to unveil and initiate the final events of future-history because He is fully God and fully human in His essence. He is the God-Man and this makes Him uniquely worthy to judge the world and execute judgement on the earth. Revelation 5:8 goes on to say,

Revelation 5:8 – 10 (NASB)
When He had taken the book, the four living creatures and the twenty-four elders fell down before the Lamb, each one holding a harp and golden bowls full of incense, which are the prayers of the saints. [9] And they sang a new song, saying, "Worthy are You to take the book and to break its seals; for You were slain, and purchased for God with Your blood men from every tribe and tongue and people and nation. [10] "You have made them to be a kingdom and priests to our God; and they will reign upon the earth."

God alone is worthy of worship. The four living creatures and the elders falling down to worship the Lamb shows that Jesus is fully God, and He is worthy of this worship because He was killed to purchase human beings to make them into a kingdom of priests.

The Bible teaches in many places that Jesus is fully man and fully God at the same time.

The Bible says that God in His essence is absolutely pure Being and perfect existence just like light is pure and powerful. In fact, focused and purified light can become a laser, powerful enough to cut steel. In the same way, God's perfect Being is absolute pure light, so His nature will consume anything impure. Human beings, of course, lack perfection because we are contaminated by sin.

Sin or evil is any lack of perfection, so it is not just "the big things" like murder. Any imperfection, no matter how small it is from a human point of view, will naturally be burned up by God's absolute purity. It is something like the difference between a paper airplane and the sun. The nature or essence of the sun is to burn and exude energy because that is the nature of its existence. A paper airplane lacks the same kind of essence as the sun. It is a different kind of existence or "being" from the sun. If a paper airplane gets too close to the sun, it will be consumed. This is not personal, as if the sun hates paper airplanes. It is simply the difference in nature between the sun and a paper airplane. In a similar way, God's absolute Being and perfection will consume anything lacking perfection and since we are imperfect, we cannot be in relationship with God in His perfection.

The good news of the Bible is that Jesus is 100% human and 100% God so He is perfect enough to solve the difference problem human beings have with the perfection of God. Jesus is the only perfect human being and in His human nature He can enter into direct contact with God the Father in God's perfection. This also means He can voluntarily be the perfect substitute for you and me, replacing our imperfection with His perfect nature. This is what the Scripture means when it says Jesus "purchased" men from every tribe and tongue and nation because anyone who trusts in Jesus from the heart will have His perfection act as a substitute for their imperfection.

God is also pure life so when Jesus, in His human nature, died, He was able to cancel out death itself. Anyone who accepts Jesus as Savior is literally purchased from death into eternal life. Revelation 5:10 says that God's purpose in giving us the good news about Jesus (the gospel) is to make us into a glorious kingdom of priests who will be part of God's rulership over the earth. Revelation 5:11 says,

> **Revelation 5:11 - 14 (NASB)**
> Then I looked, and I heard the voice of many angels around the throne and the living creatures and the elders; and the number of them was myriads of myriads, and thousands of thousands, [12] saying with a loud voice, "Worthy is the Lamb that was slain to receive power and riches and wisdom and might and honor and glory and blessing." [13] And every created thing which is in heaven and on the earth and under the earth and on the sea, and all things in them, I heard saying, "To Him who sits on the throne, and to the Lamb, be blessing and honor and glory and dominion forever and ever." [14] And the four living creatures kept saying, "Amen." And the elders fell down and worshiped.

The elder's fall down before the throne to worship because in ancient Near Eastern culture, falling to the knees and touching the face to the ground was a sign of complete submission. John 4:24 says,

> **John 4:24 (NASB)**
> God is spirit, and those who worship Him must worship in spirit and truth.

To worship the Lord in Spirit means to trust, from the heart, His absolute authority, His control over time and His right to rule. To worship Him in truth means to worship Him guided by the Bible.

The final judgements on the living and the dead are sealed, no one can open these judgements except Jesus alone; thus, how, when, in what sequence and where the events of Revelation will ultimately unfold are up to Him.

End of Days:
The Book of Revelation Explained

Chapter 11: Why there are only 4 horses but seven seals!
Revelation 6: 1-2 explained...

Revelation primarily describes events that will happen after the Rapture of the church; therefore, some Christians think the warnings about these coming events are irrelevant to us today. This is not the case, because Second Timothy 3:16 says that "all Scripture is inspired by God and beneficial for teaching, for rebuke, for correction, for training in righteousness." This is the reason it is so important to recognize the larger life principles behind the events and symbols in Revelation, principles that we can and should apply into our lives today.

The prophet Isaiah prophesied about the Messiah about 750 years before Jesus was born in Bethlehem. Unfortunately, the Jewish religious and political leadership in the first century rejected Jesus as Messiah. Many of the common people also rejected Him because they missed the fact that Isaiah and other prophets taught that Messiah would come twice.

For example, Isaiah 11:1-10 describes the coming Messiah as a great warrior who will rule the earth with fairness and wisdom. He will bring in a time of such great peace that even carnivorous predators such as lions and wolves will be at peace with other animals they once hunted as prey. The time of the rule of Messiah will be glorious. Isaiah 11:1-10 ends with these beautiful words,

> **Isaiah 11:9 – 10 (NASB)**
> They will not hurt or destroy in all My holy mountain, for the earth will be full of the knowledge of the Lord as the waters cover the sea. [10] Then on that day the nations will resort to the root of Jesse, who will stand as a signal flag for the peoples; and His resting place will be glorious.

But however wonderful this time of Messiah seems to be, there are other prophecies showing Messiah humiliated and destroyed. Isaiah 53 describes Messiah as despised, tortured and killed – yet in verse ten it says that Messiah will prolong His days. It was not until the apostles witnessed the resurrection of Jesus that anyone could really understand how Messiah could both die and yet prolong His days. Isaiah 53:3, 8 and 10 says,

> **Isaiah 53:3, 8, 10 (NASB)**
> He was despised and abandoned by men, a man of great pain and familiar with sickness; And like one from whom people hide their faces, He was despised, and we had no regard for Him... [8] By oppression and judgement He was taken away; And as for His generation, who considered that He was cut off from the land of the living for the wrongdoing of my people, to whom the blow was due?... [10] But the Lord desired to

crush Him, causing Him grief; If He renders Himself as a guilt offering, He will see His offspring, He will prolong His days, and the good pleasure of the Lord will prosper in His hand.

Since there appeared to be such a big contrast between prophecies such as Isaiah 11:1-10 and Isaiah 53, some religious leaders in the first century thought there must be two different Messiah's – one who would die sacrificially to save the people, the other who would come as a mighty warrior to save the people from their political oppressors. The New Testament, however, reveals to us that the prophets did not mean there were two Messiah's, but only one who would come twice.

What should have been clear in the first century because of Daniel chapter nine is that Messiah was coming in their day. They should have been able to recognize Jesus as Messiah by the specific healing and miracle gifts the prophets said He would do. They should have been willing to hear Him explain and make sense of the prophecies. In fact, Jesus said the healing signs He performed were specific proof backing up His claim to be Messiah. Jesus said in John 14:11,

John 14:11 (NASB)
Believe Me that I am in the Father and the Father is in Me; otherwise believe because of the works themselves.

He went on to explain that He came to fulfill the prophecies and the whole Jewish law itself when He said in Matthew 5:17,

Matthew 5:17 (NASB)
Do not presume that I came to abolish the Law or the Prophets; I did not come to abolish, but to fulfill.

If the religious leaders in the first century had looked at prophecy from a principle-based point of view, they might have seen the signs of Messiah and believed His explanation about Himself. Many Jewish people did believe, but too many others had interpreted the prophecies of the Old Testament through the lens of their own political and economic times. They wanted Messiah to solve their problem with Rome, not their problem with sin. Of course, the reason the prophets revealed that Messiah would come twice is because God knew the first century leaders would respond to Messiah in this way.

We must be careful to discern the principles that Prophecy illustrates and not be so committed to an interpretation of it that we might miss something.

Some scholars think the breaking of the seals of the book in heaven by the Lamb of God are symbolic of events that will happen after the Rapture. Others interpret these seals as events that happen before the Rapture. Both groups have Scriptural, logical, and historical reasons for their views, but the breaking of the seals is an example of the Revelation Refrain. When Jesus the Messiah breaks the seals in the spiritual world, something physical will happen on the earth. The life principle this illustrates is that we can have confidence today that God is in absolute control of future history. Some people believe they can somehow force God to act because of the intensity of their faith. Others think that if enough Christians take over positions of leadership in business and politics, that God will be forced to return to earth. The breaking of the seals shows that it is Jesus alone who will call for and allow future events to come about as He designs and when He decides to act.

Revelation chapters six and eight describe the scene in heaven where the Lord breaks each of the seven seals that are on the closed book, in the hand of God the Father. After each seal is broken, a symbolic vision follows that link to a specific event or series of literal events on earth. Some scholars believe all of these seal events happen after the Rapture; others think the Rapture could happen at any point during the seal events. Both groups agree these events will happen before the second coming of Messiah Jesus to the earth. Exactly how and when these events will play out in the near future remains to be seen. The basic outline of the seals is as follows:

- **The breaking of the First Seal**: Revelation 6:1-2. The symbol of the first seal is a rider on a white horse that comes "conquering and to conquer." This could describe what we might call "cold war" because the rider has no weapon.
- **The breaking of the Second Seal**: Revelation 6:3-4. The symbol of the second

seal is a rider on a red horse which is linked to the departure of peace from the earth.
- **The breaking of the Third Seal**: Revelation 6:5-6. The symbol of the third seal is a rider on a black horse which is linked to scarcity of resources.
- **The breaking of the Fourth Seal**: Revelation 6:7-8. The symbol of the fourth seal is a rider on a pale horse which is linked to death by sword, famine, pestilence, and wild beasts.
- **The breaking of the Fifth seal**: Revelation 6:9-11. The fifth seal is not linked to a horse and rider or other specific symbol. Instead, the fifth seal is linked to a vision of the souls of martyrs crying out to God for justice but there is no direct link to any physical event on earth. It is, in essence, a delay in the physical events on the earth.
- **The breaking of the sixth seal:** Revelation 6:12-17. The sixth seal links immediately to an earthquake, the darkening of the sun, the moon appearing like blood and stars apparently falling in the atmosphere.
- **The breaking of the seventh seal**: Revelation 8:1-6. The seventh seal is linked to an earthquake, but the seventh seal is also the start of the seven trumpet judgements.

There are various ways the results of the breaking of the seals may play out in a literal, physical way in future-history, but each of these events are further examples of the Revelation Refrain - a vision, symbol, or description of an event in heaven that affects or illustrates literal events on earth. Revelation 6:1-2 says,

> **Revelation 6:1 – 2 (NASB)**
> Then I saw when the Lamb broke one of the seven seals, and I heard one of the four living creatures saying as with a voice of thunder, "Come." ² I looked, and behold, a white horse, and he who sat on it had a bow; and a crown was given to him, and he went out conquering and to conquer.

Since the vision of a white horse is in heaven, it is symbolic. No one should expect to see a white horse riding through the morning sky in the future. Instead, the rider on the white horse is given a specific type of crown. The word for crown in Greek is στέφανος (stef'-an-os) [49] which was the crown given for victory, particularly for those who won in the public games. Many scholars believe the rider of the white horse is symbolic of the Antichrist because the rider has a bow without arrows and his crown is not the diadem crown of royalty. Since the white horse comes first in the series, this must mean the Antichrist is revealed right at the start of the seal judgements. The breaking of the seventh seal happens at the half-way point of the Great Tribulation. According to this view, the last three-and one-half years of the Great Tribulation are when the trumpet and bowl judgements described in

Revelation chapters 8 through 19 come about. In recent years, this is the most common interpretation of the seals.

There are some concerns with this interpretation. In the first place, there is no clear identification of the white horse rider as the Antichrist. People who identify the first rider as the Antichrist make no effort to identify the riders of the other horses. This is an inconsistent interpretation because Revelation does identify the Antichrist in other verses. The rider on the pale horse is named "death," and Jesus is identified as the rider of a white horse in Revelation chapter nineteen. Overall, the Antichrist is given eleven different names in the Bible (six names in the Old Testament and five in the New Testament). It seems unlikely the first seal rider is in fact the Antichrist, but not named the Antichrist directly in the text.

There is no clear explanation in the verse about when the seals begin either. Many scholars think the seals begin when the Antichrist confirms a peace treaty with Israel, but that is not clearly written in Revelation. The Scripture also does not say how long the seal events will last, or how much time will elapse between one seal and the next. It is equally possible that each event will immediately follow the one before it or there could be days or months between each event.

Since Jesus used the specific figure of speech in Matthew chapter twenty-four that means world war, I believe it is possible that World War I was the beginning of the birth pains that Jesus warned were coming. It is, therefore, possible that the birth pains begin with the breaking of the first seal, since Scripture does not specifically say the first seal corresponds with the wrath of God or the confirmation of peace treaties with Israel by the Antichrist. If this is the case, then World War I was the physical event on earth that followed the breaking of the first seal in heaven.

It seems significant that there are only four horses in the vision of the breaking of the seven seals rather than seven. This seems inconsistent with the fact there are seven trumpet judgements rather than four trumpets and three other brass instruments such as trombones. There are also seven bowl judgements rather than four bowls and three other kitchen items such as platters. So, why are there four horses and then three other symbols linked to the seven seals? Could it be that the four seals are foundational events that happen before the Rapture? After all, when the seventh seal is broken in Revelation 6:16, the people on earth suddenly cry out,

> **Revelation 6:16b – 17 (NASB)**
> …hide us from the presence of Him who sits on the throne, and from the wrath of the Lamb; [17] for the great day of their wrath has come, and who is able to stand?

Does this mean the "wrath" of God does not begin until the seventh seal? Based on Revelation 6:16-17, it is possible that the "wrath" of God does not begin until the seventh seal is broken.

Bible scholars believe that all of the seal judgements are part of the Great Tribulation and must come after the Rapture because First Thessalonians 5:9 says,

First Thessalonians 5:9 (NASB)
For God has not destined us for wrath, but for obtaining salvation through our Lord Jesus Christ.

However, if the "wrath" of God does not formally begin until the breaking of the seventh seal, this may be the reason the seven seals are divided into four and three, unlike the trumpets and the bowls. I believe it is possible that the first four seals are symbolically different because they symbolize world events that are foundational to the start of the wrath of God and the Great Tribulation.

It is possible the first "birth pain" and the first seal was World War I and that means the possibility that the Rapture could happen at any moment is very real.

It is important not to be dogmatic about any one interpretation of these events. When these events come to pass, anyone who examines how world events line up with Scripture will see how world events have been written in the Scripture all along. This is exactly what happened in the first century. Many people misinterpreted the first coming of Messiah Jesus because of a pre-conceived, dogmatic commitment, to an interpretation of Scripture that concluded that Messiah would conquer the Romans. Much of the New Testament is an explanation of how the life and person of Jesus is clearly in Old Testament prophecy for anyone to see. In the same way, we need to be open in our view about how the prophecy of Revelation will come to pass, but firm on the overriding principle that Messiah Jesus is coming again, soon!

If the formal "wrath of God" does begin with the breaking of the sixth seal, then it is possible that the Rapture could happen at any time during the breaking of the seals. Either way, Daniel 2:21 says,

> **Daniel 2:21 (NASB)**
> It is He who changes the times and the epochs; He removes kings and establishes kings.

There is a passage in the Old Testament that would lead us to think that the breaking of some of the seals might take place before the Rapture. Zechariah 6:1-8 says,

> **Zechariah 6:1 – 8 (NASB)**
> Now I raised my eyes again and looked, and behold, four chariots were going out from between the two mountains; and the mountains were bronze mountains. ² With the first chariot were red horses, with the second chariot black horses, ³ with the third chariot white horses, and with the fourth chariot strong spotted horses. ⁴ So I responded and said to the angel who was speaking with me, "What are these, my lord?" ⁵ The angel replied to me, "These are the four spirits of heaven, going out after taking their stand before the Lord of all the earth, ⁶ with one of which the black horses are going out to the north country; and the white ones are to go out after them, while the spotted ones are to go out to the south

> country." **7** When the strong ones went out, they were eager to go to patrol the earth. And He said, "Go, patrol the earth." So they patrolled the earth. **8** Then He called out to me and spoke to me, saying, "See, those who are going to the land of the north have appeased My wrath in the land of the north."

Zechariah's vision is very similar to the vision in Revelation. Zechariah says the four colored horses, which seem to have the same or very similar colors to the horses in Revelation, are the "four spirits of heaven." Apparently, the horses are symbolic of some sort of angel or spirit under God's command, released into the earth's atmosphere, that have something to do with God's "wrath in the land of the north."

In the same way, since the book of Revelation is grounded in the Old Testament, the horses found in the four seals of Revelation are possibly symbolic of a conquering and dominating spirit in the atmosphere. This would echo the vision of the horses in Zechariah that brought about an atmosphere or spiritual condition leading into God's wrath and judgement. Also, the four seals may be linked to the birth pains that Jesus prophesied about in Matthew twenty-four. Since birth pains can come before, as well as during, a birth, it is possible that the first four or five seals may be pre-conditional events leading up to the start of the wrath of God.

It is dangerous to read an interpretation of Scripture too rigidly into today's headlines. This is because headlines change, political realities shift and what seemed clear in one moment may not be as clear one hundred years later. For example, for centuries, many theologians spiritualized the Old Testament prophecies about the nation of Israel. For nearly two thousand years, Israel as a distinct, physical nation did not exist and no one could imagine how Israel could become a literal nation again. That was the "headline" of the day – Israel as a nation did not exist and the Jewish people were hopelessly scattered worldwide, therefore, the prophecies about Israel must be symbolic. But on May 14, 1948, in one day, the United Nations recognized Israel as a sovereign nation once again. The restoration of Israel is a prophecy lesson from history we should take care to remember today.

Nevertheless, it is not wrong to speculate or wonder how some of these events might take place. One group thinks the opening of the seal judgements all come after the Rapture and another group thinks the seal judgements come before the church is Raptured away. Either of these positions could be correct. What matters is the principle that God's judgement and control over the end of history will unfold in His timing and just as He wills. When it does unfold, the prophecies will line up perfectly with literal events, just as with all the other ancient Biblical prophecies that have come to pass.

This book takes the position that the opening of the first four seals will happen before the Rapture and that at least the first seal may have already been opened. Revelation 6:2 says,

Revelation 6:2c (NASB)
…and he (first horseman) went out conquering and to conquer.

Of course, there have always been dictators,

kings, and dominating generals blazing about the earth either conquering or trying to conquer. Dr. Arnold Fruchtenbaum believes the phrase "conquering and to conquer," is a figure of speech and a poetic clue. Fruchtenbaum points out that during the twentieth century's World War I and World War II, there was something different about the nature and goals of the armies and navies during those World Wars. Prior to World War I and II, throughout world history, dictators, kings and military generals from a conquering country would wage war in an effort to take possession of a target area in the name of a king, country or empire. Unlike the rest of history, with the rise of political philosophies such as Marxism, Nazism and Communism, the motivation of twentieth century wars centered less on taking possession in the name of a king and became more about the spread of a political idea or philosophy. For example, the long, "Cold War" between the United States and the Soviet Union was less about either country gaining new territory per se and more about the spreading of the philosophy of communism versus capitalism. This was a subtle shift from the past, but it led to a different kind of conflict. Because each "side" was more concerned with political philosophy than with the actual territory either side was directly colonizing, this led to regional conflicts worldwide. The Soviet Empire supplied communist rebels to destabilize an area simply because the rebels were communist, and the United States supplied another group simply because they were not communist. In the past, kings and generals fought to expand their territory for the glory and power of their own name but at the apex of the Cold War in the early 1960's,

President John F. Kennedy wanted to preserve democracy – not his own kingdom - and Soviet Premier Nikita Khrushchev was seeking to support the advancement of communism.

In a way, the struggle of the twentieth century was a gigantic strategy game, like a game of chess. It is fascinating to note that the horseman of Revelation 6:2 is given a specific kind of crown. In Greek there are several words than can be translated as "crown" in English, but the Greek "Stephanos" crown was specifically given to the victor – of a game!

End of Days:
The Book of Revelation Explained

Chapter 12: The 2nd Seal and Ezekiel's War!
Revelation Chapter 6, Part 2 explained...

In Revelation chapter six, the vision of Jesus breaking the seals is a spiritual event that links to literal events on the earth which is another example of the Revelation Refrain. The breaking of the 1st four seals release four different colored horses. There is a vision in Zechariah chapter six of different colored horses remarkably like the four horsemen of the seals in Revelation chapter six. This means it is at least possible that some of the literal events linked to the breaking of the seals is about the release of worldwide preconditions or a political and cultural mindset that sets the stage for the Great Tribulation rather than being the actual beginning of the Great Tribulation. Revelation 6:3 says,

> **Revelation 6:3 – 4 (NASB)**
> When He broke the second seal, I heard the second living creature saying, "Come." 4 And another, a red horse, went out; and to him who sat on it, it was granted to take peace from the earth, and that men would slay one another; and a great sword was given to him.

There is no hint as to the identification of the horseman in these verses and no direct indication how much time has gone by since the first seal was broken. There may be a gap in time between the breaking of the first and the second seal, or no gap in time at all, or all the literal events linked to the first four seals could happen all at once. There have always been wars and men slaying one another throughout human history. The significance of the second seal, therefore, may be that it is linked to the start of the birth pains that Jesus spoke about in Matthew 24:6 where He says,

> **Matthew 24:6 (NASB)**
> And you will be hearing of wars and rumors of wars. See that you are not alarmed, for those things must take place, but that is not yet the end. [7] For nation will rise against nation, and kingdom against kingdom, and there will be famines and earthquakes in various places. [8] But all these things are merely the beginning of birth pains.

As I have noted before, the figure of speech "nation will rise against nation, and kingdom against kingdom," is likely a reference to world war and World War I was the world's first true world war. It was called "the war to end all wars," because while there have been many wars in human history, nothing compared to the carnage of the First World War! In World War I, new battle tactics and inventions such as the machine gun, the tank and poison gas were used. The number of dead and wounded was unlike anything ever seen in human history; yet, as dreadful as this was, World War II was significantly worse, with bombers capable of carpet-bombing entire cities and the first use in war of the atomic bomb. The atom bomb is unlike anything anyone could have imagined until the twentieth century. In 1945, people could hardly believe it when a single bomb dropped by a single airplane literally vaporized 70 – 80,000 people instantly and wounded another 70,000 at Hiroshima, Japan. [50] After a second bomb was dropped at Nagasaki, Japan, the world knew we had entered an entirely unique period in human history.

Today, nuclear weapons far exceed the power of the bombs dropped on Japan in 1945. Today, a single Trident missile submarine carries forty times as much fire power as the combined munitions power used by both sides of the conflict in World War II. [51] If ever there was a time when peace was taken from the earth, it is the time between the start of World War I in 1914 and the end of World War II in 1945. Since that time, more than 150 other wars have been fought and that is more warfare than at any other time in history. Today, about 40% of all world spending is on weapons. [52] Every day, in every place on the planet, peace rests on a razor's edge.

Revelation 6:3 does not say the second horseman releases war. Instead, it says the horseman "was granted to take peace" and today peace has long since left the earth. Jesus said in Matthew 24:37,

Matthew 24:37 (NASB)
For the coming of the Son of Man will be just like the days of Noah.

Genesis 6:5 and 6:11 says that in the days of Noah,

> **Genesis 6:5b, 11 – 12 (NASB)**
> ...that every intent of the thoughts of their hearts was only evil continually... [11] Now the earth was corrupt in the sight of God, and the earth was filled with violence. [12] And God looked on the earth, and behold, it was corrupt; for humanity had corrupted its way upon the earth.

Peace has been taken from the earth and our world today is filled with evil and violence continually, unlike any other time in recorded history. In recent decades the wholesale slaughter of human beings has reached a level unimaginable in the past through the horror of abortion. Tens of millions of children are murdered before birth and a sense of lawlessness spreads everywhere.

If the breaking of some of the seals are pre-conditional events and are part of the birth pains that lead up to the Great Tribulation, then there is another prophetic event that apparently needs to be fulfilled prior to the official start of the Great Tribulation. This coming event may be part of the second seal, or a part of the lack of peace and the birth pains that lead up to the wrath of God. There is good reason to think this event could happen very soon - It is Ezekiel's war. Ezekiel 38:1-5 reads,

> **Ezekiel 38:1 – 5 (NASB)**
> Now the word of the Lord came to me saying, [2] "Son of man, set your face toward

Gog of the land of Magog, the prince of Rosh, Meshech and Tubal, and prophesy against him [3] and say, 'Thus says the Lord God, "Behold, I am against you, O Gog, prince of Rosh, Meshech and Tubal. [4] I will turn you about and put hooks into your jaws, and I will bring you out, and all your army, horses and horsemen, all of them splendidly attired, a great company with buckler and shield, all of them wielding swords; [5] Persia, Ethiopia and Put with them, all of them with shield and helmet; [6] Gomer with all its troops; Beth-togarmah from the remote parts of the north with all its troops—many peoples with you.

The word "Gog" in this prophecy does not refer to a place or even a specific person. It is a royal title similar to the ancient title of "Pharaoh" for an Egyptian king or the word "Czar" for a Russian king. [53] Ancient Jewish Rabbi's identified "Magog, Rosh, Meshech, and Tubal" as land areas currently occupied by Turkey and Russia. Persia, Ethiopia and Put are apparently where Iran, Ethiopia and Libya are today. [54] Gomer and Beth-togarmah may be parts of eastern Europe, but when the prophecy of Ezekiel was written about 580 B.C. there were no political alliances between the countries occupying those areas. Today, however, modern Iran occupies the land of the Persians. The land of Put is likely modern Somalia. Turkey and Russia either occupy or control areas traditionally identified as Rosh, Meshech and Tubal and all these countries have economic, political, or military connections. Russia, for example, is currently rebuilding its Soviet-era naval bases in Somalia and Ethiopia so they can conduct naval operations in the Indian Ocean and the Red Sea. [55] Russia also has military alliances with Iran, Syria, and Libya. While Turkey is, as of this writing, a NATO allied country, there is growing sympathy in Turkey with Russian foreign relations goals because Turkey is a majority Muslim country opposed to the nation of Israel. These connections mean that a military link between all these countries is possible. Ezekiel 38:8 says,

> **Ezekiel 38:8 (NASB)**
> After many days you will be summoned; in the latter years you will come into the land that is restored from the sword, whose inhabitants have been gathered from many nations to the mountains of Israel which had been a continual waste; but its people were brought out from the nations, and they are living securely, all of them.

The Ezekiel War will happen "after many days" and "in the latter years." The prophecy was written about 580 B.C., so our modern era is certainly many days after Ezekiel prophesied and there are a great many signs that we are in the latter years. One of those signs is that the nation of Israel has been gathered from many nations and the Jewish state was recognized as a sovereign nation on May 14, 1948. In 1948, the land of Israel was largely desert or malarial swamp land in an arid environment and had been that way for centuries. Israeli farmers invented the drip irrigation system, drained the swamps, and turned the desert into farms that are the envy of the world today.

The Nation of Israel today certainly fits the description of Israel that is found in Ezekiel. In fact, the actual mountains in the land of Israel finally fell within the boundaries of the nation in June 1967 after the Six-day war. Ezekiel's War could not have happened before 1967 and it has not happened as of this writing either. It has only been over the last five or six decades that this prophecy could be fulfilled, but the Ezekiel war has not yet happened. It must happen soon and may be a part of "peace being taken from the earth."

Some Bible scholars think the Ezekiel war will happen during the Great Tribulation or has already happened symbolically, but these conclusions do not fit the specific time indicators in the prophecy, as we will see later, and no such war has happened in the past. The prophecy also says the specific motivation of the invaders is a desire for plunder - a motivation no one could really imagine over the last two thousand years since the land had been a wasteland for millennia. Ezekiel 38:10-12 gives this motivation for plunder in more detail. Ezekiel 38:10-12 reads,

> **Ezekiel 38:10 – 12 (NASB)**
> 'This is what the Lord God says, "It will come about on that day, that thoughts will come into your mind and you will devise an evil plan, [11] and you will say, 'I will go up against the land of unwalled villages. I will go against those who are at rest, that live securely, all of them living without walls and having no bars or gates, [12] to capture spoil and to seize plunder, to turn your hand against the waste places which are now

inhabited, and against the people who are gathered from the nations, who have acquired cattle and goods, who live at the center of the world.'

Plunder are goods that a conquering army confiscates as they take control of an area. For centuries there has been speculation about what kind of plunder would motivate a modern military alliance to attack Israel, especially since verse eight says that the area will be a "continual waste" up until the time of the invasion. The mystery deepens because the land of Israel during the days Ezekiel wrote his prophecy was not exactly a breadbasket or a place where gold or silver was plentiful. In the days of Abraham, about a thousand years before Ezekiel, Israel had been a land of plenty, a land "flowing with milk and honey," but the days of that plenty were long gone by Ezekiel's time.

In today's world, farmland, or livestock or even gold and silver seem like a small motivation to tempt a full military invasion. Verse four says this motivation for plunder will be so intense the leader of the invasion force will feel dragged into it. It will be as if he has no choice! There will be spiritual hooks in his jaws pulling him into the invasion.

It is unwise to be dogmatic or rigid when reading prophecy into today's headlines. Even when things appear to make sense as modern events unfold, it is wise to stay humble. Nevertheless, there is nothing wrong with some speculation so long as the motivation is to show a reasonable, plausible, or realistic way a prophecy might come to pass. By showing how a prophecy could unfold, it may give unbelievers pause and give believers a greater confidence. In terms of Ezekiel's War, we know for certain there will be an invasion attempt of Israel, attempted by a confederacy of nations, and at least one of the participating nations will be from an area currently controlled by Russia. There is some uncertainty about the ancient names of some of the other nations in this invasion force, however, this diverse invasion force will be from areas both north and south of modern-day Israel.

As of this writing, modern Russia is allied with Syria, a nation directly north of Israel and a traditional adversary of Israel. Currently, there is a civil war raging in Syria and this has allowed Russia to develop and build-up its military presence in Syria. The Ezekiel alliance may be linking up on tonight's evening news!

In terms of a modern motivation for plunder, Russia may be motivated by changing interests in energy resources. For example, Russia today is a major supplier of natural gas and oil to Europe. Natural gas exports are a serious economic interest to Russia since the Russian economy has been so unpredictable and risky after the fall of the Soviet Union. If Russia loses or sees a major downturn in profits from exports of natural gas and oil, it could have a massive negative economic impact on the country. In fact, such a loss could shake the current political leadership out of power. It is also interesting to note that Israel just recently discovered one of largest natural gas fields in the world. It is called "the Leviathan field." This natural gas field is so large it can fuel all of Israel's energy needs for the next forty years. It will eventually make Israel a major exporter of natural gas, particularly to Europe. In fact, in January 2020

Israel signed a treaty with Cyprus, Greece, and Italy to export natural gas into Europe. [56]

The Leviathan gas field will make Israel an energy superpower, completely independent of any need to import fuel from any other country. Israel will begin exporting natural gas cheaper and in greater volume to Europe by 2025. This means that within the next few years, Russia stands to lose all, or a substantial amount, of economic input from its exports of natural gas to Europe. This will be a potential major threat to its economy, especially if there is a world economic downturn of some kind. Israel has contracted with Russian companies to help them develop the field, but the link between Russian companies and one of the largest natural gas fields in the world, may eventually suggest to Russia it would do better to take total control of the field directly. If the ongoing Palestinian political crisis in Israel ignites again, that could be all the excuse Russia and its anti-Israel allies would need to invade. The real goal of any such invasion, however, will be to take control of a major economic resource, that is, to take plunder.

In light of recent weaknesses in America and other Western countries because of the Covid-19 pandemic and economic downturns, it is interesting to notice in the prophecy how other countries will react to the northern alliance invasion of Israel. Ezekiel 38:13 says,

Ezekiel 38:13 (NASB)
Sheba and Dedan and the merchants of Tarshish with all its villages will say to you, 'Have you come to capture spoil? Have you assembled your company to seize plunder,

to carry away silver and gold, to take away cattle and goods, to capture great spoil?'"

Ezekiel 38:13 means that these other countries will only issue verbal objections to the northern alliance invasion of Israel but will not intervene militarily. In today's world, if one country invades another country there is always a risk that other nations around the world might send military resources to intervene. This is exactly what happened in 1990 when Iraq invaded Kuwait. In 1991, the United States, in response to an Iraqi invasion of Kuwait, led a coalition of dozens of other countries to send military resources in and push Iraq out of Kuwait. [57] This sort of intervention tends to discourage one country from invading another.

In Ezekiel thirty-eight, however, other countries will merely make verbal protests, probably to save face. At that future time, the world will be so anti-Israel that they will simply do nothing. For example, in the United States today there is growing sympathy for the Palestinians and increasing anti-Israel and anti-Jewish attitudes. If Russia sees Israel as a major economic threat and perceives the United States as unwilling to risk war over Israel since most of the world views Israel as the invader of the Palestinians, they might see the situation as an opportunity to destroy Israel. This would also enable them to take control of the Leviathan natural gas field. All of this is just speculation, but it is at least reasonably possible. Ezekiel 38:14-23 reads,

Ezekiel 38:14a, 16 – 23 (NASB)
"Therefore prophesy, son of man, and say to Gog, ...[16] you will come up against My people Israel like a cloud to cover the land. It shall come about in the last days that I will bring you against My land, so that the nations may know Me when I am sanctified through you before their eyes, O Gog." ... [18] It will come about on that day, when Gog comes against the land of Israel," declares the Lord God, "that My fury will mount up in My anger. [19] In My zeal and in My blazing wrath I declare that on that day there will surely be a great earthquake in the land of Israel. [20] The fish of the sea, the birds of the heavens, the beasts of the field, all the creeping things that creep on the earth, and all the men who are on the face of the earth will shake at My presence; the mountains also will be thrown down, the steep pathways will collapse and every wall will fall to the ground. [21] I will call for a sword against him on all My mountains," declares the Lord God. "Every man's sword will be against his brother. [22] With pestilence and with blood I will enter into judgement with him; and I will rain on him and on his troops, and on the many peoples who are with him, a torrential rain, with hailstones, fire and brimstone. [23] I will magnify Myself, sanctify Myself, and make Myself known in the sight of many nations; and they will know that I am the Lord.'"

The northern alliance invasion of Israel will seem successful at first. The alliance will be so vast it will seem that Israel could not possibly survive. God will allow it to seem like an unwinnable situation, so that when Israel is saved, everyone will be able to see that Israel's salvation is a miracle of God. God will cause an earthquake so violent that the whole planet will shake. This event will cause mass confusion so that the alliance against Israel will turn their weapons on each other. Some critics and unbelievers will claim that Israel will be saved by a lucky chance. Anyone who knows these Scriptures, however, or anyone who sees that a perfectly timed earthquake causing invading army to destroy itself cannot be a coincidence - they will know that God intervened.

On a side note, Ezekiel 38:22 is consistent with scientific observation also. Major earthquakes have been known to cause strange atmospheric events: flashes of light, lightning, hail, bluish flames, and spheres of light bouncing across the landscape. These atmospheric events happen when electromagnetic fields in the earth are disrupted by an earthquake. In some cases, different types of rocks can explode or even catch on fire. Some earthquakes are so severe they can launch violent clouds of dust and debris into the atmosphere that can condense into hail. [58]These events have been documented in history and studied by scientists.

Finally, Ezekiel 39:9 and verses 11-12 explain why this event is likely to happen before the Great Tribulation. Ezekiel 39:9, 11b-12 reads,

> **Ezekiel 39:9, 11b-12 (NASB)**
> Then those who inhabit the cities of Israel will go out and make fires with the weapons and burn them, both shields and bucklers, bows and arrows, war clubs and spears, and for seven years they will make fires of them... [11b] So they will bury Gog there with all his horde, and they will call it the valley of Hamon-gog. [12] For seven months the house of Israel will be burying them in order to cleanse the land.

Based on what we know from the book of Revelation, the Great Tribulation will last seven years – not seven years and seven months. In addition, the book of Revelation tells us that the first three and a half years of the Great Tribulation will be filled with terrible judgements and the second three and a half years will be so severe that if God did not end those days no humans would survive. The seven years of the Great Tribulation will not be the sort of time anyone will be burying bodies or collecting military leftovers for fuel. Also, the Ezekiel war cannot be the same war as the final battle of Armageddon because that battle happens at the end of the Great Tribulation leaving no time for seven months of burying the dead or seven further years to use up the leftover fuel. It seems more likely that the Ezekiel war is part of the preparation for the Great Tribulation, part of the birth pains. It is also likely this war is next on the prophetic calendar, and based on the speculation above, it is not out of the realm of possibility this war could happen in the near future.

**End of Days:
The Book of Revelation Explained**

Chapter 13: The Third Seal!
Revelation chapter 6, Part 3 explained...

Revelation 6: 5 – 6 (NASB)
When He broke the third seal, I heard the third living creature saying, "Come." I looked, and behold, a black horse; and he who sat on it had a pair of scales in his hand. [6] And I heard something like a voice in the center of the four living creatures saying, "A quart of wheat for a denarius, and three quarts of barley for a denarius; and do not damage the oil and the wine."

Revelation 6:5-6 does not identify the rider of the horse and there are no time markers in these verses either. We do not know if the breaking of the third seal happens immediately after the breaking of the second or if there is a time gap between them. We have no idea how long this possible gap could be nor how long the events that the breaking of the third seal describes will last. The third seal, like each of the others, is a vision of events that happen in heaven. As a vision, this means the horse, the scales, the horseman and the voice are part of the Revelation Refrain, symbols that link to actual events in the physical.

A denarius is not a coin in use today, but it represented a day's wages in the first century. Three quarts of barley is not standard grocery fare today, but in the first century it was standard famine rations for a Roman solider. Some interpreters think the third seal is a description of worldwide famine, but neither the word "famine" nor "worldwide" occur in the prophecy. Oil and wine were commonly used as medicine in the first century, but the horseman is commanded not to "damage the oil and the wine." Excluding oil and wine means this prophecy is probably about economic scarcity rather than famine since in a true famine, every item used for food would be in short supply. In fact, it says a day's wages will be necessary to buy a normally cheap barley meal so the third seal may be about major inflation, expensive goods, or economic depression.

In the late 1920's and throughout the 1930's, the world suffered an economic collapse unlike any other in human history – the Great Depression. During those dreadful years, people in many countries would work an entire day just to purchase a single meal. The Great Depression was a worldwide event where overall Gross Domestic Product on the planet dropped approximately 15%, and unemployment soared to 20-33%. It was the worst economic downturn in world history. [59] If ever there was a black horse in heaven and a day's wage to buy a single meal on earth, it was during the Great Depression in the 1930's.

In the United States, and many other countries, the one thing that was plentiful during the Great Depression was alcohol. In America during the 1920's, alcohol was technically illegal but at the height of the Great Depression in 1933, the legal prohibition against alcohol was ended. The Great Depression was a time of scarcity that did not touch the oil or the wine.

It is possible at least some of the first six seals happen before the Rapture and the start of the Great Tribulation, but no one should be dogmatic that the Great Depression was the breaking of the third seal. The Depression may have been merely a good picture to warn us what the breaking of the third seal will be like in the future.

Human beings tend to follow a pattern in terms of economic scarcity. When the economy is good and there are few shortages, people tend to become lukewarm about God, but when people face trouble, they will seek Him. Psalm 78:34 says, "when He killed them, then they looked for Him…

<u>Whether the Great Depression was the third seal or not, both this scripture passage and the lesson of history from 1929 should be a warning to us today not to put hope in physical things or put trust in money.</u>

> **<u>Revelation 6:7 (NASB)</u>**
> When the Lamb broke the fourth seal, I heard the voice of the fourth living creature saying, "Come." [8] I looked, and behold, an ashen horse; and he who sat on it had the name Death; and Hades was following with him. Authority was given to them over a fourth of the earth, to kill with sword and with famine and with pestilence and by the wild beasts of the earth.

The rider of the fourth horse is named "death" and Hades is the place of the dead, but the vision does not say what Hades looks like nor is there any suggestion about how a place like Hades can follow anyone. This means the fourth horsemen and Hades are part of a symbolic section of the Revelation Refrain. What is literal is that one fourth of the human population of the earth will die. It does not say how long it will take for one fourth of the earth's population to die, but even during the worst plagues, wars, and famines in human history, such a huge percentage of the population has never yet been killed because of one event or short series of events. [60] [61] If this were to happen today, it would mean the deaths of at least two billion people in a very short time span.

There are four causes of death listed with the fourth horseman – sword, famine, pestilence, and wild beasts – but it is not clear how many are killed by which cause. It could be that a war brings about most of these deaths and the war leads to famine, disease and untamed wild animals that kill the rest.

Revelation 6:9 – 11 (NASB)
When the Lamb broke the fifth seal, I saw underneath the altar the souls of those who had been slain because of the word of God, and because of the testimony which they had maintained; [10] and they cried out with a loud voice, saying, "How long, O Lord, holy and true, will You refrain from judging and avenging our blood on those who dwell on the earth?" [11] And there was given to each of them a white robe; and they were told that they should rest for a little while longer, until

the number of their fellow servants and their brethren who were to be killed even as they had been, would be completed also.

It is unclear who these martyrs are from the text alone, but it seems likely that these are believers killed for their faith after the Rapture because it says these are the "souls of those who had been slain because of the Word of God," and they are still in a disembodied state. At the Rapture, all believers who died before the Rapture and all who are alive during the Rapture event will be transformed into immortal, resurrection bodies. Since these are souls that still wait for a physical resurrection, they must be believers who die for Christ after the Rapture and during the Great Tribulation. This interpretation is further confirmed by Revelation chapter seven, which says there will be many people after the Rapture who will be saved. Revelation 7:13 says,

> **Revelation 7: 13 – 14 (NASB)**
> Then one of the elders responded, saying to me, "These who are clothed in the white robes, who are they, and where have they come from?" [14] I said to him, "My lord, you know." And he said to me, "These are the ones who come out of the great tribulation, and they have washed their robes and made them white in the blood of the Lamb.

Revelation 6:9 is another example of the Revelation Refrain because it is a vision of the throne room of God. Verses 6-11 are symbolic because they describe events in heaven, and it does not say what a soul looks like nor does the text explain why they need to be given white robes. White robes are usually symbolic of being washed clean from sin, so these souls in Revelation 6:9 still await being cleansed and raised from the dead. It also does not say how long these souls will need to wait or how long they have been waiting up to this point. What is apparently literal is there will be a gap in time, a "little while" more, until Jesus returns to avenge His followers who have died for their faith in Him and there will be more martyrs before the end. The fifth seal seems to be something like a short delay, a kind of "deep breath before the plunge." With the breaking of the sixth seal, people will finally realize the wrath of God has come. It does not say how long it will take for the souls of the martyrs to make their appeal to God or how long it will take for God to give them His reassurance.

Revelation 6:12 – 17 (NASB)
I looked when He broke the sixth seal, and there was a great earthquake; and the sun became black as sackcloth made of hair, and the whole moon became like blood; [13] and the stars of the sky fell to the earth, as a fig tree casts its unripe figs when shaken by a great wind. [14] The sky was split apart like a scroll when it is rolled up, and every mountain and island were moved out of their places. [15] Then the kings of the earth and the great men and the commanders and the rich and the strong and every slave and free man hid themselves in the caves and among the rocks of the mountains; [16] and they said to the mountains and to the rocks, "Fall on us and hide us from the presence of Him who

sits on the throne, and from the wrath of the Lamb; [17] for the great day of their wrath has come, and who is able to stand?"

Revelation 6:12-17 is another example of the Revelation Refrain because John uses the words "like" and "as' to describe what he sees in the vision. It is how these events will appear from the point of view of a man watching from a distance. What is literal is a major earthquake, severe atmospheric upheaval, and the reaction of people on the earth.

The word "star" in Greek is ἀστήρ (as-tare') [62] and while it can mean the stars in the night sky, it more generally means any atmospheric light, not necessarily the precise astronomy term "star" as we mean it today. We know from the context that he means something falling from the sky that looks like the stars in the night sky. The actual stars in the night sky remain intact because we see in Revelation 8:12 that the stars are still in the sky. This is a description of what a "man on the ground" might see in the atmosphere and feel on the earth if something like a super volcano were to erupt. For example, John says "every mountain and island were moved out of their places" so this will be a worldwide, earth shattering earthquake causing volcanic events that will throw trillions of tons of ash and soot into the sky blocking the rays of the sun. From the ground, the sky will appear as black as sackcloth. The ash will also create a prism-like effect in the atmosphere so the moon would appear blood-red, particularly at sunrise and sunset. Falling volcanic debris from the upper atmosphere will fall like stars from the sky and the atmospheric shockwave from the explosion passing through the clouds of high-altitude volcanic ash will be so intense it will look like the sky is being split down the middle.

Something similar to the sixth seal event has happened in recorded history with much the same results. On August 27, 1883, at the Island of Krakatoa in Indonesia, a volcano erupted after a massive earthquake. The quake opened a crack in the earth and billions of gallons of sea water slipped into the opening. The water sinking into this crack was suddenly flash boiled into super-heated steam by magma from deep within the volcano. Since the steam was under immense pressure, the island exploded, literally tearing it instantly to shreds. The blast was heard 3,000 miles away! Sailors reported ruptured ear drums 40 miles out and an estimated 36,000 people were killed. The atmospheric pressure wave appeared to witnesses to split the sky in two. The pressure wave from the explosion bounced around the entire planet four times, burning ash fell with streaks of light from the sky, the sun was darkened by at least one third and ash in the upper atmosphere resulted in red sunsets so vivid and blood-red that New York fire trucks were called out believing something in the city must be on fire. [63] Everything that happened at Krakatoa fits the description of Revelation 6: 12-17 to the letter.

The volcanic explosion of Krakatoa stunned the world in the late nineteenth century, but the earthquake and explosion in Revelation 6:12 will make Krakatoa seem like a little firecracker. The Revelation 6:12 explosion will move every mountain and every island on the planet, probably because the event will shift every tectonic plate on earth! Everyone will suddenly recognize that the challenging events the world has witnessed up to this point were just warnings. This event, they will say, is the "wrath of God!" Every human being on earth will be stunned, no one will be able to ignore it and every person - the great, the small, the rich and the poor, will know that no one can stand against God.

There have been natural events in recorded history that fit the description of the sixth seal, so there is no reason to doubt this prophecy will unfold in the future.

End of Days: The Book of Revelation Explained

Chapter 14: Why fear the future?
Revelation 7: 1-17 explained...

The Rapture could happen before the seal events, or it could happen at any time during the first five seal events. When the sixth seal is broken, everyone on earth will realize the wrath of God is being poured out on the earth. Revelation 7:1 says,

> **Revelation 7:1 (NASB)**
> After this I saw four angels standing at the four corners of the earth, holding back the four winds of the earth, so that no wind would blow on the earth or on the sea or on any tree.

The words "after this" are a clue because there is some flexibility in the Greek grammar. It means that some of the events in chapters 7 through 9 may be "interludes," (also called "periscopes" by theologians) which give more detailed descriptions of events but are out of a sequence.

For example, chapter seven is apparently an interlude, adding information and details about events that happen just before the seventh seal is opened. This chapter describes people who convert to Christ after the Rapture and must therefore suffer through the judgements of God upon the earth. Chapter seven is also another example of the Revelation Refrain because it begins with a vision in heaven. In a visionary context, the description of angels "standing at the four corners of the earth holding back the four winds" and "the four corners of the earth" are figures of speech from the first century representing the four cardinal directions – North, South, East, and West.

Even today we use "accommodative" language, that is, figures of speech, like this to describe our point of view even though we "know" the technical truth. For example, most people still use the concept of "sunrise" and "sunset" even though we know scientifically that the sun does not "rise" or "set." Instead, we know that the earth turns relative to our point of view. Most people understand the use of "point of view" language in our modern age since every weather app on our smart phones and every weather person on our television sets still lists the times for "sunrise" and "sunset." Accommodative language is common and useful in the human experience, so just because the Bible describes something so apparently unscientific as "the four corners of the earth" does not mean the Bible teaches that the earth is square. It is simply using point of view language. Besides, ancient mariners and astronomers for the most part, knew the earth was round, and the Greeks had in fact already calculated the approximate size of the planet (with some accuracy) long before Jesus was born. Finally, the context of this chapter is part of the Revelation Refrain, something "visionary" and "symbolic" illustrating a physical reality, so a figure of speech is not out of character. Revelation 7:2 continues to use point of view and visionary or symbolic language in verse two which reads,

> **Revelation 7:2-3 (NASB)**
> And I saw another angel ascending from the rising of the sun, having the seal of the living God; and he cried out with a loud voice to the four angels to whom it was granted to harm the earth and the sea, ³ saying, "Do not harm the earth or the sea or the trees until we have sealed the bond-servants of our God on their foreheads."

No one knows what the "seal of the living God" looks like, how big it is or even how the writer knows what he is seeing. Obviously, the Holy Spirit is revealing the meaning behind what the writer sees, but John does not write down the exact details. Revelation 7:4 reads,

> **Revelation 7:4 – 8 (NASB)**
> And I heard the number of those who were sealed, one hundred and forty-four thousand sealed from every tribe of the sons of Israel: ⁵ from the tribe of Judah, twelve thousand were sealed, from the tribe of Reuben twelve thousand, from the tribe of Gad twelve thousand, ⁶ from the tribe of Asher twelve thousand, from the tribe of Naphtali twelve thousand, from the tribe of Manasseh twelve thousand, ⁷ from the tribe of Simeon twelve thousand, from the tribe of Levi twelve thousand, from the tribe of Issachar twelve thousand, ⁸ from the tribe of Zebulun twelve thousand, from the tribe of Joseph twelve

thousand, from the tribe of Benjamin, twelve thousand were sealed.

The 144,000 are specifically from the "sons of Israel," and God lists off the number that will come from each tribe, so there can be no doubt that these 144,000 men are Jews. In Scripture, there are at least nineteen different lists of the twelve tribes in twenty-nine different passages. [64] Each is slightly different because each list was intended to emphasize a different issue and yet keep the symmetry of twelve tribes. Sometimes a list will combine Ephraim and Manasseh, calling it the tribe of Joseph. Some of these lists add the tribe of Levi, but Levi is usually left out because they did not own land and were responsible for priestly duties in the kingdom. In all cases, the point is not the exactness of the tribal lists but the specific concept of the number twelve.

Since each list also depends on the context, there has been a great deal of speculation about why the tribe of Dan is not listed here in Revelation chapter seven. Some scholars think it is because idolatry was brought into Israel through the tribe of Dan. This is not specifically written in Scripture and there were tribes, such as the tribe of Ephraim, that also brought idolatry into Israel. Dan is also listed in the millennial tribal list found in Ezekiel chapter forty-eight, so descendants from the tribe of Dan will not be lost. Today, of course, most Jewish people do not know which tribe they come from anyway.

Some critics argue that since the lists of tribes sometimes differs that the Bible contradicts itself. This is not true because each tribal list is intended to emphasize a different point. In Revelation seven, the point is that God alone will seal these 144,000. No one today can claim to be part of the 144,000 because only God will know who they are, and it is God alone who seals them. None of these men will be Gentiles (non-Jewish) so any modern Gentile group (such as Jehovah's Witnesses) who claim they know who the 144,000 are must be wrong. Any "replacement" teachers are also wrong because God lists off the specific tribes from which He will seal these men. Revelation 7:9 reads,

> **Revelation 7:9 – 12 (NASB)**
> After these things I looked, and behold, a great multitude which no one could count, from every nation and all tribes and peoples and tongues, standing before the throne and before the Lamb, clothed in white robes, and palm branches were in their hands; [10] and they cry out with a loud voice, saying, "Salvation to our God who sits on the throne, and to the Lamb." [11] And all the angels were standing around the throne and around the elders and the four living creatures; and they fell on their faces before the throne and worshiped God, [12] saying, "Amen, blessing and glory and wisdom and thanksgiving and honor and power and might, be to our God forever and ever. Amen."

After the sealing of the 144,000, John also sees a "great multitude" of people, far more than just the 144,000, who will turn to Jesus during the Great Tribulation. It is clear from these verses that no people group on earth will be left out from hearing the Gospel. In the past, no one could imagine how such a thing could happen since there are so many remote places in the world. Today, the foundations needed to fulfill this prophecy are in place because we have technologies so advanced there is no place on the planet where information cannot flow freely. The message of Jesus, enhanced by the mystery and suddenness of the Rapture, will be known throughout the earth and an untold army of believers will respond. John sees them waving palm branches because in the first century, palm branches were a sign of victory.

The people will cry out saying, "Salvation to our God," but since God does not need saving, this phrase is a figure of speech. It is like saying, "Good for you" when someone wins a trophy. It means, "God is the source of our salvation, and we recognize this truth." In fact, John explains this in verses thirteen through seventeen which read,

Revelation 7:13 – 17 (NASB)
Then one of the elders responded, saying to me, "These who are clothed in the white robes, who are they, and where have they come from?" [14] I said to him, "My lord, you know." And he said to me, "These are the ones who come out of the great tribulation, and they have washed their robes and made them white in the blood of the Lamb. [15] For this reason, they are before the throne of God; and they serve Him day and night in His temple; and He who sits on the throne will spread His tabernacle over them. [16] They will hunger no longer, nor thirst anymore; nor will the sun beat down on them, nor any heat; [17] for the Lamb in the

center of the throne will be their shepherd and will guide them to springs of the water of life; and God will wipe every tear from their eyes."

The Scripture does not exactly say what the 144,000 will do or what being sealed really means, but in Scripture a seal or sealing, such as being anointed with oil, is usually the mark of a special calling or task. Immediately after describing the 144,000, John describes a crowd of believers in white robes that is much larger than 144,000. Later, in Revelation chapter 14, we find out that "no lie" was found in the mouth of the 144,000 either. From these two facts, many scholars conclude that the 144,000 will be preachers. These 144,000 Jewish men turn to Jesus as their Messiah immediately after the Rapture! It seems likely that the sudden disappearance of Christians, the rise of the Antichrist and the judgements being poured out on the earth will give their preaching great credibility.

Even in the present, before the Rapture, there are many stories of people from remote tribes looking for God who have had a dream, or see a vision, find a Bible, or meet a missionary. One way or another, people who are looking for God will find Jesus, because God is not unfair. Acts 17:25 says,

Acts 17:25b – 28 (NASB)
He Himself gives to all people life and breath and all things; [26] and He made from one man every nation of mankind to live on all the face of the earth, having determined their appointed times and the boundaries of their habitation, [27] that they would seek God,

if perhaps they might feel around for Him and find Him, though He is not far from each one of us; **28** for in Him we live and move and exist, as even some of your own poets have said, 'For we also are His descendants.'

Although we do not have all the details because God alone is the judge, there will be people saved from every nation, even during the Great Tribulation – because God loves even His enemies.

End of Days:
The Book of Revelation Explained

Chapter 15: Without Excuse!
Revelation Chapter 8 explained...

Revelation says that even when people know God is judging the earth, they will harden their hearts against Him. This is a consistent truth found in the Bible. People routinely harden their hearts against God's leading, and the more irrational they become, the louder the Lord will get until His voice just plain hurts!

While Christians should not expect to feel the wrath of God, God may allow us to feel the wrath of man and the wrath of nature (so to speak). After all, the people of God have felt these things many times in history from persecution, wars, and natural disasters. For example, the book of Exodus tells us the people of God were under the wrath of man when Pharaoh, the king of Egypt, treated them brutally. Exodus 1:13 says,

> **Exodus 1:13 – 14 (NASB)**
> The Egyptians used violence to compel the sons of Israel to labor; [14] and they made their lives bitter with hard labor in mortar and bricks and at all kinds of labor in the field, all their labors which they violently had them perform as slaves.

In Exodus, once Pharaoh was confronted by Moses for the first time, things did not immediately get better for the children of Israel. It seems that the people expected things to get better right away, but Pharaoh made things worse for the people of Israel. In fact, the book of Exodus tells us that the first few plagues affected everyone in the country – Egyptians and Hebrews. It was not until the fourth plague that there was any separation between what the pagan Egyptian people were experiencing and what the people of God were going through. This means the children of Israel were allowed to feel the wrath of nature when the Nile River was turned into blood, when the country was overrun with frogs and when lice spread across man and beast. Nevertheless, this process of increasing plagues was part of God's plan to judge the Egyptians and deliver His people. Within the judgement process, there came a point after the fourth plague where God began to separate His people. It says in Exodus 8:22,

> **Exodus 8:22 – 23 (NASB)**
> But on that day I will set apart the land of Goshen, where My people are living, so that no swarms of flies will be there, in order that you may know that I, the Lord, am in the midst of the land. I will put a division between My people and your people. Tomorrow this sign will occur.

Apparently, during the first four plagues, Pharaoh used his own freewill to defy the God of Israel, but afterward we read that God hardened Pharaoh's heart, because God had given the king a chance to change of his own freewill. God allowed the minor suffering of the Nile turning to blood and the annoyance of frogs and lice to demonstrate by these mighty miracles that He was the true God. Pharaoh could have turned to the true God but since he refused, God confirmed his freewill choice. In short, it was as if God was saying "Okay, king! That's what you want – that's what you'll get!"

The truth is, when someone refuses God's call repeatedly, there comes a point where God's patience dries up and His wrath against human rebellion begins. The first three plagues did cause suffering, and the fourth plague of swarming flies was a final warning, but since the king of Egypt refused to turn to God, the full wrath of God began to fall upon him and his people. The fifth plague killed livestock, the sixth infected people with vicious, oozing boils, the seventh was a hailstorm the likes of which had never been seen before and it destroyed nearly every growing food stock in the land. The eighth was an invasion of locusts that ate everything the hail did not destroy, threatening starvation and death. The ninth was a blackout so severe the darkness could be felt so that people literally gnawed on their fingers because of the oppression. The wrath of God that started with the fifth plague was obviously considerably more severe than the plagues leading up to it but there was a separation between the people of Egypt and the people of God after the fourth plague. In the same way, Revelation chapter eight shows a shocking increase in the intensity of the judgements God sends, but there is also a separation between what the followers of Antichrist experience and what God's people experience. Revelation 8:1 says,

Revelation 8:1 (NASB)
When the Lamb broke the seventh seal, there was silence in heaven for about half an hour.

In heaven, time may be experienced differently, so there is no way to know if "about half an hour" in heaven is exactly thirty minutes as it is on this earth. Whatever "about half an hour" may mean in terms of time here on earth, what is significant is the silence. Throughout the breaking of the first six seals heaven will be filled with worship and music, shouts and peals of thunder, stunning voices and angels and elders falling to their faces. Here, however, is an eerie silence. It is a final gulping breath before the plunge. Revelation 8:2 reads,

Revelation 8:2 – 4 (NASB)
And I saw the seven angels who stand before God, and seven trumpets were given to them. ³ Another angel came and stood at the altar, holding a golden censer; and much incense was given to him, so that he might add it to the prayers of all the saints on the golden altar which was before the throne. ⁴ And the smoke of the incense, with the prayers of the saints, went up before God out of the angel's hand.

Revelation chapter eight is another example of the Revelation Refrain. The context of Revelation 8:1-4 is symbolic because it is a vision of the spiritual realm. It is symbolic because the text does not explain what prayers look like or how John knows the prayers of the saints are added to the incense. It is possible the Holy Spirit simply revealed this to John, but other Scripture (Psalm 141:1-2) does describe the smoke of normal, physical incense as symbolic of human prayer. Revelation 8:5 says,

> **Revelation 8:5 – 6 (NASB)**
> Then the angel took the censer and filled it with the fire of the altar, and threw it to the earth; and there followed peals of thunder and sounds and flashes of lightning and an earthquake. ⁶ And the seven angels who had the seven trumpets prepared themselves to sound them. The first sounded, and there came hail and fire, mixed with blood, and they were thrown to the earth; and a third of the earth was burned up, and a third of the trees were burned up, and all the green grass was burned up.

Prayer is not useless and Revelation 8:5 shows that the prayers of the saints have a profound effect on physical events. The fire on the altar in heaven is symbolic of God's holy purity and since this is being mixed with the prayers of the saints, it shows that God's response to our prayers is always at the right time and in the right way.

The prayers of the saints, mixed with the holy purity of God's perfect timing, results in "thunder, and sounds and flashes of lightning and an earthquake" and "hail and fire, mixed with blood" that is "thrown to the earth" resulting in "a third of the earth" being burned up. Revelation does not tell us exactly how this will literally be accomplished, but the description resembles a violent volcanic eruption. Volcanic eruptions throw burning ash into the atmosphere that can condense as rain or hail accompanied by lightning strikes. Some eruptions can cause hurricane-force pyroclastic flows of burning lava pieces, white hot ash, and gas. [65] A pyroclastic flow can travel at a high rate of speed along the ground accompanied by a vast, burning cloud in the atmosphere pushing a shock wave that will obliterate nearly everything in its path. Such a cloud could flash-boil a human body causing the body to explode. Imagine such a cloud hitting a large population center – it would literally cause hail and fire to mix with blood as the flow raced along at hurricane speed.

Revelation 8:6 says this event will be so massive that one-third of the planet including one-third of the trees and other vegetation will be consumed. While there have been many volcanic eruptions in recorded human history, nothing on this scale has happened since the Great Flood, but it is not impossible. Not only do we have evidence that volcanic events of this magnitude have happened in the past, there are potential volcanic eruptions just waiting in the earth today that could do this kind of damage. For example, if the massive volcano at Yellowstone National Park in Wyoming were to erupt today, it is estimated it would cause an ash cloud at least six miles high. This is enough ash to cause global temperatures to drop considerably and the ash would fall covering most of Wyoming, Montana, Utah, Nevada, and Colorado in a layer three feet deep in red-hot ash. In addition, a pyroclastic flow or other form of ash cloud would reach from the center of the blast in Wyoming as far away as Los Angeles and Chicago, extend north past

Calgary and effectively burn most of the United States.

The land surface area of the earth is 57,308,738 square miles. One-third of this land surface would be approximately 18,911,883.5 square miles and there are roughly 3.17 million square miles of land surface in the United States. [66] This means the destruction described in Revelation chapter eight will be like destroying America six times over!

In whatever way this happens, Revelation 8:6 says this hail and fire burning one-third of the earth will be mixed with blood. It is unclear if this mixing is a reference to the blood-red color of the ash cloud or if it will be a literal rain of blood, but it is not a physical impossibility for something like this to happen. Blood, after all, is 90% water. If a large amount of blood were evaporated from the flash boil of millions of bodies during a volcanic pyroclastic explosion, the liquid could then be drawn up into the atmosphere by hurricane-force winds. It could then mix with rainwater and fall back to the surface as rain "mixed with blood." Also, there is a natural phenomenon known today as "blood rain" that occurs when the spores of the microalgae *Trentepholia annulate* mix with evaporated water. [67] When the evaporated water condenses into rain, the appearance is essentially identical to blood. Revelation 8:6 is part of the Revelation Refrain, so it could be blood red algae spores or actual blood, but what is certainly literal is the destruction of one-third of the trees and grass on earth.

The idea that Revelation chapter eight may describe a volcanic eruption of some kind is made stronger by the description of the events that follow the sounding of the first trumpet. Revelation 8:8-11 says,

> **Revelation 8:8-11 (NASB)**
> The second angel sounded, and something like a great mountain burning with fire was thrown into the sea; and a third of the sea became blood, [9] and a third of the creatures which were in the sea and had life, died; and a third of the ships were destroyed. [10] The third angel sounded, and a great star fell from heaven, burning like a torch, and it fell on a third of the rivers and on the springs of waters. [11] The name of the star is called Wormwood; and a third of the waters became wormwood, and many men died from the waters, because they were made bitter.

The symbolic part of the Revelation Refrain is the vision of heaven and the angel sounding his trumpet. Then it says "something like" a great mountain burning with fire was thrown into the sea. The word "like" means John is describing what he saw, and this is the only way he could think to describe it. There is no way to know exactly what he saw, but a massive volcanic eruption certainly would throw chunks of burning lava high into the atmosphere that could fall back into the sea and look like a burning mountain of fire. Another possibility might be a comet or meteor falling into the ocean and both these sorts of events have happened in recorded human history.

For example, on June 30, 1908, in Tunguska Siberia, witnesses reported that a burning star fell from the sky and exploded. The explosion flattened 80 million trees over an 830 square mile area. Witnesses said the fireball was as bright as the sun and the blast created a shockwave so intense it shattered windows hundreds of miles away. The explosion happened in a very remote area, but research several years after the event still found hundreds of square miles of devastation. The Tunguska blast was apparently an asteroid, meteor or comet that broke apart and exploded about fifteen miles above the surface. Scientists estimate it was moving at approximately 33,500 miles per hour. [68]

In ancient history, another atmospheric blast like Tunguska happened at the north end of the Dead Sea in the lower Jordan region of what is today the kingdom of Jordan. This event took place around 1,750 - 1,850 B.C., in the Middle Bronze Age and left a path of destruction so complete that the entire region remained uninhabited for 500 – 700 years. Prior to this atmospheric blast, the area had rich fertile soil, well-watered by perennial rivers and washes. This region once hosted the city-states of Sodom, Gomorrah and other villages and towns. These settlements were all destroyed in an instant according to the evidence in the soil as well as the eyewitness account found in Genesis 19:24. Archaeological evidence shows that the shock wave from this event, funneled by the surrounding mountains into a tornado-like siphon high into the atmosphere, drew tons of super-heated salt brine into the air from the Dead Sea. In Genesis nineteen, anything perpendicular, such as a tree or person, in the path of this super-heated salt brine was coated with salt. This is why Genesis says that Lot's wife was "turned into a pillar of salt." The resulting destruction of the atmospheric blast also caused massive ground water contamination that lasted for centuries. [69] What is described in Revelation eight has already been seen on a smaller scale at the Dead Sea and Tunguska. There is no reason to believe these events are not literal.

However violent and destructive these judgements appear, God is still merciful because only one-third of the earth is destroyed. God could simply obliterate the whole planet in one mighty stroke. Instead, His wrath is poured out in a controlled way in order to allow people a chance to repent and turn to Him. This is the reason a great multitude of people will turn to the Lord during the Great Tribulation as we have seen in Revelation chapter seven. Revelation 8:12 says,

> **Revelation 8:12 (NASB)**
> The fourth angel sounded, and a third of the sun and a third of the moon and a third of the stars were struck, so that a third of them would be darkened and the day would not shine for a third of it, and the night in the same way.

If the sun were to literally lose one-third of its mass, planet earth would freeze solid, but the prophecy only says the sun, moon and stars will be "darkened." It does not necessarily mean the sun, moon or stars will suffer any loss of mass in a literal way. Instead, it likely means the view of them from the surface of the earth will appear one-third less bright than normal. Since Revelation does not say how long it will be between the events described in chapter eight, it is possible all four of these trumpet judgements are linked. If the first trumpet judgement is a vision of a volcanic eruption or comet strike, then vast amounts of dust and ash blasted into the upper atmosphere will block light from the sun, moon, and stars just as it says in verse twelve. A similar phenomenon happened with the eruption of Krakatoa in 1883, an eruption that caused daylight to reduce by about one-third worldwide.

Scripture does not tell us about any time intervals between the first four trumpet judgements. It could be they will happen one after the other. It also does not say how long it will take for each event to happen or how long the effects will last. What we do know is the darkening of the sun, moon and stars recorded here will be temporary because in Revelation chapter sixteen the power of the sun will be significantly increased. Evidently there is some break between the events of the first four trumpets and the fifth trumpet because Revelation 8:13 says,

Revelation 8:13 (NASB)
Then I looked, and I heard an eagle flying in midheaven, saying with a loud voice, "Woe, woe, woe to those who dwell on the earth, because of the remaining blasts of the trumpet of the three angels who are about to sound!"

Some ancient manuscripts of Revelation 8:13 use the Greek word angel (ἄγγελος) [70] and others use the Greek word eagle (ἀετός). [71] It is possible this is evidence of a misspelled word creeping into the ancient copies of the text, but it seems most likely the word should be "angel." This angel will explode across the sky, shouting louder than thunder a final warning to the people of the earth. The surviving population of the planet will have already seen and heard the Rapture and the preaching of the 144,000 Jewish evangelists. They will have seen how the book of Revelation is lining up with what is happening in the world. They will have endured the disasters, and now they will see and hear an angel shouting in the sky. There will be no excuse for anyone to reject the message of Jesus!

Revelation 8:13 says that God will throw off restraint and make a last-ditch effort to reason directly with humanity. For millennia God has limited the appearance of the supernatural; but toward the end of the Great Tribulation, He will send an angel through the sky that no one can deny – and yet they will still reject Him! Jesus illustrated this stubborn tendency when He told the story of the rich man and Lazarus in Luke chapter sixteen. In that story, the rich man in hell pleads with Abraham to send someone back from the dead to warn his brothers about hell. The rich man believed that if his brothers were to see a man raised from the dead they would turn to God and be saved from future torment. But Abraham said that even if the rich man's brothers were to see a man raised from the dead, they would not believe because their deeds are evil. It is a Biblical truth that evil, self-absorbed desires eventually take root in the mind blocking out rational thought. The more irrational a person becomes, the greater the person's spiritual blindness. Even with an angel shouting the truth in the sky, even with 144,000 people preaching the truth and the miracle of the Rapture in recent memory, people will still reject God!

Freewill is an awesome, powerful thing so you should take care not to harden your heart against God's leading or you risk becoming increasingly irrational and unreachable over time.

End of Days:
The Book of Revelation Explained

Chapter 16: Non-negotiable!
Revelation 9 explained...

Some people dismiss the book of Revelation as first century apocalyptic literature intended to encourage Christians under persecution by the Roman Empire 2,000 years ago. They think Revelation is just an illustration of good overcoming evil in a comic-book like exaggeration. They do not think there is anything literal to be found in its pages. The Revelation Refrain of symbol illustrating or linking to physical events, and the claim of the text itself, shows that Revelation is not all symbol, nor is it all literal. There are literal future events illustrated by the various symbols. These symbols can be understood by cross-referencing the Old and New Testaments and also from the wording of the text itself. This Revelation Refrain pattern continues in Revelation chapter 9 which reads,

> **Revelation 9:1-2 (NASB)**
> Then the fifth angel sounded, and I saw a star from heaven which had fallen to the earth; and the key of the bottomless pit was given to him. [2] He opened the bottomless pit, and smoke went up out of the pit, like the

smoke of a great furnace; and the sun and the air were darkened by the smoke of the pit.

It is clear from the wording of this passage that the star is symbolic since it is called "him" and "he" is given a key. No one can give a physical key to a literal star since it is a gigantic ball of plasma in space! It is not uncommon in Scripture, however, to call angels "stars." The Greek grammar for the words "which had fallen" is in the perfect tense, so a more literal translation could be "the star having fallen." [72] In other words, this is a picture of a fallen angel!

So far in Revelation the physical or literal judgements that happen on the planet can be explained by some natural phenomenon, so there is no reason to doubt they will happen in a literal way. This entire passage, however, seems to be a vision of supernatural events. What happens in the literal or physical is a bit more difficult to explain.

In the first place, a true bottomless pit could only be at the center of the earth. At earth's center, gravity would probably be convoluted or suspended, and every direction would be both "up" and "down." In Scripture, prior to the resurrection of Jesus, the place of the dead is called "Hades." Luke chapter sixteen describes Hades as being divided between a place of comfort and a place of imprisonment and torment. Jesus told the story of a rich man who died and found himself in the place of torment. In that story, He taught there is a separation between the place of comfort, and the place of torment, in Hades. It is unclear from Scripture if Jesus was telling a parable as an illustration of a point or if He meant to explain a fact or both, but Luke 16:26 does say,

> **Luke 16:26b (NASb)**
> ...between us and you there is a great chasm fixed, so that those who wish to come over from here to you will not be able, and that none may cross over from there to us.'

Other Scripture implies that the place of comfort in Hades was emptied after the resurrection of Jesus when He took the souls of believers waiting there into heaven. The other half of Hades, however, is still a place of confinement and torment. Eventually, all of Hades will be cast into the Lake of Fire (Revelation 20:14). In Hades today, some fallen angels who rebelled against God in the days of Noah are confined in chains. In fact, in Revelation 9:1, we see this pit being opened because some of the fallen angels confined there will be released as part of the great day of Judgement. Jude 6 says,

> **Jude 6 (NLT)**
> And I remind you of the angels who did not stay within the limits of authority God gave them but left the place where they belonged. God has kept them securely chained in prisons of darkness, waiting for the great day of judgement.

In Luke chapter eight, Jesus healed a man who had been possessed by a legion of demons. These demons were terrified of being sent into the abyss or pit and asked that Jesus would allow them to go into a herd of pigs instead. Clearly, this pit or abyss is a place even demons fear. There is today a misunderstanding about the devil and demons. Contrary to popular opinion, Satan is not the ruler of hell as if he sits on a throne ordering demons to do his bidding. This is not a Biblical teaching at all. In the end, Satan, Hades itself and all fallen angels already confined in that abyss will be cast forever into the Lake of Fire. It is a future punishment that Satan himself fears. Revelation 9:3 reads,

> **Revelation 9:3 – 6 (NASB)**
> Then out of the smoke came locusts upon the earth, and power was given them, as the scorpions of the earth have power. [4] They were told not to hurt the grass of the earth, nor any green thing, nor any tree, but only the men who do not have the seal of God on their foreheads. [5] And they were not permitted to kill anyone, but to torment for five months; and their torment was like the torment of a scorpion when it stings a man. [6] And in those days men will seek death and will not find it; they will long to die, and death flees from them.

Normal locusts do not kill and even if they did, how could anyone "not permit" them to hurt grass or any green thing when that is exactly what normal locust do? These are obviously not normal locusts, and they are clearly under supernatural control. Since John uses the words "like the smoke of a furnace" and "as scorpions," and these demonic creatures come from a spiritual place, it is possible that this describes a demonic invasion from the spiritual realm that has effects of mental torment and madness in the physical. This seems especially likely since verse six says that for five months people will wish for death under the torment of these creatures but will not be able to die. This does not necessarily mean people are incapable of physical death. To wish for something is a mental process, so it seems likely that this is a mental torment so extreme everyone will be confused and rationally incapable of even considering a suicide attempt. Revelation 9:7 reads,

> **Revelation 9:7 – 11 (NASB)**
> The appearance of the locusts was like horses prepared for battle; and on their heads appeared to be crowns like gold, and their faces were like the faces of men. **8** They had hair like the hair of women, and their teeth were like the teeth of lions. **9** They had breastplates like breastplates of iron; and the sound of their wings was like the sound of chariots, of many horses rushing to battle. **10** They have tails like scorpions, and stings; and in their tails is their power to hurt men for five months. **11** They have as king over them, the angel of the abyss; his name in Hebrew is Abaddon, and in the Greek he has the name Apollyon.

There has been a great deal of speculation about exactly what are these creatures. We do know from other Scripture that there are angels and demons in the spiritual realm, and these spiritual beings have some limited interaction with the physical world. For example, some sicknesses can be caused or influenced by demons (Job 2:7). We know that God has sent angels into the physical as messengers and in Second Kings 19:35, a single angel killed 185,000 Assyrian troops in a single night. We do not know the exact rules or restraints on demons or angels from God, nor are we exactly certain what they may look like, since these beings are normally invisible to us. But since these locust-like beings in Revelation chapter nine come from the spiritual abyss, where other fallen angels are imprisoned, the entire context of the passage seems to mean that John is seeing into the spiritual realm. In fact, the king of these creatures is a spiritual being, an angel named Abaddon in Hebrew or Apollyon in Greek. Normal, physical locusts do not have a king, nor do they have a spiritual leader from the angelic realm with a name. This means that Revelation 9:1-11 is consistent with a spiritual attack, and what John writes in these verses is what the demonic horde looks like in the spiritual realm. The physical or literal result of their activity is madness and mental pain so intense it will feel like being stung by a scorpion. People will want to die!

Another reason we can conclude this is a spiritual attack that manifests itself in the mental state of these people in the future is that the attack is limited to a period of five months. The text does not tell us if everyone can see these beings as the torture continues but as suddenly as it begins, this attack will end. Revelation also does not tell us what happens to the demons. It does not say they are destroyed but they simply disappear from the text! This fact is consistent with interpreting this passage as a spiritual attack that affects the minds of people on the earth because the madness ends abruptly, and the locust-like demons disappear.

An important Biblical principle to recognize is that while the name of the fallen angel in command of this horrific demon horde is named "Abaddon" and "Apollyon," which means "destroyer," it is God who allows their release. [73] It is also God who commands their limits. They cannot kill anyone, and it is God who limits their activity to five months. God is completely in control just as he was in the book of Job. In Job's case, Satan was not allowed to touch the man without God's direct consent, because Satan is under God's control. In fact, Satan complained about this in Job 1:10 where it is written,

> **Job 1:10 (NASB)**
> Have You not made a fence around him and his house and all that he has, on every side?

The book of Job and this prophecy in Revelation reminds us that Satan is not the opposite of God in terms of God's nature, essence, or power. Satan is a created being under God's ultimate control. Satan and his followers can whisper lies from the spiritual realm, but they cannot physically touch a believer without God's direct consent.

<u>Satan is not all powerful, all knowing or everywhere present, even in an evil sense, because only God has all power, all knowledge and only God is present everywhere.</u>

> **Revelation 9:12-15 (NASB)**
> The first woe is past; behold, two woes are still coming after these things. [13] Then the sixth angel sounded, and I heard a voice

from the four horns of the golden altar which is before God, **14** one saying to the sixth angel who had the trumpet, "Release the four angels who are bound at the great river Euphrates." **15** And the four angels, who had been prepared for the hour and day and month and year, were released, so that they would kill a third of mankind. And the four angels, who had been prepared for the hour and day and month and year, were released, so that they would kill a third of mankind.

The text does not say the altar itself was speaking, only that the voice seemed to come from the altar. In Revelation chapter eight, the altar is shown as the place where incense is added to the prayers of the saints, so this is likely symbolic of the fact that God not only hears the prayers of His people, but He responds at the right time, in the right place, and the right way. This entire prophecy makes it clear that God will make things right in the end and He remains in control of judgement and destruction.

There is no evidence in Scripture that angels are bound, chained, or imprisoned unless they are fallen angels. These four fallen angels are not only bound, but they are also chained to a specific physical location for a specific purpose and time. Since John hears a voice from the heavenly altar and sees the angels released, the physical or literal part of this prophecy is the death of one-third of the human race.

This is significant because in the last trumpet judgement, no one could die for five months. It is unclear if there is any gap in time between the five months of torment and the release of the four fallen angels of death. It seems likely there is at least some time gap because to measure "five months" there must be a specific beginning and ending point. This gap may only be a matter of days but at this point in the Great Tribulation, this gap, however long, is more evidence of God's mercy. After five months of mental anguish, people come to their senses, they know this is a judgement from God and they will have another chance to repent.

God has measured out His righteous indignation over the rebellion of men, giving them time between these judgements to change their ways. In Revelation 9:15, God will allow the fury and hatred of fallen angels who hate humans as much as they hate God, to be poured out on the human race. It is little wonder that Jesus said in Mark 13:20,

Mark 13:20 (NASB)
And if the Lord had not shortened those days, no life would have been saved; but for the sake of the elect, whom He chose, He shortened the days.

In Revelation chapter six, one quarter of earth's population died. Here in chapter nine, one-third more will die, which means that over one-half of the population will by then be destroyed. If the Great Tribulation begins within the next decade, this means roughly a little over four billion people could perish!

The Revelation Refrain continues in verse 16 - 19 as John again sees something in the heavenly, spiritual realm that has a direct, literal impact on the earth. Since verses twelve through fifteen describe a heavenly vision, but the physical link is to the actual deaths of people on the planet. It follows that verses sixteen through nineteen is a description of what certain demonic forces look like in the spiritual realm and what those forces link to in the physical. Revelation 9:16 reads,

> **Revelation 9:16 - 19 (NASB)**
> The number of the armies of the horsemen was two hundred million; I heard the number of them. [17] And this is how I saw in the vision the horses and those who sat on them: the riders had breastplates the color of fire and of hyacinth and of brimstone; and the heads of the horses are like the heads of lions; and out of their mouths proceed fire and smoke and brimstone. [18] A third of mankind was killed by these three plagues, by the fire and the smoke and the brimstone which proceeded out of their mouths. [19] For the power of the horses is in their mouths and in their tails; for their tails are like serpents and have heads, and with them they do harm.

One reason it is likely this description of the horsemen is not literal is the sudden jump in the text from a narrative about four angels over to a description of two-hundred million horsemen. Not only that, but John also specifically says he sees these horsemen in a vision. The text does not say who the horsemen are, where they came from or if they are physical or spiritual.

The four angels are released and allowed to kill one-third of the earth's population, but this one-third of humanity is specifically killed by fire, smoke, and brimstone - not by the horseman themselves. Based on this fact, and since John sees the horsemen in a vision, it is likely the lion-headed creatures are the demonic force behind the physical manifestation of fire, smoke, and brimstone. It is like seeing the physical and the spiritual of the great whirlwind in the book of Job that killed Job's children. In the physical, the whirlwind in the book of Job probably looked like any other tornado. If we could have seen into the spiritual realm, however, we might have seen some horrific looking demonic creatures stirring up the physical winds. We do know from the book of Job, and other Scripture, that demonic forces are sometimes released to cause physical storms and other calamities. Since these two hundred million horsemen are under the command of the four fallen angels, it seems likely John is describing the spiritual side of what is behind a massive explosion of fire, smoke and brimstone that kills billions of people.

There has been a great deal of speculation about the horsemen of Revelation chapter nine. One popular view is that these horsemen are actually two-hundred million Chinese soldiers because Revelation sixteen prophecies about "kings of the east" invading during the last battle of Armageddon. In 1965, Chinese dictator Mao Zedong boasted that China could form a two-hundred-million-person army, so some Bible teachers added Revelation chapter nine to Revelation chapter sixteen and came up with Chinese soldiers. [74] The context of Revelation chapter nine, however, is John seeing the spiritual forces behind an explosive destruction.

Besides this, the term "kings of the east" in Scripture normally refers to Mesopotamia and Persia – not China. Not only this, but the words "200 million" in Greek use the term μυριάς (myrias) which can mean 10,000 or it can mean "innumerable host." [75] Some scholars translated "myrias" as 10,000, they did the math and came up with two-hundred million. Since the term can also mean "innumerable host," however, it could be a figure of speech. It may not be a literal number, especially since this is likely a description of the spiritual realm. In other words, it could be essentially saying, "there will be a gazillion of 'em!"

Since the context is a vision, there is little reason to think grotesque horse-like, lion-headed, multi-colored monsters with snakes for tails will be a physical reality. The context shows this is what these demons look like in the spiritual realm. This is especially likely because it is the fire, smoke, and brimstone – not snake bites or lion teeth - that kill anyone. Thus, the fire, smoke and brimstone are the physical reality that follows the vision and that is the Revelation Refrain once again.

It is interesting to note that bombs and guns spout fire. Keep in mind that John had never seen bombs or guns. He only knew his vision of lion-headed demons resulted in what appeared to him as spouts of fire that kill. This means it is possible this passage describes the demons in the spiritual realm that will drive the final army of the Antichrist to rally and oppose Jesus at the battle of Armageddon. This battle is described in Daniel chapter eleven and Revelation chapter sixteen. Revelation 9:20 says,

Revelation 9:20 – 21 (NASB)
The rest of mankind, who were not killed by these plagues, did not repent of the works of their hands, so as not to worship demons, and the idols of gold and of silver and of brass and of stone and of wood, which can neither see nor hear nor walk; [21] and they did not repent of their murders nor of their sorceries nor of their immorality nor of their thefts.

Whether the locusts or horsemen are seen in the physical or not, the literal result is five months of madness followed by one-third of the population dying from fire. Many people will still not turn from their evil ways, but since the text reads "the rest of mankind," at least some of them will turn to the Lord. But why would anyone harden their heart after five months of pain followed by so much death?

The answer is that our human sin nature is overwhelmingly self-centered. People can be tempted to worship demons after a lifetime focused on gratifying the sinful nature. This is because the more anyone gratifies selfish desires, the more irrational they become trying to justify their actions. Eventually a person becomes essentially unreachable because they cannot even think rationally. This process is what Jesus said is the law of planting and harvesting (sowing and reaping). He said that what you plant in your life is what will grow in your life. If a person plants irrational self-indulgence, then irrational selfishness will only increase until it is thirty, sixty or even a hundred times greater than what was planted. In C.S. Lewis' book "Mere

Christianity," Lewis explained this process as follows:

> Every time you make a choice you are turning the central part of you, the part of you that chooses, into something a little different than it was before. And taking your life as a whole, with all your innumerable choices, all your life long you are slowly turning this central thing into a heavenly creature or a hellish creature: either into a creature that is in harmony with God, and with other creatures, and with itself, or else into one that is in a state of war and hatred with God, and with its fellow creatures, and with itself. To be the one kind of creature is heaven: that is, it is joy and peace and knowledge and power. To be the other means madness, horror, idiocy, rage, impotence, and eternal loneliness. Each of us at each moment is progressing to the one state or the other. [76]

The law of planting and harvesting is the key to understanding why some people will become so self-focused they would rather worship demons than God. It seems likely this future situation will be a form of the idea "if you can't beat 'em, join 'em." Even today it may be tempting to think that if you join the rioters in the streets then the rioters will not destroy your house! But this does not happen because trying to pacify a hard heart, does not change the heart. In the future, people will believe that if they worship demons, the demons will leave them alone. They will follow this irrational thought process because they have committed themselves to pursuing their self-absorbed desires. They have hardened their hearts against following God, and they believe that pacifying or giving into their tormentors will cause the tormentors to back off. But these demons have the ultimate hard heart and just like terrorists, they will only get worse.

Over the centuries, God has allowed good things like the sun and the rain, good food and clean water to bless even those who hate Him. He allows this so that perhaps, by seeing these blessings, some people will turn to follow Him in life. But God also allows human beings true freewill. They can, and so often do, cause misery to each other. God allows this not just for the sake of freewill but so that perhaps, by suffering and realizing it is human choice that causes this suffering rather than God, some people will turn to follow Him. Both good and evil are allowed so that free will can exist. This is the state of the world because if God does not allow both good and evil, both blessing and judgement, then people cannot be truly free. And without true freedom of choice, there can be no real love between God and human beings. This is the reason, in the end, even when God's judgement falls, He will continue to allow a person to turn. His goal is that people will freely choose to follow Him.

God will allow anyone to turn to Him, even up to the last moment, but people who harden their hearts against God and His ways will only become more irrational and unreachable over time.

End of Days:
The Book of Revelation Explained

Chapter 17: God is a warrior-king!
Revelation 10 explained...

Revelation 10:1 (NASB)
I saw another strong angel coming down out of heaven, clothed with a cloud; and the rainbow was upon his head, and his face was like the sun, and his feet like pillars of fire...

Chapter nine prophecies about the spiritual and physical events resulting from the sounding of the sixth of seven trumpets. Revelation chapter ten is an interlude, a break in the narrative between the sixth and the seventh trumpet events. We are not told how long this interlude will last. The Revelation Refrain between what is spiritual or symbolic linked to what is physical continues in this chapter, and there is evidence of at least some gap between the literal events which may last days or weeks.

In Revelation 10:1, John sees a mighty angel descend from heaven, covered in a cloud and a rainbow. In context, this is a visionary, symbolic event rather than literal. Just as with the rest of the Revelation Refrain, there are clues in the text as to what this means. In Scripture, a cloud is usually a symbol of judgement, and a rainbow is a symbol of God's promise and glory. For these reasons, some

Bible scholars believe this is a vision of Jesus since before He was born in Nazareth, Jesus appears in the Old Testament with the title "the Angel of the Lord." There are some problems with this interpretation since the text is unclear about the exact identity of this angel. Besides this, the Greek word here for "another" is ἄλλον (allon) which means "another of the same kind;" [77] thus, this angel is another of the same kind of angels the vision has described already. It seems more likely this is a very high-level angel - perhaps the archangel Michael. As the archangel, Michael stands in the presence of God, so he reflects the glory of God. What is certain is that this angel is sent in power and judgement. Revelation 10:2 reads,

> **Revelation 10:2 – 3 (NASB)**
> …and he had in his hand a little scroll which was open. He placed his right foot on the sea and his left on the land; ³ and he cried out with a loud voice, as when a lion roars; and when he had cried out, the seven peals of thunder uttered their voices.

The words "little scroll" here are different in Greek than the words translated as "scroll" in Revelation 5:1. This word could be translated as "booklet" rather than a larger, sealed scroll. What matters is that the angel holding the little scroll is given full authority over both the land and the sea. He is authorized as a spokesman for God and has the power of God's authority to declare a new chapter in the history of creation. In fact, in verse three, this angel cries out with a voice like a lion, and the word for "cry out" is κράζω (krazo) in Greek, which means to "croak or scream." [78] In other words, this is a crazy, terrifying, authoritative, barbaric battle cry. It is an angel of God screaming "God has had enough! This is the time for the final war!"

In our culture today, many people have a false view of God and His nature. Too many people view God as a passive, slightly senile, old man. Others see God as disconnected or unconcerned about events on earth. Both views are false. The Bible does tell us God cares! He is love itself! He has awesome patience with the rebellion of men because He wants to give everyone as many chances as possible to freely turn to Him. But there is another Biblical truth about the nature of God. However loving and kind He is, no one should forget that God is also the greatest warrior in the cause of what is right and good. It is a dangerous thing to discount the righteous justice of the King.

Scripture teaches that God is pure Being – the great "I Am." As human beings, we only participate in existence, but God is existence itself. Other things exist only because He exists eternally and brought everything else into being. He has no beginning and no end. He is the first and He is also the last. Whatever is good and complete and pure in this world is only a reflection of what God is in the pure sense of His nature. When we experience something that is good, it is only good because it comes from the creative hand of God, who is goodness itself. In the same way, when we recognize justice, it is only because God is justice itself.

God is unchangeable, eternal, and perfectly self-existent. All other things that exist are dependent beings and finite because all other things came into existence at some point in the past. God is immaterial, immense beyond comprehension, all-power, all-knowing, perfect wisdom, pure light, absolute unity of being in perfect tri-unity of person. God alone is the way, the truth, and the life. This is the God of the Bible, and He is completely unlike the distant or weak version of God too many people make up in their own imaginations. When this angel from God roars "enough" with a roaring, awful, majestic cry, then everyone will know that it is indeed a fearful thing to fall into the hands of the living God. In this shocking moment, God will declare He has had enough and His final judgement will no longer be delayed.

God is pure Being and He is not disconnected or unconcerned with current events because He remains absolutely in control of time.

> **Revelation 10:4 - 7 (NASB)**
> When the seven peals of thunder had spoken, I was about to write; and I heard a voice from heaven saying, "Seal up the things which the seven peals of thunder have spoken and do not write them." [5] Then the angel whom I saw standing on the sea and on the land lifted up his right hand to heaven, [6] and swore by Him who lives forever and ever, who created heaven and the things in it, and the earth and the things in it, and the sea and the things in it, that there will be delay no longer, [7] but in the days of the voice of the seventh angel, when he is about to sound, then the mystery of God is finished, as He preached to His servants the prophets.

The words of the mighty thunders are not recorded because God does not tell us everything. God holds onto His own mystery and awe because no one gives Him advice and He is worthy of awe. When He says there will be no more delay, He means there is no longer any time for human beings to turn from their wicked ways. The time of freewill ends here and every human being at that point will be locked into the choice each person has made. This future moment will be the same as when God confirmed the freely chosen rebellion of Pharaoh, king of Egypt, in the days of the Exodus. In Exodus, Pharaoh freely hardened his own heart, but the day came when God accepted and confirmed Pharaoh's choice, because everyone is eventually given more of the heart they have freely chosen.

Many scholars think the wording in the Greek language suggests the seventh trumpet has within it all the bowl judgements. This means that all seven of the bowl judgements will probably be unleashed at once. Revelation chapter ten prophecies about the final unleashing of God's righteous anger at the rebellion of man, all poured out as Jesus splits the sky and smashes His enemies on the last day.

Revelation 10:8 - 11 (NASB)
Then the voice which I heard from heaven, I heard again speaking with me, and saying, "Go, take the book which is open in the hand of the angel who stands on the sea and on the land." **9** So I went to the angel, telling him to give me the little book. And he said to me, "Take it and eat it; it will make your stomach bitter, but in your mouth it will be sweet as honey." **10** I took the little book out of the

angel's hand and ate it, and in my mouth it was sweet as honey; and when I had eaten it, my stomach was made bitter. [11] And they said to me, "You must prophesy again concerning many peoples and nations and tongues and kings."

Revelation 10:8-11 is the Revelation Refrain pattern of something symbolic that illustrates and links to something that is literal. The eating of the book is symbolic since John, in a vision, takes it from the hand of an angel. In Scripture, eating a teaching or a prophecy is symbolic of taking it into yourself like food. So, whenever a person reads the Bible, the teaching it contains should be taken into the heart, that way it can sustain a person from within.

The Scripture in the Bible should be to Christians our spiritual food just as steak and potatoes are food.

After eating the booklet, John is told to prophesy again. This means that what he just ate symbolically in the vision is linked to the literal action of prophesying or preaching to the Jewish people. As another example of the Revelation Refrain, this vision is probably linked to the same symbolic use of eating a scroll that is seen in the Old Testament in Ezekiel 3:1, which reads,

Ezekiel 3:1 – 3 (NASB)
Then He said to me, "Son of man, eat what you find; eat this scroll, and go, speak to the house of Israel." [2] So I opened my mouth,

and He fed me this scroll. ³ He said to me, "Son of man, feed your stomach and fill your body with this scroll which I am giving you." Then I ate it, and it was sweet as honey in my mouth.

Since the symbol of an eatable scroll tasting like honey is consistent with other Scripture, it makes sense to interpret this to symbolize how completely the prophet is expected to take God's teaching into himself. Both these passages of Scripture in Revelation and Ezekiel show us that God's Word is both sweet and bitter. It is sweet to hear about the goodness and forgiveness of God, but this is only half the message. It is easy to camp on the sweet parts of God's revelation and forget that God is also the King of the universe and the righteous judge of every created thing. There is a coming day of judgement that will be bitter for those who rebel against God.

End of Days:
The Book of Revelation Explained

Chapter 18: Reach!
Revelation 11 explained...

The book of Revelation follows a consistent pattern with the Revelation Refrain and the symbols are either explained in the text itself or link directly to other visions and symbols in the Old Testament. Since the symbols are seen in a vision, they only illustrate or picture something that is literal. The text itself provides clues to what is symbolic and what is literal. For example, Revelation 11:1 says,

> **Revelation 11:1 – 2 (NASB)**
> Then there was given me a measuring rod like a staff; and someone said, "Get up and measure the temple of God and the altar, and those who worship in it. [2] Leave out the court which is outside the temple and do not measure it, for it has been given to the nations; and they will tread under foot the holy city for forty-two months.

What is significant here is that John is told by "someone" to measure the temple of God but the "someone" is not identified, and John does not actually measure anything. In fact, there are no measurements of a temple to be found in the book of Revelation. But is it possible these measurements were simply left out? Or is this an example of John being disobedient in some way? If so, why is there no record of God or an angel rebuking John for not doing as he was told?

To understand this, it is best to let Scripture interpret other Scripture. In Ezekiel chapters 40 - 43, the prophet Ezekiel is told in a vision to measure a temple and all the measurements are given. In fact, the measurements are magnificent and huge, much larger than the temple of Solomon that was destroyed in 586 BC. Ezekiel's measurements are also larger than the second temple built after the exile of the Jewish people to Babylon in 586 BC. The second temple was destroyed in 70 A.D., so the temple Ezekiel measured cannot be either the first or the second temple, but Ezekiel's temple cannot be the temple that will stand during the Great Tribulation either. This is because Ezekiel's temple will never be defiled. However, the temple in Revelation will be defiled by the Abomination that causes Desolation that will be set up by Antichrist. Ezekiel 43:7 says,

> **Ezekiel 43:7 (NASB)**
> He said to me, "Son of man, this is the place of My throne and the place of the soles of My feet, where I will dwell among the sons of Israel forever. And the house of Israel will not again defile My holy name…

The temple Ezekiel describes will be a new temple built after the Great Tribulation. It is the temple of the Millennium, a place of memorial and remembrance, where the nations of the earth will come to hear the wisdom of Messiah Jesus. The reason the Great Tribulation temple in Revelation is not measured is because it will not be a temple built under the blessing or direction of God. In the Old Testament, measurements were used as a symbol of ownership. Even today, real estate agents must describe in a sales contract the exact measurements of a property, rather than just an address, so legally anyone can know exactly what is owned by whom. In the same way, God showed the prophet Zechariah, in Zechariah chapter two, a vision of an angel measuring Jerusalem because God owns the city.

In Revelation 11:1-2 however, John is told by "someone" to measure the temple, but he does not do it. The lack of measurement probably symbolizes that the temple built by the Jewish people for use during the Great Tribulation does not belong to God, will not be directed by God, and does not represent His holiness. The Great Tribulation temple will be built in unbelief. The builders in that future day will not believe that Jesus is Messiah so their temple will be an effort to reinstate the animal sacrifices and laws of Moses. This is an insult to the fact that Messiah Jesus has fulfilled the law of Moses by His death and resurrection.

At the start of the Great Tribulation, a majority of the Jewish people will still reject Jesus as their Messiah. At the mid-point of the Great Tribulation, the Antichrist will show his true intentions when he defiles their new temple. He will stand in the holy place and declare that he alone is God. When this happens, the Jewish people will suddenly see that the prophecies of the book of Revelation and the preaching of the 144,000 are correct. They will realize Jesus is indeed their Messiah and the final battle will begin.

The Revelation Refrain continues in Revelation chapter eleven. The lack of measuring of the temple in the vision links to the literal fact that there will be a third temple that God does not endorse. There is no temple in Jerusalem as of this writing, but there will be a third temple built there in the future. In Israel today most Jews are non-religious. Most secular Jews do not want to see a third temple built because they know constructing such a building will only cause more problems with the Muslim world. Orthodox Jews in Israel are also generally opposed to seeing a third temple built because most of them believe that only the Messiah can build such a temple.

There is a small minority of Jewish people, members of a group called "the Temple Institute," who are committed to the construction of a third temple. [79] They study the Old Testament regulations and have already rebuilt most of the priestly garments, furniture, and utensils for a new temple. This group is small and dedicated, but as of this writing, there is still a great deal of opposition to the idea of building a temple.

One reason for this opposition is that Muslims are opposed to the building of any Jewish temple because it would need to be built on the Temple Mount. This spot in Jerusalem is also the location of the Islamic Dome of the Rock and the Al Aqsa Mosque. Some people think that either or both of these mosques would have to be destroyed to build a third Jewish temple. Clearly the Islamic world is not going to support that idea any time soon.

There are, however, four theories about where the original temple of Solomon stood. Two of these theories place the temple either just north of the Dome of the Rock or just to the south, but no one knows for certain. It is possible the original temple site might not be under the Dome of the Rock or the Al Aqsa Mosque at all. Archaeologists continue to study the area, but religious feelings and political pressure make any work on the Temple Mount difficult and controversial.

With so much political and religious opposition today, it is difficult to see how anyone will be able to build a third Jewish temple in Jerusalem. For most of the last 2,000 years, many Bible scholars could not conceive of any way a literal third temple could be built. For centuries, there was no nation of Israel, the Jewish people were spread all over the earth, and there are two Muslim mosques on the Temple Mount. For these reasons, many scholars tried to spiritualize any Biblical hint that a third temple would be built. This all changed on May 14, 1948. During the Six Day War speculation about a literal third temple took on new life when the Jewish people took control of the city of Jerusalem in June 1967 for the first time since the Romans destroyed the city in A.D. 70. The possibility a third temple will soon be rebuilt, in fulfillment of the prophecies in Revelation, is more of a possibility today than ever before.

Revelation goes on to describe the ministry of God's two special witnesses. Revelation 11:3 says,

Revelation 11:3 (NASB)
And I will grant authority to my two witnesses, and they will prophesy for twelve

hundred and sixty days, clothed in sackcloth."

Twelve hundred sixty days, based on Jewish lunar thirty-day months, is forty-two months. This is the same period as the three and a half years described in Daniel chapter nine and marks the midpoint of the Great Tribulation. Daniel chapter nine explains that the Antichrist will stun the world with many false miracles. He will then confirm a peace treaty with Israel, but he will break this treaty after three and a half years when he stands in the third temple and declares that he is God. At this point it might be a good idea to review the future timeline to see where the two witnesses fit into future-history.

The church age has been unfolding in seven stages over the last two thousand years which John prophesied about in Revelation chapters one through three. The church age is the gap Daniel prophesied about in Daniel chapter nine. This gap falls between the first set of sixty-nine sets of seven years that he prophesied about, and the last set of seven years that we know are called the Great Tribulation. The gap between Daniel's 69th and 70th week of years began in 33 AD, after Jesus died, rose from the dead and ascended into heaven. It will continue until the Antichrist confirms his treaty with Israel. His confirmation of a peace treaty will ignite Daniel's 70th seven-year period, the period known as the Great Tribulation.

The New Testament teaches that the bodies of born-again Christians will be transformed instantly, "in the twinkling of an eye," into eternal resurrection bodies. This event is called "the

Rapture," and it will happen at some unknown point before the Great Tribulation. The Rapture can happen at any time, so it is possible that the events symbolized by the breaking of the first four or five seals on the scroll in the hand of God the Father, described in Revelation chapters five through seven, could be pre-requisite events that set up the Great Tribulation. People will not realize the wrath of God is upon them until the breaking of the sixth seal. It is also possible that all the seal events will happen during the first half of the Great Tribulation. The seals are found in Revelation chapters six and eight. They are,

> **The First Seal** (6:1-2): A White horse "conquering and to conquer." This could be cold war.
>
> **The Second Seal** (6:3-4) A Red horse. Peace departs – A time of lawlessness worldwide.
>
> **The Third Seal** (6:5-6): A Black horse. "A quart of wheat for a denarius" – A time of scarcity or economic depression.
>
> **The Fourth Seal** (6:7-8): A Pale horse. Death by sword, famine, pestilence, and wild beasts – A time of worldwide chaos.
>
> **The Fifth Seal** (6:9-11): The Martyrs cry - A time of delay. This may be a time of increased persecution of God's people.

The Sixth Seal (6:12-17): Earthquake and atmospheric upheaval – A time of natural convulsions on earth.

The Seventh Seal (8:1-6): Another earthquake – A time when the seven Trumpet judgements begin.

The sixth seal is the moment in the future when people on the earth will cry out, "it is the wrath of God." Since First Thessalonians 5:9 says "For God has not destined us for wrath, but for obtaining salvation through our Lord Jesus Christ," most conservative Bible scholars think the Rapture must happen before the sixth seal events. Some scholars do think the Rapture will happen before any of the seal events, but either way the Great Tribulation is the final seven years described in Daniel chapter nine. What is clear is that the 144,000 Jewish evangelists will teach about Jesus after the Rapture. In fact, it is possible the Rapture may be what convinces them that Jesus is the Jewish Messiah. It is at this point, after the Rapture, during the preaching of the 144,000 and the first three-and-a-half years of the Great Tribulation, that the preaching of the two witnesses will also begin.

In Revelation, there is a break in the timeline description in chapters nine through eleven to give more detail about various events. In some cases, it is unclear how long some of the trumpet judgements will last, or if there is any time gap between the end of one judgement and the start of the next. The Trumpet judgements are found in Revelation chapters eight, nine and eleven. They are,

The First Trumpet (8:7): One-third of plants on earth burn up.

The Second Trumpet (8:8-9): One-third of ocean life is destroyed.

The Third Trumpet (8:10-11): One-third of fresh water is contaminated.

The Fourth Trumpet (8:12): One-third of the atmosphere is darkened.

The Fifth Trumpet (9:1-11): An invasion of demons but no death (1st woe)

The Sixth Trumpet (9:12-19): A 2nd invasion of demons causing one-third of the population to be killed (2nd woe)

The Seventh Trumpet (11:15-19): The opening of the seven final bowl judgements (3rd woe).

When the Antichrist breaks his peace agreement with Israel and declares himself to be God, he will at that point take control of Israel and the city of Jerusalem. The Antichrist will then begin the greatest persecution of the Jewish people in history. This is the reason Revelation 11:2 says,

Revelation 11:2 (NASB)
Leave out the court which is outside the temple and do not measure it, for it has been given to the nations; and they will tread

under foot the holy city for forty-two months.

"The nations" is a reference to Gentile (non-Jewish) control. At the end of this forty-two-month period (3.5 years), the final bowl judgements will be poured out and the remaining Jewish people hiding in the hills will all turn and believe that Jesus is their Messiah. Once they do this, the Lord Jesus will return to save them! The Antichrist will then be defeated, the Great Tribulation will end and the Millennial rule of Jesus the Messiah on earth will begin. This is the basic outline of events, but much of it could unfold in different ways, so some of these events will not be fully understood until after they are fulfilled.

We can say for certain that the signing, or confirming, of a peace treaty between Israel and the Antichrist will happen after the Rapture. That event is the starting gun of the Great Tribulation. It is during the first half of these last seven years that the two witnesses will be speaking in Jerusalem while the 144,000 are a witness in the rest of the world. Revelation 11:3 reads,

> **Revelation 11:3 – 7 (NASB)**
> And I will grant authority to my two witnesses, and they will prophesy for twelve hundred and sixty days, clothed in sackcloth." [4] These are the two olive trees and the two lampstands that stand before the Lord of the earth. [5] And if anyone wants to harm them, fire flows out of their mouth and devours their enemies; so if anyone wants to harm them, he must be killed in this way. [6]

These have the power to shut up the sky, so that rain will not fall during the days of their prophesying; and they have power over the waters to turn them into blood, and to strike the earth with every plague, as often as they desire. 7 When they have finished their testimony, the beast that comes up out of the abyss will make war with them and overcome them and kill them.

Although it is not exactly clear, it seems most likely that the two witnesses will be operating in the city of Jerusalem because that is where they will finally be killed in the end. There has been a great deal of speculation about the identity of these two men. Some believe that since the prophet Elijah was taken up into heaven without experiencing physical death and Elijah had the power to call down fire from heaven and Jesus said in Matthew 17:10 that Elijah would come first, that one of these two men must be Elijah returned from heaven. But Jesus also pointed out that John the Baptist had already come in the spirit of Elijah and the religious leaders of the day had missed him. This means the verse saying "Elijah comes first" does not necessarily mean Elijah the man will literally return from heaven.

Other scholars think that since Moses was given power to turn water into blood and bring plagues on the land of Egypt that Moses must be the second witness. As possible proof for this speculation, some Bible teachers point out Matthew 17:1 where Jesus was transfigured into glory. During His transfiguration, Jesus was seen talking with Elijah and Moses, so they believe these two prophets will be the two witnesses.

Still others point out that like Elijah, Enoch (who lived in the days before Noah's Flood) was also possibly translated into heaven without physically dying. Enoch and Elijah are the only two people recorded in the Bible who were translated into heaven without dying in the physical. For this reason, some scholars think the two witnesses are Enoch, representing the days before the Flood, and Elijah, representing the days after the Flood.

These two witnesses could be Elijah and Moses or Elijah and Enoch, but the most important point is that the text in Revelation simply does not say. The identity of these two men is not revealed, but whoever they are, they are very precious to God. God calls them the two olive trees and the two lampstands that stand before the Lord. Whatever their identity, these men have a specific task to do. Part of that task is to be faithful in their witness all the way to their deaths. Revelation 11:8 reads,

> **Revelation 11:8 – 9 (NASB)**
> And their dead bodies will lie in the street of the great city which mystically is called Sodom and Egypt, where also their Lord was crucified. [9] Those from the peoples and tribes and tongues and nations will look at their dead bodies for three and a half days, and will not permit their dead bodies to be laid in a tomb.

The context of Revelation 11:8-9 has changed from the visionary (two olive trees and two lampstands before the Lord) to the literal or physical (their dead bodies in the street). The identity of the great city is clear because even though at this point in future-history it will be a city as evil and unclean as Sodom and Egypt, it is still the place where Jesus was crucified and that can only be the city of Jerusalem.

For centuries, the clear line between what was symbolic and what was literal in these verses in Revelation was unknown because no one could imagine how "Those from the peoples and tribes and tongues and nations will look at their dead bodies for three and a half days." The technology that could allow the whole earth to see these bodies in the street was unknown until the 20th century. Even recently, technology has advanced again with satellite and internet technology so that literally everyone on earth could tune in and see images from Jerusalem in real time. Revelation 11:10 says,

> **Revelation 11:10 (NASB)**
> And those who dwell on the earth will rejoice over them and celebrate; and they will send gifts to one another, because these two prophets tormented those who dwell on the earth.

It is possible that unbelievers in the first half of the Great Tribulation will believe that the trumpet judgements (and maybe the seal judgements) are brought about by the command and control of the two witnesses. What is clear is that people will be afraid of the witnesses. When the Antichrist declares himself to be God, and then successfully kills these miracle-working witnesses, many people will conclude that the Antichrist is God because, in their view, "only a god could kill them." Later in Revelation we find out that the Antichrist will have a second in command, a media-propaganda specialist who will market and promote him. It makes sense that the success of the Antichrist in killing the witnesses will be a future marketing triumph. But God will get the last laugh. It is written in Revelation 11:11,

> **Revelation 11:11 - 12 (NASB)**
> But after the three and a half days, the breath of life from God came into them, and they stood on their feet; and great fear fell upon those who were watching them. [12] And they heard a loud voice from heaven saying to them, "Come up here." Then they went up into heaven in the cloud, and their enemies watched them.

The false prophet will try to market the death of the witnesses as proof that the Antichrist's claim in the temple to be God is true. Since everyone on the planet is tuning in to see their bodies lying in the streets of Jerusalem, no one will miss God raising them from the dead and calling them into heaven with a loud voice. At that point, anyone who thinks the Antichrist is a god will probably think twice. Since this will happen at about the half-way point of the Great Tribulation, this is the crucial turning point for the human race. To this point, God has allowed His wrath to be poured out at a measured rate, that is, only a third of the sea is destroyed, only a third of green vegetation has been consumed and so on. To this point, God has allowed time gaps between His judgements to allow human beings yet another chance to freely turn away from their rebellion over to His Lordship. To this point, God has protected the ministry and the lives of the two witnesses, and probably the 144,000 also. God will do all of this in one last effort to give human beings a chance to freely repent. But here, in Revelation eleven, the final warning is given that the end of all things has been decided and God's final judgements will be poured out all at once. Revelation 11:13 says,

Revelation 11:13 - 19 (NASB)
And at that time there was a great earthquake, and a tenth of the city fell; seven thousand people were killed in the earthquake, and the rest were terrified and gave glory to the God of heaven. [14] The second woe is past; behold, the third woe is coming quickly. [15] Then the seventh angel sounded; and there were loud voices in heaven, saying, "The kingdom of the world has become the kingdom of our Lord and of His Christ; and He will reign forever and ever." [16] And the twenty-four elders, who sit on their thrones before God, fell on their faces and worshiped God, [17] saying, "We give You thanks, O Lord God, the Almighty, who are and who were, because You have taken Your great power and have begun to reign. [18] And the nations were enraged, and Your wrath came, and the time came for the dead to be judged, and the time to reward Your bond-servants the prophets and the saints and those who fear Your name, the small and the great, and to destroy those who destroy the earth." [19] And the temple of God which is in heaven was opened; and the ark

of His covenant appeared in His temple, and there were flashes of lightning and sounds and peals of thunder and an earthquake and a great hailstorm.

After the resurrection of the two witnesses, there will be a mighty earthquake. Once again, it is important to see the Revelation Refrain and the difference between what is happening in heaven, in the spiritual, and what is happening on the earth in the physical. The announcement that the third woe is coming quickly is probably part of the vision of events in heaven, not a literal announcement that people will hear on the earth. It is also possible there is some gap in time between the resurrection of the two witnesses and the final pouring out of the seven bowl judgements. This is so, because the death and resurrection of the two witnesses coincides with the Antichrist claiming to be God in the temple, which happens at the midpoint of the Great Tribulation, but the midpoint of the Tribulation is still three and half years before the day the Lord will physically return to the earth. If the final bowls are poured out all at once, or nearly all at once, there could be a gap between the mid-point and the final bowl judgements of nearly three and a half years.

In verse fourteen it warns that the third woe is coming quickly and then verse fifteen to eighteen are a sort of "flash-forward." In other words, the warning that the third woe is coming quickly is a warning that at the end of this gap between the mid-point of the Tribulation and the return of Jesus, the dead will be judged, and the kingdom of the Messiah will begin. Greek scholars point out that the grammar and construction of the sentences describing the third woe indicate that all seven of these final judgements will be released in one big flood. Adding this up, it seems likely the final period between the death and resurrection of the two witnesses and the final pouring out of God's wrath just as Jesus returns, will be the last possible moment people can make up their minds about who they will serve. It is during this period that the Antichrist will demand a decision from everyone by requiring the whole world to take an oath of allegiance to him by taking his mark in their right hand or their forehead – or die!

There is a powerful principle illustrated in these prophetic verses. Over and over again, the Bible makes it plain there really is a spiritual world and an eternal state of existence that is coming upon every human being. What we do here and now in this life determines the reward we will or will not receive in the eternal state. Whatever rewards the Lord decides to give to us are rewards that last forever.

<u>Revelation vividly illustrates why we should take Jesus seriously when He warned us in Matthew 6:20 to build up treasures in heaven rather than focusing our attention on temporary rewards here on earth.</u>

Some people today read about the coming judgements of the Great Tribulation with dread, but if you are a believer today, you will not experience the terror of those days. If you are reading this after the Rapture because you were left behind, remember that staying faithful to Jesus and refusing to take the mark of allegiance to the Antichrist will guarantee you a great eternal reward. Today, many

Christians fear that they will not have any great reward because they are not serving as pastors or missionaries or evangelists leading thousands of people to Christ. If you read this because you were left behind, you may think something similar because you need to keep a low profile just to survive. But God rewards faithfulness, not the measure of your influence or fame.

God does not make mistakes, nor does He make junk. There are no "throw-away" servants in His kingdom. If you have freely chosen to follow Jesus, then no matter what station God has allowed you to have in this life, your life matters to God. He cares about you, or He would not have allowed you to exist in the first place. This means that how you live out the station in life He has allowed for you is what matters in the end. Imagine a housewife living in the 19th century, a woman who did not change her world by writing any books or leading millions to Christ. The Bible teaches that her faithfulness is what will be rewarded. Such a woman will be just as rewarded as the greatest of evangelists, if she was faithful to be the best servant of the Lord she could be in her place in life. If she was gracious, and kind, and loved her neighbors and took care of the sick, then she was a witness in her world. In heaven, she will be honored to shine in the eternal glory of Jesus because she was faithful to what He called her to do and be in this life.

In the same way, it is your faithfulness today that matters and will be rewarded. If you read these words before the Rapture, then focus yourself on being the best witness you can be with how you live your life. If you read these words after the Rapture, and survival requires you to hide, you can still be faithful not to give into the terrible pressure you will feel to take the mark of allegiance to the Antichrist. You will be tempted to take his mark because he will destroy your ability to buy or sell. You may experience famine and fear, but if you are faithful in your allegiance to Jesus, He will give you just as great a reward for simply being faithful as He will give to the greatest evangelist.

Decide to devote yourself to be the best witness you can possibly be within whatever station the Lord allows you to be in – because the reward is in the doing, not in the size of your influence.

End of Days:
The Book of Revelation Explained

Chapter 19: Persist!
Revelation 12 explained...

Romans 12:1 - 2 (NASB)
A great sign appeared in heaven: a woman clothed with the sun, and the moon under her feet, and on her head a crown of twelve stars; ² and she was with child; and she cried out, being in labor and in pain to give birth.

The Revelation Refrain continues with a description of something in the spirit that links to something literal and physical and the symbolic is again rooted in the Old Testament. The woman clothed with the sun is a vision because it says she is a "sign" that appears in heaven. In fact, this passage in Revelation is a sort of summary of earth history to date. It is not a description of a future timeline but rather a sort of catching up of the narrative with the bigger picture of Scripture as a whole.

In the book of Revelation there are seven scenes called "signs." Only three of these signs are called "great signs," because each of the great signs are symbolic of one-third of earth's history. This is not just any history or even a history of civilizations or cultures. These signs sum up history as it relates to the great plan of God to pay for the sins of the world, and to judge anyone who rejects God's free offer of salvation. The first of these great summing-up history signs is this woman clothed with the sun.

In Revelation 12:5, the woman clothed with the sun gives birth to a child who will rule the nations with a rod of iron. This is an Old Testament reference to the Messiah. We can conclude that the child is Jesus, and the woman is the nation of Israel, who gives birth to the Messiah. This interpretation is further strengthened by the fact that the sun, moon, and stars are symbols found in the Old Testament referring to the nation of Israel. For example, in Genesis 37:9, Jacob recognizes his son Joseph's dream about the sun, moon and stars bowing down to him is a reference to himself, his wife and his family. Jacob said in Genesis 37:9,

> **Genesis 37:9 – 11 (NASB)**
> Then he had yet another dream, and informed his brothers of it, and said, "Behold, I have had yet another dream; and behold, the sun and the moon, and eleven stars were bowing down to me." [10] He also told it to his father as well as to his brothers; and his father rebuked him and said to him, "What is this dream that you have had? Am I and your mother and your brothers actually going to come to bow down to the ground before you?" [11] And his brothers were jealous of him, but his father kept the matter in mind.

The woman clothed with the sun is also crowned with twelve stars, one star for each of the twelve tribes of Israel. These symbols show that Israel through the ages has been like a woman in labor giving birth to salvation through the Messiah for mankind. God planned from before the creation of the world that human beings would have freewill because each of us has sinned and we all need to be saved. This is the great story of the ages, summed up here in a vision of a woman giving birth. The summary continues in Revelation 12:3 which reads,

> **Revelation 12:3 – 4 (NASB)**
> Then another sign appeared in heaven: and behold, a great red dragon having seven heads and ten horns, and on his heads were seven diadems. [4] And his tail swept away a third of the stars of heaven and threw them to the earth. And the dragon stood before the woman who was about to give birth, so that when she gave birth he might devour her child.

This vision is an intense picture of the vicious age-long conflict between Satan and the child of the woman. Revelation 20:2 says that Satan is called "the dragon, the serpent of old, who is the devil and Satan." Satan waited to kill the child of Israel, the promised Messiah, ever since he successfully tempted Adam and Eve to rebel against God's command in the Garden of Eden. At that time, God promised that one day a special child would be born who would destroy the work of Satan and bring healing to the rift between human beings and God. Genesis 3:15 says,

Genesis 3:15 (NASB)
And I will make enemies of you and the woman, and of your offspring and her Descendant (her seed); He shall bruise you on the head, and you shall bruise Him on the heel.

Genesis 3:15 links directly to Revelation 12:4 because throughout Biblical history, human beings have been called the "seed of a man," not the "seed of a woman." Genesis 3:15, however, says there will come a man who is the seed of a woman alone. In Luke 1:34, an angel explains to Mary, the mother of Jesus, that her son will be the "seed of the woman." Luke 1:34 reads,

Luke 1:34 – 35 (NASB)
But Mary said to the angel, "How will this be, since I am a virgin?" [35] The angel answered and said to her, "The Holy Spirit will come upon you, and the power of the Most High will overshadow you; for that reason also the holy Child will be called the Son of God.

Mary's firstborn son Jesus is a miracle of God. He is the seed of a woman. Genesis 3:15 says Satan will only ever "bruise his heel," meaning that Satan can only hurt Jesus physically and temporarily. In fact, when Jesus died on the cross it may have looked to Satan as if he had won the day - but Jesus rose from the dead, so Satan's attempt to hurt Jesus the Messiah was only temporary. Jesus, however, by rising from the dead accomplished the eternal salvation of anyone who puts their trust in Him. In this way, Jesus has literally crushed the enemy's plan, stomping him on the head!

In Scripture, angels are often symbolized as stars. Revelation 12:4 illustrates that when Lucifer rebelled against God, he became Satan and one-third of the angels followed him in his rebellion. Revelation 12:3 also shows Satan with seven heads and ten horns. This symbolism is explained in Revelation chapters thirteen and seventeen. The heads and horns are also seen in the book of Daniel, so it is clear they are symbolic of the Antichrist. We learn from the book of Revelation that the Antichrist will be so possessed by Satan that if you see the Antichrist, then you are seeing Satan himself. This sums up the meaning of the woman clothed with the sun, the child, and the dragon. Revelation 12:5 goes on to say,

Revelation 12:5 – 6 (NASB)
And she gave birth to a son, a male child, who is to rule all the nations with a rod of iron; and her child was caught up to God and to His throne. ⁶ Then the woman fled into the wilderness where she had a place prepared by God, so that there she would be nourished for one thousand two hundred and sixty days.

We know from the New Testament that Jesus was caught up into heaven forty days after the resurrection. According to this summary vision of the plan for Messiah and the Jewish people, at some point after Messiah Jesus goes to heaven, the nation of Israel, symbolized by the woman, will flee "into the wilderness." The word "then" in verse six must skip over the entire church age because we will find out in Revelation, and by reference to a few prophecies in the Old Testament, that a remnant of the Jewish people will flee from the wrath of the Antichrist. God will set aside a special wilderness retreat for their protection. This escape will happen immediately after the Antichrist declares in the temple that he is God. A remnant of the Jewish people will see the Antichrist's declaration for what it is – a revelation that the Antichrist is not a friend of Israel but is instead the devil himself. Their eyes will be opened, but the Antichrist will begin the worst persecution of the Jewish people in history. The remnant, however, will flee into the wilderness where they will wait out this persecution for three and a half years, just as Revelation 12:6 explains.

The flight of the Jewish remnant into the wilderness has not happened as of this writing, but it has been prophesied to happen in Revelation chapter twelve, Daniel 11:36, Isaiah 16, Isaiah 33:13 and Micah 2:12. These prophecies describe a special place where God will miraculously care for and protect these Jewish refugees from the persecution of the Antichrist. In fact, the prophecies indicate God will care for them as He did in the days of the Exodus when God sent miracle provisions of food and water. Dr. Arnold Fruchtenbaum believes the clues in these prophecies show that the wilderness refuge is most likely the ancient city of Petra. Petra is an amazing ancient city carved into sheer rock walls. Since the houses are essentially carved out caves, these houses of stone are not in ruins but can still be occupied. It is an abandoned city of stone, threaded through a maze of canyons covering an area the size of Manhattan, New York.

It is estimated these empty caverns can house over two hundred thousand people. The ancient people of Petra had also created a complicated water system that funnels spring and rainwater into cisterns. This water system is still functional today. Also, Petra has only one narrow entrance making it very protected and remote. [80] Whether or not Petra is the actual place the Jewish remnant will flee, other prophecies make it clear that the Antichrist will persecute Jewish people worldwide. He will also pursue this remnant until other military pressures draw him away from the remnant so that they will successfully escape into this wilderness stronghold.

The Old Testament prophecies about the Jews in the last half of the Great Tribulation say they will call out to Messiah to be rescued from the persecution of the beast (Antichrist). Since as of this writing, most Jews do not believe Jesus is Messiah, this means they will eventually recognize how Jesus fits the prophecies of the Old Testament. When they call to Him, He will return in power and great glory to rescue them from the Antichrist and bring final judgement to anyone following the Antichrist. In fact, Jesus said the end of all things would only happen when Israel, as a nation, accepts Him as Messiah. Jesus said this in Matthew 23:38 which reads,

Matthew 23:38 – 39 (NASB)
Behold, your house is being left to you desolate! [39] For I say to you, from now on you will not see Me until you say, 'Blessed is He who comes in the name of the Lord!'"

At the time Jesus said this, the leaders of the nation of Israel had rejected Him as Messiah. Jesus was paraphrasing Psalm 118:26, which the Jewish Rabbis had said for centuries was a reference to Messiah. Jesus meant that once Israel as a whole nation called out to Him as Messiah, He would return and rescue them. Revelation 12:7 goes on to say,

> **Revelation 12:7 – 9 (NASB)**
> And there was war in heaven, Michael and his angels waging war with the dragon. The dragon and his angels waged war, [8] and they were not strong enough, and there was no longer a place found for them in heaven. [9] And the great dragon was thrown down, the serpent of old who is called the devil and Satan, who deceives the whole world; he was thrown down to the earth, and his angels were thrown down with him.

Based on Old Testament symbolism, the woman clothed with the sun, is the nation of Israel and the Jewish people. The dragon with seven heads and ten horns ready to devour the woman's newborn Son is Satan, who will eventually indwell the man called Antichrist.

In the Revelation Refrain in Revelation 12:7, there is also the symbolic vision of heaven at war between Satan and his angels against Michael and his angels. This links to the literal fact that Satan will be cast down to the earth. This links to Ephesians 2:2, which says that Satan is "the Prince of the power of the air," and Job 1:12, 1 Kings 22:21 and Zechariah 3:1 that say Satan wanders around the earth yet still has access to heaven. In fact, Revelation 12:10 says that Satan is the accuser of Christians, and he accuses us day and night before the throne of God. Of course, it is unclear why Satan has access to heaven at all. One possible reason is that human beings have been given freewill, and in order for our will to be truly free, there must be a real possibility of failure. In order to fail, there must be a real accusation also! In other words, for Jesus to wash away our sins, there must be an accusation of sin. Perhaps Satan accuses believers of sin but each and every time he does, Jesus steps in to say, "My blood is sufficient to cover that." But here in Revelation chapter twelve, Satan's access to accuse Christians is finally revoked. God will no longer listen to accusations against His people because the blood of Jesus has proven to be enough.

Satan's future-history has long been known. According to Ezekiel 28:14-16, Satan was originally called Lucifer and he was a beautiful Cherub angel in charge of music and worship. In his pride, Satan chose to rebel against God! While he is still beautiful to look at, which is why the Bible says he can appear as an angel of light, and despite the fact that he is very smart, he is also irrational and insane. For centuries he has accused and stirred up evil directly and through the agency of the fallen angels who follow him, but here in Revelation chapter twelve his access to heaven is ended and he will be thrown down to the earth itself.

Once Satan is thrown to the earth at the mid-point in the Great Tribulation, he will try to kill every person who opposes his Antichrist. Satan is already insane, but at this point he will go berserk. Every Jewish person and every Christian will be his target in his unhinged hatred of God and his fear that his time is short. During this persecution rampage by the Antichrist, it will bring about the ultimate and final choice for every person on earth. Everyone will be forced to choose between Satan, through his possession of the Antichrist, and God. The Antichrist will have already used false signs and wonders. He will have already killed the two witnesses to try and bolster his claim to be God, but since the true God has taken the two witnesses into heaven, the veil is thrown off. At this point, the Antichrist will spew a river of lies and propaganda promising that anyone who swears allegiance to him by taking his mark, will be able to overcome God. He will promise to give his followers the immorality they want to keep their sin, and many will believe him. Romans 1:18 says that people are already without excuse for not believing and following God, but at this point in future-history after all they have seen, heard, and felt God will confirm their choice by hardening them even further. Second Thessalonians 2:9 says it this way,

> **Second Thessalonians 2:9 – 11 (NASB)**
> …the one whose coming is in accord with the activity of Satan, with all power and signs and false wonders, [10] and with all the deception of wickedness for those who perish, because they did not receive the love of the truth so as to be saved. [11] For this reason God will send upon them a deluding influence so that they will believe what is false…

Pharoah began by resisting God of his own free will and he had every chance to humble himself and turn to God. Eventually, God essentially said, "fine! You have chosen resistance. I will now confirm your choice and use your stubbornness to prove I am the one true God. I will smash the gods of Egypt one at a time and everyone will see that I Am God." It will be the same in this future history for anyone who continues to follow the Antichrist.

Revelation 12:10 – 17 (NASB)
Then I heard a loud voice in heaven, saying, "Now the salvation, and the power, and the kingdom of our God and the authority of His Christ have come, for the accuser of our brethren has been thrown down, he who accuses them before our God day and night. [11] And they overcame him because of the blood of the Lamb and because of the word of their testimony, and they did not love their life even when faced with death. [12] For this reason, rejoice, O heavens and you who dwell in them. Woe to the earth and the sea, because the devil has come down to you, having great wrath, knowing that he has only a short time." [13] And when the dragon saw that he was thrown down to the earth, he persecuted the woman who gave birth to the male child. [14] But the two wings of the great eagle were given to the woman, so that she could fly into the wilderness to her place, where she was nourished for a time and times and half a time, from the presence of the serpent. [15] And the serpent poured water like a river out of his mouth after the woman,

so that he might cause her to be swept away with the flood. ¹⁶ But the earth helped the woman, and the earth opened its mouth and drank up the river which the dragon poured out of his mouth. ¹⁷ So the dragon was enraged with the woman, and went off to make war with the rest of her children, who keep the commandments of God and hold to the testimony of Jesus.

The context of Revelation 12:10-17 is a vision and is, therefore, symbolic, but it links to the literal reality that the remnant of the Jewish people will hide from the persecution of the Antichrist in a mountain wilderness stronghold. Symbolically, Exodus 19:4 says that God saved Israel on Eagle's wings which means that "eagle's wings," in a symbolic context, is about God saving His people using miracles. In Exodus, God sent manna from heaven and water from a rock to save His people. In this future-history, God will do similar miracles and save His people once again.

Now that Satan has been thrown down and the Jewish remnant has retreated to Petra, Satan will stir up persecution against the Jews through Antichrist symbolized as "water like a river out of his mouth after the woman." In Scripture, water used in a symbolic way often refers to military action. This is probably symbolic of genocidal commands from the Antichrist and bold military action against God's people, but since God is saving His people by miracles once again, some sort of natural disaster will intervene. In the book of Numbers, God caused the earth to open up and consume Korah and his followers (Numbers 16:32). Revelation 12:16 could be something similar that will happen to the army pursuing the Jewish remnant. It could also mean that Gentile (non-Jewish) people will come to the aid of Jewish people by hiding them, just as many non-Jewish people did during the holocaust in World War II. Either way, the point is that the remnant of the Jews will be supernaturally protected until Jesus returns.

End of Days:
The Book of Revelation Explained

Chapter 20: The Beast!
Revelation 13 explained...

Prophecy in the Bible is like a map that only shows large landmarks. Prophetic "maps" leave out the curves or the length of road between the landmarks meaning it is not always revealed what length of time will happen between major events. It is also something like viewing a range of mountains stretching away from you into the distance. This view will only show the peaks of the mountains, but not the valleys and hills in-between. Occasionally, prophecy will also focus in on a landmark or peak, like a "cut-scene" in a movie where the main story pauses so the viewer can get more detail about something important. For example, from about halfway through the eleventh chapter through the end of the thirteenth chapter, there is a "cut scene" giving the reader some more detail about the Antichrist. Revelation 13:1 reads,

> **Revelation 13:1 - 2 (NASB)**
> Then I saw a beast coming up out of the sea, having ten horns and seven heads, and on his horns were ten diadems, and on his heads were blasphemous names. ² And the beast which I saw was like a leopard, and his feet

were like those of a bear, and his mouth like the mouth of a lion. And the dragon gave him his power and his throne and great authority.

The Revelation Refrain continues in the chapter thirteen "cut-scene." The beast and what happens to him is a vision or symbol because it is an otherworldly description of a creature and because John uses the word "like" in verse two. John also says that the beast gets his power from the dragon, a creature we already know is symbolic of Satan. Daniel chapters two and seven also describe this creature. The specific parts of the Revelation thirteen beast link to Daniel's vision of four distinct monsters in Daniel chapter seven and to Daniel's vision of a statue in Daniel chapter two. They are all illustrations of the same thing. Daniel chapter seven specifically says that the beasts represent different kingdoms that will form in the centuries after Daniel's time. These clues explain that the beast, the dragon, and the description of what happens to him in this passage, are symbolic rather than literal.

To understand what Revelation thirteen links to in the literal future, we need to look back at the prophecies from the book of Daniel. Daniel was written in the sixth century B.C. His vision of a statue and of four beasts in Daniel chapter two and chapter seven, link to future kingdoms that would dominate over the land of Israel until the coming of Messiah. These would have been the future for Daniel, but they are in the past for us. By examining the world empires that came upon the earth after the sixth century, and kingdoms that had a direct impact or influence on the land of Israel up until the coming of Messiah, we can see how these literal kingdoms link to Daniel's vision. We also know, from Daniel, that there will be a gap in time between the first and second comings of Messiah. This means there will be a final kingdom in the days of the second coming and Revelation thirteen gives us more detail about this final kingdom. This is the reason that parts of all four kingdoms in Daniel's vision are also parts of the last kingdom which is also prophesied about in Revelation thirteen.

The four beasts in Daniel chapter seven are a lion with eagle's wings (verse 3), a bear, (verse 5), a leopard with wings (verse 6) and a beast with iron teeth (verse 7). In Daniel's vision, this final beast with iron teeth sprouts ten horns and this is the link between Daniel's beast and the beast in Revelation thirteen. In Daniel, the ten horns on the final beast rise or grow as Daniel watches. He sees three of the ten horns get torn up but another one rises that has eyes like a man. Revelation thirteen gives more detail about this final "horn," and we see that it is the Antichrist. Daniel 7:23 says,

> **Daniel 7:23 – 24 (NASB)**
> "This is what he said: 'The fourth beast will be a fourth kingdom on the earth which will be different from all the other kingdoms, and will devour the whole earth and trample it down and crush it. [24] As for the ten horns, out of this kingdom ten kings will arise; and another will arise after them, and he will be different from the previous ones and will humble three kings.

Revelation thirteen says that the Antichrist is a composite beast that has aspects or parts of all the kingdoms that Daniel described. Dr. Arnold Fruchtenbaum believes this means that the significance of the kingdoms that came before the Antichrist are not about geography, but rather about the type of government each kingdom represented. [81] In other words, each of the kingdoms that Daniel prophesied about had a different kind of government, so the prophecy likely means that the final "kingdom" will have parts of all the others. The final kingdom of the Antichrist will not be characterized by a capital city or a country of origin. Instead, it will be a specific governmental type, such as the difference between communism and capitalism.

Daniel's vision of a metal statue and his vision of four beasts prophesies about the same thing as Revelation chapter thirteen. God tends to confirm His revelation in two or three different ways.

Daniel's four beasts represented the kingdom of Babylon, which existed in Daniel's day, the Mede-Persian Empire which started at the end of Daniel's career, the Greek Empire and finally the Roman Empire. The symbols fit this historical outline, and this is the reason many Bible scholars believe the final world empire will be a "revived Roman empire." But if the prophecy is about the type of government each of these kingdoms represented, then the capital city or country of each empire is not what matters in the prophecy.

Dr. Fruchtenbaum points out that this interpretation carries some weight because we also see these four kingdoms in Daniel's vision of a statue. [82] In Daniel's vision of the mighty statue, the head is made of gold, the breast of silver, the thighs of bronze and the legs of iron. It also has ten toes made partly of iron and partly of clay. The ten toes symbolize the same thing as the ten heads of the beast in Revelation thirteen. Each of the statue's materials has a different quality. Each material is progressively less valuable (gold is worth more than silver and so on) and each is progressively stronger (gold is so soft you can bruise it with your teeth, but iron will break your teeth.)

In Daniel 2:38, Daniel says that the head of gold is the king of Babylon, so gold represents pure monarchy. Babylon was a vast kingdom ruled by a single man. In that type of government, the king of Babylon was above the law. This is later confirmed when Daniel sees the vision of four beasts in Daniel chapter seven. The beasts and the statue parts are the same. In Daniel 7:4, the beast is a lion with the wings of an eagle. This symbolizes great power and swift action. In a pure monarchy, such as the kingdom of Babylon, the king spoke with ultimate authority and his orders were carried out without delay.

In Daniel 2:32, we learn that the breast and arms of the statue, made of silver, represent the kingdom that followed Babylon. We know from history this was the composite kingdom of the Medes and Persians. The two arms correspond to the division of this kingdom between two groups – the Medes and the Persians. This was not a pure monarchy like Babylon even though it was ruled by a king. It was not a pure monarchy because the king was not above the law, but the law was above the king. This is the reason we read in Daniel chapter six how Darius, the Mede-Persian king in the later days of Daniel's career, was manipulated by corrupt officials into signing a law where no one could worship any god other than the king for thirty days. This manipulation of the king was done to try to trap Daniel because his enemies knew that Daniel only prayed to the God of Israel. The king himself was bound by the law – something that did not bind the king of Babylon. Daniel 6:8 reads,

> **Daniel 6:8 (NASB)**
> Now, O king, establish the injunction and sign the document so that it will not be changed, according to the law of the Medes and Persians, which may not be revoked.

Daniel chapter seven reinforces this concept that the Mede-Persian empire was not a pure monarchy because the bear that represents this empire is lopsided. The bear is lopsided because the law could conflict with the king but also because the Medes-Persians used local rulers to govern, and these local rulers often rebelled causing instability in the empire.

Daniel 2:32 says the third part of the statue was a belly and two thighs made of bronze. Bronze is a strong, shiny, gold-colored metal, but just because bronze has a gold color and shines, that does not make it gold. In the same way, history shows that the third empire after Babylon was the Greek empire. This empire spread primarily by the conquest of Alexander the Great. Alexander did not have a legal right to rule – he ruled by straight conquest, powerful and swift. He looked like gold, but he was just bronze. The statue had two thighs because Alexander's empire was divided between east and west, but in Daniel 7:6, the Greek empire is also represented by a leopard with four wings, swift to kill. Alexander conquered most of the known world in less than twenty years, but at his death his empire was divided in rulership between his four generals, just as the leopard in Daniel's vision had four wings. As a type of government, the Greek empire ruled by conquest regardless of legality. The Greeks also used local leadership to rule various districts.

Daniel 2:33 says the fourth part of the statue was two legs of iron. In history, this corresponds to the two parts of the Roman Empire, east and west. The Romans ruled with an iron hand. Like the Greeks before them, they expanded by military conquest but unlike the Greeks or the Mede-Persians, the Romans used Roman people to rule over local officials. They did not trust the locals. Dr. Fruchtenbaum points out how the Roman system expanded and ruled by imperialism and colonialism. Imperialism looks to convert a local population into the culture of the conqueror by planting colonies in conquered territory.

In Daniel's vision, the final imperialist, colonial system of government and expansion that began with the Romans will develop in several stages. This corresponds to the feet being made partially of clay and partially of iron. This two-part mixed stage of development will eventually split into ten parts, just as there are ten heads on the beast in Revelation chapter thirteen.

The Roman Empire first split into an eastern and western branch, the western branch based in Rome and the eastern branch based in Constantinople (now Istanbul, Turkey). As the Roman Empire dissolved, other kingdoms continued the system of military expansion followed by colonies from the home country. The colonies were populated by people from the home country, they ruled over local officials from the conquered area and exploited the local resources. This system was also a mix of the imperialist, colonial mindset (the iron) with an attempt to pacify or be of some benefit to the local people the colonizers were exploiting (the clay). Unfortunately, iron and clay do not mix, so the history of colonialism by European and Asian powers is a history of local exploitation, rebellions, genocide, and instability. The United States, for example, was once a colony of the British Empire, but fell apart by revolution. Daniel 7:23 describes this instability where it says,

Daniel 7:23 (NASB)
...The fourth beast will be a fourth kingdom on the earth, which will be different from all the other kingdoms and will devour the whole earth and tread it down and crush it.

The word "different" in this passage means "diverse" because European and Asian powers set up colonies in different ways and different places all over the earth. History shows that the imperialist, colonial system did indeed crush opposition and ate up kingdoms worldwide. For example, at the height of British colonialism, it was said that the sun never set on the British Empire because there were British colonies in every time zone and on every continent on earth. This system devoured the whole earth, tread it down and crushed it because when European and Asian powers went to war, all their colonies also went to war. This is why during World War I and World War II, the entire earth was at war at the same time.

Some Bible scholars think that the ten toes of the statue in Daniel chapter two, the ten horns of the beast in Daniel chapter seven and Revelation chapter thirteen, mean that the final world empire of the Antichrist will be a revival of the Roman Empire. They think it will be based in the city of Rome, in Italy. But if the statue in Daniel chapter two illustrates or prophesies about types of government, rather than specific kingdoms based on geographical capital cities, then it means the system of colonial, imperialist rule will spread throughout the world (it has!). It will then split into ten parts or jurisdictions that the Antichrist will begin to dominate (it has not). The split into ten parts has not happened yet, but the coming ten-part division will not be about the city of Rome or a revival of the Ancient Roman Empire in an exact, literal sense. Rome may yet be part of the ten parts, but regardless of how it will be divided up, the Antichrist will move to dominate that system. This may be the reason Revelation says the final world ruler will have parts of each of the government systems that came before him. Revelation 13:2 says,

> **Revelation 13:2 (NASB)**
> And the beast which I saw was like a leopard, and his feet were like those of a bear, and his mouth like the mouth of a lion.

> And the dragon gave him his power and his throne and great authority.

The word "like" means this is symbolic and not literal. Verse one says the Antichrist comes from "out of the sea," and throughout Scripture the sea is symbolic of the Gentile (non-Jewish) world - so the Antichrist will not be Jewish! Secondly, he will be like a pure monarch (the lion's mouth and the head of gold) in that his word will be absolute law as soon as he declares something. He will also demand allegiance by force of law (the bear's feet) but he will expand his influence by conquest (the leopard) and crush all opposition with an iron fist.

In the future, there will come a day when an economic, military, or natural disaster will seduce the world into trying out a one-world government. This one-world government will collapse almost immediately into ten world jurisdictions under ten colonial, imperialist leaders. According to Daniel chapter seven, three of these jurisdictions or kingdoms will be "torn up" meaning that Antichrist will overcome them militarily. The other seven will, at that future point, simply give into his leadership. Since he is like a king, he will rule by direct announcement of his will. Like a bear, he will crush free speech and freedom of worship. Like a leopard, he will swiftly move to destroy any opposition to his will. Like the Romans who went before him, He will use only absolutely loyal governors and generals to enforce his command. Unlike any other ruler in history, however, he will be empowered by Satan himself. They will give him unusual power, even the power to do what everyone will assume are miracles. Revelation 13:3 says,

Revelation 13:3 – 6 (NASB)
I saw one of his heads as if it had been fatally wounded, and his fatal wound was healed. And the whole earth was amazed and followed after the beast; ⁴ they worshiped the dragon because he gave his authority to the beast; and they worshiped the beast, saying, "Who is like the beast, and who is able to wage war with him?" ⁵ A mouth was given to him speaking arrogant words and blasphemies, and authority to act for forty-two months was given to him. ⁶ And he opened his mouth in blasphemies against God, to blaspheme His name and His tabernacle, that is, those who dwell in heaven.

During the Antichrist's rise to world power, and probably just before he declares that he is God in the Jerusalem temple, he will suffer an apparently fatal wound to the head. Somehow, this wound will be healed. There is some argument among Bible scholars about whether this will be an actual resurrection or a deception of some kind. Since this is a future event, it remains to be seen. One way or another, many people will believe and accept his claim to be God because of his recovery from this wound, his power to overcome the two witnesses, his charisma and the work of the false prophet who will act as his spokesman and promoter.

Modern people should not be so vulnerable to his deception, but these prophecies illustrate a powerful truth about human nature - human beings cry out for leadership, particularly when things are harsh. A charismatic leader and a powerful speech can sway a crowd into a frenzy, so no one should underestimate the power of well-crafted public speaking. The Bible says the Antichrist will be boastful, full of arrogant words about his personal greatness, and blasphemies. He will make a persuasive case that his accomplishments, and the great need in the world, should convince people he is God. He will promise that anyone who devotes themselves to him will enjoy the solution to the world's problems that only he will be able to solve. Over and over again, he will point to his power to subdue other world leaders. He will gloat over his ability to kill the two witnesses and whether by deception or not, he will claim his miraculous recovery from an assassination attempt shows he is master over death itself.

After his declaration in the temple and his recovery, the Antichrist will openly offer himself as a direct alternative to all other religious faiths. He will persuade people that every religion really teaches essentially the same thing. He will claim to be the embodiment of whatever is best about any religion. In ancient times the Roman emperors proclaimed that citizens could worship any god they wanted so long as their highest allegiance was to the emperor. This is the reason they built temples to themselves. In the same way as the emperors before him, the Antichrist will try to end the conflict between religions by claiming that anyone can keep their religion so long as they proclaim that their highest allegiance is to him. In fact, the word "Antichrist" does not mean "against Christ." It means "instead of Christ."

The Antichrist will offer to end economic conflict by establishing a single world economy. He will offer to end the environmental crisis by taking total control of business and industry worldwide. He will offer to solve all religious conflict by establishing an overruling single religion over all others. People facing economic, environmental, and political chaos will flock to his flag. Human beings without an allegiance to God from the heart will always sacrifice personal freedoms and rights for the hope of security and success. This is a pattern in human history. Dictators and kings, tyrants and despots have always rallied the crowds with the promise of safety and future prosperity. What has happened in the past will happen again.

The apostle John, under the inspiration of the Holy Spirit said in First John 4:3,

> **First John 4:3 (NASB)**
> ...every spirit that does not confess Jesus is not from God; this is the spirit of the antichrist, which you have heard is coming, and now it is already in the world.

The patterns of history tend to repeat, so while the prophecies point ahead to the rise and reign of the Antichrist, the spirit of Antichrist will rise from time to time in various places all over the earth. Many Roman Emperors were driven by a spirit of Antichrist as were dictators such as Joseph Stalin, Mao, and Adolf Hitler. The spirit of Antichrist has already been at work, the final Antichrist is inevitable, and the world's population today is being conditioned to accept his imperialist rule. Today, people are trained by public education and the propaganda of our media and entertainment systems to accept the ongoing public narrative without question. People are persuaded to believe that human government is the answer to human problems. The average person is trained and pressured to sacrifice freedom for community safety!

When the public cannot debate an issue, when freedom of speech is suppressed, or when people will not speak up for fear of a mob crushing them, it is the path toward imperialism. Christians need to be sober minded, willing, and prepared to speak the truth in love, because the time is short. The spirit of Antichrist can stir up another mini-Antichrist before the Rapture of the church. People without God as the true ruler of their lives will naturally look to a human ruler for answers. Considering what the final Antichrist will be like, Christians must be on guard, never taking freedom for granted. Revelation 13:7 says,

Revelation 13:7 (NASB)
It was also given to him to make war with the saints and to overcome them, and authority over every tribe and people and tongue and nation was given to him.

Some scholars think the use of the word "saints" in Revelation 13:7 means the church will not be removed (Raptured) before the events in Revelation chapter thirteen. This cannot be the case, however, because Jesus said in Matthew 16:18 that the gates of hell would not overcome the church. Revelation 13:7 says that the Antichrist will overcome these saints; so, these saints cannot refer to the church today. This is not a contradiction because the word "saints" is used of all believers in the true God, including believers from the church age which began with the resurrection of Jesus. The word "church" also includes people who will choose to believe in Jesus after the Rapture as well as Old Testament believers in the Most High God. In fact, Daniel uses the term in Daniel 7:21 which reads,

> **Daniel 7:21 – 22 (NASB)**
> I kept looking, and that horn was waging war with the saints and prevailing against them, ^{22} until the Ancient of Days came and judgement was passed in favor of the saints of the Highest One, and the time arrived when the saints took possession of the kingdom.

These saints in Revelation thirteen will be believers who turn to Jesus during the Great Tribulation, after the Rapture. During the Great Tribulation there will be a harsh, final line drawn between those who stay true to Jesus and those who give allegiance to the Antichrist. Revelation 13:8 says,

> **Revelation 13:8 – 10 (NASB)**
> All who live on the earth will worship him, everyone whose name has not been written since the foundation of the world in the book of life of the Lamb who has been slaughtered. ^{9} If anyone has an ear, let him hear. ^{10} If anyone is destined for captivity, to captivity he goes; if anyone kills with the sword, with the sword he must be killed.

> Here is the perseverance and the faith of the saints.

John quotes Jesus when he challenges the reader to have an ear and really hear what the Spirit is revealing here. This prophecy illustrates that there must be no compromise or rationalization about a person's personal allegiance. True believers will not worship the Antichrist regardless of consequences and there will be consequences. The Antichrist will wage war against anyone who will not submit and swear religious, political, and economic allegiance to him.

Even today, before the Rapture and the rise of the Antichrist, this principle remains the same. Christians must resist the temptation to give into the world system or compromise with the world's way of thinking or acting no matter the consequences. The world's philosophy celebrates compromised lifestyles and values that directly contradict what God has revealed in the Bible.

Revelation 13:10 illustrates that whatever a person plants in life is what is going to grow. When a person chooses to be in submission to anyone or anything other than Jesus, then that person is choosing a path of captivity to ungodly attitudes, beliefs, and actions. That person will continue on that path getting more of the same, but it is the faithfulness of the believer that he or she does not follow the same path. It takes perseverance and spiritual grit to resist the lure of the world. Revelation 13:11 says,

Revelation 13:11 (NASB)
Then I saw another beast coming up out of the earth; and he had two horns like a lamb and he spoke as a dragon.

Whenever the Scripture uses the earth symbolically, it means the world system and the secular worldview. Revelation 13:11 says that a false prophet will one day support, defend, and promote the Antichrist. The false prophet will be a product of a secular worldview, so the vision shows him coming up from the earth. He is seen as having two horns like a lamb because he will come across as gentle and lamb-like in the way he will market the Antichrist's program to unify all world religions. He will sound reasonable and caring. He will probably teach that every religion is basically the same, but that the Antichrist is the central figure every religion in history has pointed to over the centuries. He will call Antichrist the Messiah and people will believe his lies, but as it says in this prophecy, his words will originate from Satan himself.

The foundation for this argument is already well at work in the world today. The idea that every religion is basically true is increasingly popular in America. While this idea seems so loving and reasonable, it is false. Not all religions can be true because they contradict each other, and opposite ideas cannot be true in the same way and in the same sense. For example, if all religions are true, then Christianity must also be true, but the Christian faith declares without apology that there is one and only one God and that Jesus is the only true God. This contradicts other religions that teach that all of reality is God or that there are many gods or that Jesus is just one of many spiritual authorities. Both concepts cannot be true at the same time and in the same way because they are opposites. Revelation 13:12 goes on to describe the teaching of the false prophet in greater detail. It says,

> **Revelation 13:12 – 14 (NASB)**
> He exercises all the authority of the first beast in his presence. And he makes the earth and those who live on it worship the first beast, whose fatal wound was healed. [13] He performs great signs, so that he even makes fire come down out of the sky to the earth in the presence of people. [14] And he deceives those who live on the earth because of the signs which it was given him to perform in the presence of the beast, telling those who live on the earth to make an image to the beast who had the wound of the sword and has come to life.

The false prophet who will promote and market the Antichrist will be "given" an ability to perform apparent miracles. There is some debate among scholars as to whether these will be real miracles or deceptions. One way or another, the false prophet will do amazing things that will boost his popularity and help him market the Antichrist into "celebrity-of-the-world status." Modern people, educated in science and technology, will be deceived by these signs into directly worshipping the Antichrist.

This final deception is part of God's plan to draw the final line between freewill and God's judgement. People at this point in the Great

Tribulation will have been given every possible chance to choose God instead of the Antichrist just as Pharoah in the book of Exodus had every chance to reject the false gods of Egypt. Just as God hardened Pharoah, confirming his freewill choice, so the Lord will use the stubbornness of this future generation to prove in the end that the Antichrist is a false god; yet they will still refuse to turn to Jesus and be saved. They will be beyond redemption. Second Thessalonians 2:9 says,

> **Second Thessalonians 2:9 (NASB)**
> ...the one whose coming is in accord with the activity of Satan, with all power and false signs and wonders...

Revelation 13:12-14 is a warning to us today - just because people claim to have dreams from God or claim to perform healings and use the Bible as the basis of their proclamations, does not make them true servants of God. During the Great Tribulation, the Antichrist and the false prophet will use signs, wonders, and apparent miracles to market themselves. They will twist the Scriptures to try and boost their teachings, but the mark of a true prophet of God is found in Deuteronomy 13:1 which says,

> **Deuteronomy 13:1 – 3 (NASB)**
> If a prophet or a dreamer of dreams arises among you and gives you a sign or a wonder, [2] and the sign or the wonder comes true, of which he spoke to you, saying, 'Let's follow other gods (whom you have not known) and let's serve them,' [3] you shall not listen to the

words of that prophet or dreamer of dreams…

Real healings, prophetic dreams, signs, and wonders from God in the present day, will never be done to confirm a teaching that contradicts the Bible.

Revelation 13:15 – 16 (NASB)
And it was given to him to give breath to the image of the beast, so that the image of the beast would even speak and cause as many as do not worship the image of the beast to be killed. [16] And he causes all, the small and the great, and the rich and the poor, and the free men and the slaves, to be given a mark on their right hand or on their forehead…

As the Antichrist rises in political power and religious leadership, both he and the false prophet will eventually twist his religious teaching into idolatry. In some way, perhaps through computer artificial intelligence or through the internet, the false prophet will create an interactive image of the beast. Whatever this image is, it will communicate a propaganda message from the Antichrist to a traumatized population. No one knows exactly how he will spin his message, but it will involve his claim to be God.

Eventually, however, after his own recovery from a head wound and after he kills the two witnesses, the Antichrist will throw off all restraint because his support base will begin to slip when people will see the two witnesses raised from the dead and taken up into heaven. The resurrection of the two witnesses will weaken his political and religious support. Once the average person sees the resurrection of the two witnesses, the Antichrist and his false prophet will need to spin some sort of explanation propaganda to maintain power. However, he and the false prophet will spin the narrative, since the population will be conditioned to accept whatever narrative comes from the ruling authorities, many will fall for it. It is likely he will fear a loss of support, so he will attempt to crush all opposition by restructuring world trade. Revelation 13:17 says,

> **Revelation 13:17 – 18 (NASB)**
> …and he provides that no one will be able to buy or to sell, except the one who has the mark, either the name of the beast or the number of his name. [18] Here is wisdom. Let him who has understanding calculate the number of the beast, for the number is that of a man; and his number is six hundred and sixty-six.

The mark of the beast relates to the ancient Hebrew or Greek alphabets. The letters in these alphabets are also related to numbers. For example, in ancient koine Greek, the first letter of the alphabet is α (Alpha) and Alpha corresponds to the number 1. The second letter is Beta (β) which corresponds to the number 2 and so on. In ancient Hebrew, the first letter of the alphabet is Aleph (א) which corresponds to the number one, then Bet ב = (2) and so on. [83] This number / letter system could be used to write messages. For example, in the ancient

Roman city of Pompeii, an inscription was found that reads, "I love her whose number is 545." [84]

Unfortunately, some speculations about the mark of the beast have generated considerable fear. Some people have even refused to take medicines by injection over fear they might be deceived into receiving the mark of the beast, but the text makes it clear this mark is a deliberate act of allegiance to the Antichrist. This means it cannot be a secret branding or injection of some kind that anyone could receive by accident. It is possible this mark could be a tattoo or microchip that is invisible to the natural eye, but it is specifically "either the name of the beast or the number of his name," not the name, address and bank account number of the person who takes the mark. Banking or credit information might be added into the mark, since it is directly linked to permission to do business, but the mark itself is directly linked to the individual's freewill choice of loyalty to the Antichrist. This means it cannot be taken by accident.

The specific name of the Antichrist or his number is unclear from this text. While Hebrew and Greek have numbers associated with the letters of the alphabet, it is unclear if the prophecy refers to a calculation of the name in Hebrew, Greek or some other language. Speculation about the name of the Antichrist has led to many unfounded fears over the years. For example, in the 1980's some people were very concerned that President Ronald Reagan might be the Antichrist because each part of his name, Ronald Wilson Reagan, has 6 letters which comes out to 666. President Lyndon Johnson's name also can add up to 666 but Johnson died in 1973. The truth is that roughly one in every 10,000 names can add up to 666 depending on what spelling and what language is used to make the calculation. [85]

There is no need for wild speculations or fear about either the mark of the beast or his name. His identity will not be clear until after the Rapture. The requirement that everyone take the mark to be able to buy or sell will not happen until after he openly declares in the temple that he is God. At that point in future-history it will be obvious who he is and what taking the mark will mean.

End of Days:
The Book of Revelation Explained

Chapter 21: Satisfaction!
Revelation 14 and 15 explained...

Revelation chapter thirteen says that at the midpoint of the Great Tribulation, the Antichrist will demand everyone swear loyalty to his religious, economic, and political rulership by taking a mark that includes his name and the number of his name. At that future point, his political, economic, and religious support will be threatened, probably because of the resurrection of the two witnesses that the whole world will witness. He will then throw off all restraint and embark on a campaign to destroy any opposition. He will persecute to the death almost two-thirds of the Jewish people. The remaining Jewish remnant will be miraculously protected in the ancient wilderness fortress of Petra. Christians, and anyone else who refuses to swear allegiance to him by taking the mark will also be put to death. This persecution will be the worst attack against the Jewish people in the history of the human race, which is why the Old Testament prophet Jeremiah, in Jeremiah 30:7, described the Great Tribulation as "the time of Jacob's distress." At the end of this three and a half years of persecution, the Lord Jesus Christ will return. Revelation 14:1 says,

Revelation 14: 1 – 5 (NASB)
Then I looked, and behold, the Lamb was standing on Mount Zion, and with Him 144,000 who had His name and the name of His Father written on their foreheads. ² And I heard a voice from heaven, like the sound of many waters and like the sound of loud thunder, and the voice which I heard was like the sound of harpists playing on their harps. ³ And they sang a new song before the throne and before the four living creatures and the elders; and no one was able to learn the song except the 144,000 who had been purchased from the earth. ⁴ These are the ones who have not defiled themselves with women, for they are celibate. These are the ones who follow the Lamb wherever He goes. These have been purchased from mankind as first fruits to God and to the Lamb. ⁵ And no lie was found in their mouths; they are blameless.

The 144,000 were first introduced in Revelation chapter seven. They will be celibate Jewish men fully devoted to Jesus as their Messiah. The word for celibate in Greek is μολύνω (mo-lü'-no) [86] which means "to contaminate, or defile through fornication or adultery" but this Scripture does not imply that women are unclean or that normal, married sexual relations are impure. The word means that any sexual activity outside of heterosexual marriage is unclean, so, these Jewish men are celibate because they are not married and they have not given into the temptations of fornication or adultery. Revelation 14:6 goes on to say,

> **Revelation 14:6 – 7 (NASB)**
> And I saw another angel flying in midheaven with an eternal gospel to preach to those who live on the earth, and to every nation, tribe, language, and people; ⁷ and he said with a loud voice, "Fear God and give Him glory, because the hour of His judgement has come; worship Him who made the heaven and the earth, and sea and springs of waters."

Normally, the fact the prophet sees "another angel flying" would be the start of the Revelation Refrain of something symbolic linked to something that is literal. In this case, however, the word "midheaven" is μεσουράνημα (me-sü-rä'-na-mä) which means "the highest point of the sun at midday." [87] In other words, this angel is flying in the physical atmosphere, so the context suggests the flight of this angel will be a literal, physical event. Since this happens at the end of the Great Tribulation, this will be the very last opportunity for people to turn to God. This event is where God will pull out all stops, allowing the supernatural experience of an angel in the sky calling to everyone on earth. It is possible this is the fulfillment of Jesus' prophecy in Matthew 24:14 where He said,

> **Matthew 24:14 (NASB)**
> This gospel of the kingdom shall be preached in the whole world as a testimony to all the nations, and then the end will come.

Some scholars think this prophecy in Matthew 24:14 relates to the spread of the gospel by missionaries or technology and this might be correct. Many missionaries have used this verse as motivation to go to the most remote parts of the earth. It is also possible that this prophecy could be linked to Revelation 14:6-7 because the context of Matthew chapter twenty-four is about the Great Tribulation. Either way, God will make certain that every person will hear the good news about Jesus in their own language

"This gospel of the kingdom shall be preached in the whole world as a testimony to all nations" was something nearly inconceivable for centuries. For many years no one could imagine how this could be accomplished. Even during the great missionary movement during the nineteenth century, missionaries were limited to travel by ship or on horses or on foot. Up until the twentieth century there were also limits on languages and literacy of the people missionaries traveled to visit. All these barriers are things of the past today.

In our modern era, it seems like technology doubles in efficiency and speed every year or so, and this observation is sometimes called "Moore's Law." [88] As of this writing, computer software can essentially translate almost any language into any other language with the press of a button. Today, there are satellite "clouds" in low earth orbit able to beam the internet to every corner of the earth. By the end of the next decade, there will not be a place on earth that a solar powered laptop, tablet, or phone, with the right receiver, cannot access the internet. For example, the American telecom and space company SpaceX is currently building an internet satellite cloud that will be accessible anywhere on the planet and the poorest, most remote groups on earth are already tuning in. In remote parts of northern Haiti, the poorest country in the western hemisphere, people living in grass huts with packed mud floors are using solar powered cell phones every day. In the highlands of the remotest parts of Papua, New Guinea, portable solar panels, and cell phone technology allow missionaries to download audio versions of the Scriptures, read in local languages, so the locals can hear the gospel. The technology is now available where the gospel is being preached to the whole earth. If the prophecy in Matthew chapter twenty-four is not about the angel preaching in Revelation 14, but is about the gospel being preached before the Rapture, this prophecy is being fulfilled right now.

Revelation 14:8 (NASB)
And another angel, a second one, followed, saying, "Fallen, fallen is Babylon the great, she who has made all the nations drink of the wine of the passion of her sexual immorality."

After the first angel preaches the gospel message calling everyone to worship God rather than the Antichrist, there will come another angel who will show the contrast between what God offers and what the Antichrist represents. This contrast is clear because the word "Babylon" is used in this passage just as our culture uses the word "Hollywood." Hollywood is both a city in California and symbolic of the movie and entertainment industry. In the same way, Babylon is both a city and symbolic of the Antichrist's false philosophy and religion.

Throughout the Bible, the city of Babylon is symbolic of a system of false, human-centered religion, based on a philosophy tracing back to the earliest post-Flood human city called "Babel." In Genesis, Babel was the center of human civilization immediately after the Flood. God had commanded the descendants of Noah to spread out over the whole earth, but they refused and built the city of Babel. In their rebellion, they created a religious system that became the mother of all other false religious systems throughout human history. Revelation 14:9 says,

> **Revelation 14:9 – 12 (NASB)**
> Then another angel, a third one, followed them, saying with a loud voice, "If anyone worships the beast and his image, and receives a mark on his forehead or on his hand, [10] he also will drink of the wine of the wrath of God, which is mixed in full strength in the cup of His anger; and he will be tormented with fire and brimstone in the presence of the holy angels and in the presence of the Lamb. [11] And the smoke of their torment ascends forever and ever; they have no rest day and night, those who worship the beast and his image, and whoever receives the mark of his name." [12] Here is the perseverance of the saints who keep the commandments of God and their faith in Jesus.

These three angels are the final warnings in the final moments of the final days of the Great Tribulation before Jesus returns. This will be a unique moment in human history, an experience so awesome and captivating that no human being will miss it. It is the final straw, the line in the sand where God will declare through His angels, in every language and in a public way, that no one can deny that the final choice between turning to God or loyalty to the Antichrist has come. Anyone who chooses to continue in loyalty to the Antichrist is now warned that they will get the full blast of the wrath of God and the eternal torment of hell on top of it if they continue in their rebellion.

The Bible warns over and over again that people are going to hell unless they are saved by Jesus. The Bible also says the torments of hell will last forever. Modern critics think that hell is cruel, inhumane, and unfair, but the truth is, hell is actually fairness itself. This is true because there is a difference between "fairness" and "mercy."

To illustrate, there is a story about a college professor who warned his students at the start of the term about three upcoming research papers. He told the students over and over again that they would deserve an automatic failing grade if they turned in any of the papers even one minute later than the requirement. On the day the first paper was due, twenty students turned in their papers on time, but ten students did not. The professor questioned the ten failing students about whether they understood the requirements, and each admitted they were fully aware of the rules. The professor explained that he would give them mercy and allow them to turn in their papers late. On the day the second paper was due, fifteen students turned in their papers, but fifteen did not. The fifteen were worried but they hoped they would get the same treatment as the first group and, in fact, the professor did the same thing. He questioned whether they understood the requirements, found that each of them was completely aware of the rules, but once again he extended mercy to let them turn in the paper late. Finally, on the day the final paper was due, only ten turned in the paper on time and twenty students did not. They were not worried at all since they had seen the professor give mercy to the first and the second group of late students. But this time they were outraged when the professor gave each of them a failing grade. They were so outraged they murmured and clamored until a leader of this group openly said aloud that the situation was "unfair."

"Unfair?" asked the professor.

"Certainly," replied the students. "You let us off the first and the second time."

"Let you off?" said the professor. "No. I extended mercy to you."

"What do you mean," they asked?

"Well, the standards were absolutely clear, and you understood those standards," he replied. "I was only under an obligation to give you a failing grade but because I am the one who makes the rules, I am able to offer mercy. But if you want justice, that's different. Justice can only be what is right according to the rules. If that is what you want, then I will change the grades on the first two papers to "fail." After all, those are the standards and you understood what was required...Or you can accept what mercy I have offered. Which will you have?"

In the same way, no human being ever asked to be born. The Bible teaches that our existence is dependent on the Creator. This life, our existence, our awareness of reality around us, all belong to the Creator. In short, this life is His class. He has the right to the set the rules and every human being has fallen short of the standards He has set. God has no obligation to give mercy to anyone, but because of His great love, He does offer us mercy. It is for this reason that Hell is necessary. This is so because "fair" means to treat everyone the same according to a standard. To be fair to human beings, created with the amazing capacity to exercise freewill, there must be a place where people who do not want to love God may go. The Bible teaches that God does not force His love on anyone. God only offers a persuasive argument that people should freely accept His mercy so those who do not want to love God must be released somewhere independent of God. It would not be fair to force anyone into relationship with God if they do not want to be near Him. Former atheist C.S. Lewis explained the attitude of those condemned to hell this way:

> There are only two kinds of people in the end: those who say to God, "Thy will be done," and those to whom God says, in the end, "thy will be done." All that are in Hell, choose it. Without that self-choice there could be no Hell. [89]

The true God is light and love and goodness and relationship. He is all these things in a pure sense. On the other hand, "evil" is only a lack of what is good, so if a person, of their own freewill, chooses to reject God, then in the end they reject all these good things in their pure existence also. Hell is, therefore, utterly dark because it a place apart from God and God is light. Foolish people in the modern world who reject God and arrogantly say they would rather go to hell and party with their pagan friends than submit to God, are deceived. There are no parties in hell because a party would be joyful, and God is joy itself. There will be no friendships in hell because it is a place apart from God and God is relationship itself.

Nevertheless, however horrible hell is, people will freely and fairly choose to exist there. They will forever receive what they have chosen because they spent a lifetime rejecting God. In fact, Lewis suggested in his quote above, that while people in hell will hate hell, they will hate the idea of laying down their pride to serve God even more. As time stretches out into a bleak eternity, they will reinforce in their hearts their hatred of God as they rehearse their reasons for rejecting Him...over and over again...forever and ever.

Why does hell exist forever? For the same reason that heaven exists forever. Heaven is God's home, and He is eternal. As human beings created in God's image, we are only like God, not exact duplicates, or copies, so we are not eternal because we have a beginning and God has no beginning. We start to exist at some point in time, but once we begin to exist, since we are made in His eternal image, we will continue to exist as long as God exists. This is what the Scripture means when it says in Revelation 14:12:

> **Revelation 14:12 (NASB)**
> "Here is the perseverance of the saints who keep the commandments of God and their faith in Jesus."

As long as God exists, those who have turned in faith to Jesus to wash their sins away, will be forever kept in the beauty and bliss of His presence. To be fair, those who reject God must also exist forever in the place they have chosen that is apart from Him. The rebels in hell are also created in the image of God, therefore, the punishment of existence apart from God must endure as long as God exists.

God's mercy is always 100% undeserved so mercy can never be earned, or it would not be mercy - it would be payment. Mercy is also always 100% the prerogative of the professor of the class, because it is his class. Just as the students may not like the professor or may wish they had a professor more in line with how they think things should be, these feelings do not change the situation because it is not their classroom. Revelation 14:13 says,

> **Revelation 14:13 (NASB)**
> And I heard a voice from heaven, saying, "Write: 'Blessed are the dead who die in the Lord from now on!'" "Yes," says the Spirit, "so that they may rest from their labors, for their deeds follow with them."

So, while God will not force anyone into relationship with Him, there is a deadline when freewill ends and God's offer of mercy ends also - human death! God will delay His justice for a lifetime, as long as possible, to give everyone a chance to freely turn to Him because God loves people. God created human beings to enjoy relationship with Him forever and those who freely choose to submit to Him as Lord will receive that benefit, so we are blessed if we die in the Lord. Jesus also said this in John 14:1, where it is written,

> **John 14:1 – 3 (NASB)**
> "Do not let your heart be troubled; believe in God, believe also in Me. ² In My Father's house are many rooms; if that were not so, I would have told you, because I am going there to prepare a place for you. ³ And if I go and prepare a place for you, I am coming again and will take you to Myself, so that where I am, there you also will be.

Heaven is a special place for anyone who freely turns to God. Jesus said there are many mansions there and the word mansion is μονή (mo-nā') in Greek. [90] It means "dwelling or abiding place" so it is a place of total rest, comfort, and completeness. It is everything that hell will lack. Revelation 21:4 says that in this perfect existence...

> **Revelation 21:4 (NASB)**
> "...and He (God) will wipe away every tear from their eyes; and there will no longer be any death; there will no longer be any

mourning, or crying, or pain; the first things have passed away."

It is difficult for us to imagine what heaven will be like, but the beauty that still fills our cursed planet is a way to get a small glimpse of heaven. God is beauty itself in a pure sense, so He created sunrises and sunsets, mountains, and stars to reflect His glory. In this world, decay infects all these things and yet even the death of leaves on the trees in autumn are often so beautiful they take our breath away. The riot of stunning color in dying leaves every autumn, the deep blue of the sky and the stars reflected on the surface of a lake in the night, are just a tiny view of God's beauty. He created brilliant colors even in the depths of the sea, long before human beings invented scuba tanks to be able to see them. Even in judgement - God is good.

The Bible does not teach that heaven is a boring mob of disembodied spirits in white robes playing harps while seated on clouds. The God who invented puppies and parakeets is not boring nor does He lack inventiveness and since God is not boring, heaven cannot be boring either. It was God who invented laughter. God designed taste buds so that even people who hate Him can enjoy ice cream. It is God who manufactured adrenaline so even people in a fallen world can still get a rush out of a roller coaster ride. It is God who made the nerves so we can feel and taste and touch and smell. God made endless ways to make us smile and He let all of that continue even after human beings rebelled against Him. The sun still shines on people who hate Him. The rain still falls, and the crops still grow in lands committed to the worship of other gods.

Ultimately, the greatest joy of any joy, is God Himself. In God's presence there will be endless discovery. His new creation will be "world within world," [91] without end. In heaven, we may wonder if we ever really lived at all. "The day I die will be the best day I've ever lived." [92]

Revelation 14:14-16 (NASB)
Then I looked, and behold, a white cloud, and sitting on the cloud was one like a son of man, with a golden crown on His head and a sharp sickle in His hand. [15] And another angel came out of the temple, calling out with a loud voice to Him who sat on the cloud, "Put in your sickle and reap, for the hour to reap has come, because the harvest of the earth is ripe." [16] Then He who sat on the cloud swung His sickle over the earth, and the earth was reaped.

Revelation 14:14-16 is the Revelation Refrain once again. The title "Son of Man" is a title Jesus used to refer to Himself. It comes from Daniel chapter seven. Daniel used this phrase to describe the Messiah so Revelation 14:14 is a vision of Jesus. This section is also symbolic because people do not literally sit on clouds or swing sickles over a planet, and John also sees an angel coming out of the temple in heaven calling to the man seated on the cloud. All these clues tell us this is symbolic.

Overall, Revelation chapter fourteen is about the warning of angels concerning the final consequences of rejecting God. Revelation 14:14-16 illustrates the law of planting and harvesting coming true because a sickle is a huge blade that farmers used to cut ripe crops when they matured. The Bible frequently reminds people there is an absolute spiritual law of planting and harvesting (also called sowing and reaping). This law is true in a positive and negative sense. What anyone plants, either literally in a field or figuratively in terms of the actions they "plant" in their lives, whatever is planted is what will grow in the end. The harvest is always about getting the result of what is planted. Galatians 6:7 says,

Galatians 6:7 (NASB)
"Do not be deceived, God is not mocked; for whatever a person sows, this he will also reap."

In the context of Revelation chapter fourteen, the final consequences or harvest of what rebellious humanity has planted over the centuries is about to be gathered. It is now the utter end! In fact, in Greek the word "ripe" is ξηραίνω (ksa-ri'-no) which means "withered, dry, or over-ripe." [93] This will be the time when everyone gets the result of what they planted in life – and the harvest is overripe! By this future point, everyone will have had enough time to make a final choice, but the evil of human beings is now so great, there is no time left to delay. Revelation 14:17 stretches out the picture of final judgement, so over-ripe it is like a grape that will explode with juice at the slightest touch.

Revelation 14:17 – 20 (NASB)
And another angel came out of the temple which is in heaven, and he also had a sharp sickle. [18] Then another angel, the one who has power over fire, came out from the altar;

and he called with a loud voice to him who had the sharp sickle, saying, "Put in your sharp sickle and gather the clusters from the vine of the earth, because her grapes are ripe." [19] So the angel swung his sickle to the earth and gathered the clusters from the vine of the earth, and threw them into the great wine press of the wrath of God. [20] And the wine press was trampled outside the city, and blood came out from the wine press, up to the horses' bridles, for a distance of 1,600 stadia.

There are some scholars who think the blood that comes out of the wines press is literal blood. While God can do anything that is possible, 1,600 stadia comes out to approximately two hundred miles and a horse's bridle could be anywhere from four to six feet off the ground. This would be hundreds of thousands of gallons which is why some scholars think this only means that blood will splash up as high as a horse's bridle over this distance. But worrying about how far or deep this river of blood will be is unnecessary, because the context of the chapter is symbolic vision. We know this because of the Son of Man seated on a cloud, the angel coming out of the temple in heaven and the Son of Man swinging a sickle over the earth – all symbolic and seen in a vision. The visionary nature of these verses is reinforced by the fact that vines and clusters of grapes were not harvested by first century farmers with sickles. Grapes were harvested by hand in that day, so this entire vision is a dream about God's wrath pouring out like a tidal wave of blood.

But what better way to picture the terrifying anger of God finally poured out all at once with the power of a flood? His final wrath will be so intense it will flood against those who reject Him like a river of blood two hundred miles long and deep enough to drown a horse. It is a fearful thing to fall into the hands of the living God. Revelation 15:1 says,

<u>Revelation 15:1 – 8 (NASB)</u>
Then I saw another sign in heaven, great and marvelous, seven angels who had seven plagues, which are the last, because in them the wrath of God is finished. ² And I saw something like a sea of glass mixed with fire, and those who were victorious over the beast and his image and the number of his name, standing on the sea of glass, holding harps of God. ³ And they sang the song of Moses, the bond-servant of God, and the song of the Lamb, saying, "Great and marvelous are Your works, Lord God, the Almighty; Righteous and true are Your ways, King of the nations! ⁴ Who will not fear You, Lord, and glorify Your name? For You alone are holy; For all the nations will come and worship before You, For Your righteous acts have been revealed." ⁵ After these things I looked, and the temple of the tabernacle of testimony in heaven was opened, ⁶ and the seven angels who had the seven plagues came out of the temple, clothed in linen, clean and bright, and their chests wrapped with golden sashes. ⁷ And one of the four living creatures gave the seven angels seven golden bowls full of the wrath of God, who

lives forever and ever. **8** And the temple was filled with smoke from the glory of God and from His power; and no one was able to enter the temple until the seven plagues of the seven angels were finished.

In Revelation 15:1-8, the Revelation Refrain continues. The context is still visionary and symbolic because it says it is a "sign in heaven." While it is not a literal description of events on earth, it is an illustration that God's anger at rebellion and sin is measured, rational and enough. Unlike human anger, which is always a reaction, God's anger is always measured and under control. In fact, since God is eternal and unchanging, His anger eternally exists in an unchanging way against rebellion and sin. His wrath is not a reaction, it is a reality that never changes.

One way to visualize this is to picture a waterfall that has different colored lights shining onto the water as it continually flows over the edge of the fall. This kind of waterfall would appear to have different streams of water of different colors. The flow of the water does not change but if a person were to stand under the waterfall at any given place, a different color of water would fall over his or her head. Where the person stands determines what color water hits his or her head, but the waterfall does not change.

In a similar way, God's nature eternally exists, a little like water continually falling over the edge of a colored waterfall. This means a person experiences God depending on where they stand in relation to Him. In other words, if a person stands underneath the part of the waterfall that appears red under the shining light, symbolizing God's eternal anger at sin and rebellion, then that person experiences the wrath of God. If a person repents of his or her sin, it is as if the person moves from under the red stream of the waterfall over to a flow of a different color. If purple symbolizes God's mercy, then a person standing under the purple part of the waterfall experiences the mercy of God. The flow of water does not change, just as God's nature never changes, but a person can, of their own freewill, change his or her position in relation to God. This is the power, the beauty, the responsibility, and the terror of the freewill God created into human beings made in His image.

In the same way, God's wrath toward sin never changes. His wrath exists eternally, but here in Revelation chapters fourteen and fifteen, the earth and its inhabitants have shifted in position. Since the days of Adam and Eve, the world has been under God's patience. He has allowed freewill and the rebellion of men because He wants to give all people a chance to repent. But in this future time, the whole earth will shift to being under God's judgement and wrath.

In the end, there will be no complaint or accusation against God that will have any merit. Everyone will see in the last days that God's patience was exactly long enough. There will be no question or disapproval about His anger or His timing. It is important for Christians to remember this principle as we wait for the Rapture of the church and the final days of earth's future-history. In the moment it can be emotionally difficult to understand why God allows suffering or does not respond the way we might want to a prayer. This prophecy illustrates the hope of His wisdom and timing. In the end, when we see God as He is, then we will understand fully. In the end, we will be satisfied with His justice and His plan because He will make things right. When we see that glorious day, there will be nothing left for us to do except cry out in worship just as they do in Revelation 15: 3-4,

> ### Revelation 15:3b – 4a (NASB)
> Great and marvelous are Your works, Lord God, the Almighty; Righteous and true are Your ways, King of the nations! [4] Who will not fear You, Lord, and glorify Your name?

End of Days:
The Book of Revelation Explained

Chapter 22: Why God's kindness is so amazing!
Revelation 16 explained...

It is difficult for some people to see how God can be a "God of love" when Revelation says God is going to pour out buckets of blood on the planet. Why should anyone believe God is going to punish people just for being imperfect? In some cases, such as child molesters and murderers, God's wrath makes sense to us, but why do bad things happen to everyday good people? This is a common concern, and this question does not necessarily come from Bible critics. Christians wonder about this also when we read how the wrath of God will be horrific, like bowls of horror being poured out.

The first part of the answer is that God is the Creator of the heavens and the earth and as the Maker, He has the right to make the rules concerning His design. When anyone violates those rules, there will be a consequence. The second part of the answer has to do with the nature of God's perfect Being, that is, His essence.

The Bible reveals that God's perfection, His essence, is like the purity of light. In fact, absolutely pure light, focused in any one spot, becomes a laser that can cut steel! The nature of light exists in a certain way – it is what it is and cannot be anything else. Light has a nature that pours out into the universe all the time. For example, the sun is a source of light, and it pours out light twenty-four hours a day, seven days a week, without ceasing. That is the nature, or essence, of the sun. Also, the nature of the sun's energy and light is such that it will consume anything that does not share its own nature. This is the reason a paper airplane will be burned up if it gets too close to the surface of the sun. The sun would not consume a paper airplane because it is angry at paper airplanes or because it is being unfair. It would consume a paper airplane because paper is not of the same nature as the sun. The sun's light has a consuming power just because the sun is what it is.

In a similar way, God's holiness, purity, and perfection pours out of His Being. The Bible says,

Deuteronomy 4:24 (NASB)
For the Lord your God is a consuming fire…

Just like the sun has a consuming power because it is what it is, God's perfection is also a consuming power because God is who He is – His perfection is like pure light, so concentrated and absolute it can cut steel. Since human beings are not perfect, we do not have the same nature as God, therefore, we would be consumed if we drew too close to God's perfect Being. We are essentially paper airplanes trying to fly near the surface of the sun! God has provided a way for us to be in His presence through the death and resurrection of Jesus. In a way, the blood of Jesus can be our "Son-Screen." There is no reason anyone must fall under the consuming power of the wrath of God. God has made it possible for anyone to freely ask Jesus for His mercy and forgiveness. But God's nature is what it is! If people continue to rebel, no matter how "good" they may appear from our human point of view, they are still imperfect in comparison to God's holiness. This means all human beings are of a different nature than God's infinite perfection so they will be consumed by God's holiness. In fact, Revelation chapter sixteen describes what will happen when God's holiness is no longer restrained. It reads,

> **Revelation 16:1 (NASB)**
> Then I heard a loud voice from the temple, saying to the seven angels, "Go and pour out on the earth the seven bowls of the wrath of God.

The final seven bowl judgements are described in Revelation chapter sixteen in order, but the sense of the Greek wording in chapters 14 through 16 is that these final judgements will all be poured out at once. Prior to these bowl judgements, the environmental judgements in the seal and trumpet judgements were measured or restrained in some way. In most of those judgements it will be only one third of something destroyed or one fourth of the population affected. Here, with the bowl judgements, there will be no sense of measurement or restraint. So, why are these judgements so unrestrained?

Some people think of God as a vindictive deity who just squashes people with storms and earthquakes, like a kid squashing ants. If prophecy, and particularly the book of Revelation, is taken out of context, God might seem this way, but prophecy fits into a context within the whole of Scripture. The Bible teaches that God has put a barrier between His perfection and holiness and the sin and rebellion of human beings so that we are not consumed by His nature. God has done this to allow for our freewill, but this also means allowing human rebellion for thousands of years. In the end, the time of human freewill will end and then the barrier between God's holy nature and this earth will be brought down. In that future day, just as the sun would consume a paper airplane, God's nature will consume all unholiness.

Revelation 16:1 is another example of the Revelation Refrain – something symbolic linked to something literal. The angels pouring out "bowls of the wrath of God" are symbolic because it happens in heaven and the text does not explain what "wrath" in the bowl is exactly. Is it a substance like water? Does it have a color? It does not say how large the bowl is or how much of this material is poured out. All it says is that whatever color or substance is in the bowl, it represents the wrath of God and it has a direct, literal effect on the earth. Revelation 16:2 says,

> **Revelation 16:2 (NASB)**
> So the first angel went and poured out his bowl on the earth; and a harmful and painful sore afflicted the people who had the mark of the beast and who worshiped his image.

The literal result is oozing, loathsome sores breaking out on people, but it is important to note that only those who are in alliance with the Antichrist are affected by these sores. There have been judgements in Revelation so far that have affected everyone on the planet, even believers. This is often the case in history also. There have been many plagues and wars and economic depressions God has allowed that have hurt everyone, believers or not. This is because we live in a fallen, cursed, and broken world where bad things can affect everyone. God has promised those who put their trust in Him that no matter what difficult time we may be allowed to face in this life, He will make everything right in the end. While there is no promise in God's Word that believers will never face difficult times, there are many promises that God will make it up to His followers. Still, there are also times of judgement in history where God's people have been exempt. In the book of Exodus, the first 3 plagues affected everyone, but there came a point at the 4th plague (Exodus 8:22) when God made a separation between His people and the Egyptians. God will do the same thing at this point in future-history. Revelation 16:3 reads,

> **Revelation 16:3 (NASB)**
> The second angel poured out his bowl into the sea, and it became blood like that of a dead man; and every living thing in the sea died.

In Greek, it is unclear whether the sea actually turns to blood or only appears blood red. The text does say it "became blood like that of a dead man" and uses the word "like." No one will know for certain until this event takes place in the future. Whether it means the oceans will turn to actual blood or not, the result is the same and everything dies.

The bowl judgements are poured out all at once, just before the second coming of Jesus at the end of the Great Tribulation. The plagues from the bowls will likely last for a few days or weeks because once "everything in the sea" dies, the plankton in the oceans will die as well. Since the plankton cycle in the ocean accounts for about 50% of the Oxygen in earth's atmosphere, within days of this cycle completely ending, every person and every animal on planet earth will be gasping for breath. [94] Since God is pouring out His final judgement, the plagues must happen just before the Lord's return because He will need to correct these natural imbalances quickly so the people of God will not suffer also. Revelation 16:4 says,

> **Revelation 16:4 – 7 (NASB)**
> Then the third angel poured out his bowl into the rivers and the springs of waters; and they became blood. [5] And I heard the angel of the waters saying, "Righteous are You, the One who is and who was, O Holy One, because You judged these things; [6] for they poured out the blood of saints and prophets, and You have given them blood to drink. They deserve it." [7] And I heard the altar saying, "Yes, Lord God, the Almighty, true and righteous are Your judgements."

At this point in future-history, human beings have literally heard from God directly. His angel has just proclaimed visibly and audibly in the sky a final invitation to everyone to turn to Him. Anyone who rejects that evidence truly deserves the judgements that will fall. Not only does God destroy every living thing in the oceans, but He makes all fresh water on earth undrinkable. Again, these final judgements are poured out all at once at the very end of the Great Tribulation. Human beings normally cannot live for more than a few days without water so God will separate His people from those suffering from these plagues. Of course, the God who created the heavens and the earth is powerful enough to turn all of earth's drinking water into blood.

As the Creator and owner of the universe, God also has every right to determine how the creation should operate, which is the reason the angel cries out, essentially saying…

> "God, your justice is right on. You have rightful ownership of everything, and you have the right and the wisdom to decide when enough is enough."

Creation itself is an act of God's grace and grace is undeserved favor. In God's eternal essence, He needs nothing and does not need to do or create anything. Within His perfect, Triune Being, He eternally experiences perfect relationship, so God does not need to create anyone because He is lonely. Within Himself, the Father perfectly loves the Son and the Holy Spirit, the Son perfectly loves the Father and the Holy Spirit, and the Holy Spirit perfectly loves the Father and the Son.

Nevertheless, while God within Himself has no needs, God's nature is also free and creative. He freely chose to create creatures in His image and in the image of God humans have the capability of interpersonal relationship just as God is a relational being. Like God, humans are free and have a capacity to be creative.

Still, by nature, all created creatures are less than God. Human beings are only in His image, not an exact duplicate. No creature, no human and no spiritual being, such as an angel, actually deserves to be in any personal relationship with God. The Bible teaches, however, that God invites human beings into relationship with His perfect, eternal self. None of us deserve this. It is amazing, undeserved, grace - so when creatures who do not deserve to exist at all, refuse to accept a relationship with God who created them, there will be a well-deserved consequence. When creatures who are dependent for their existence on God's good will freely rebel against Him to pollute His good creation with greed and pollution and selfishness and death, God has every right to be angry. This is the reason these final bowl judgements are so horrific. The gloves will have come off. God's justified anger against human rebellion will be fully unleashed. Revelation 16:8 says,

Revelation 16:8 (NASB)
And the fourth angel poured out his bowl upon the sun, and it was given power to scorch people with fire. 9 And the people were scorched with fierce heat; and they blasphemed the name of God who has the power over these plagues, and they did not repent so as to give Him glory.

It is God who fired up the sun in the first place when He designed and created it. In this future moment, God will turn up its temperature and the reason for God's judgements are spelled out in this verse. People will know these judgements are from God, but it will not change their attitudes. Why will people continue in their rebellion despite these judgements? Why is it that hard times and horrific consequences will not change a rebellious heart? If these judgements do not change people, why does God unleash them?

The truth is, none of these judgements in Revelation are intended to force people to "be good." None of these judgements are intended just to torture people either. In fact, these judgements are not punishments as we think of the term "punishment." When we think of punishment, we think of consequences of actions intended to cause the punished person to consider his or her ways, so they can reconsider their actions and, hopefully, decide to make things right. Instead, the Revelation judgements are the natural results of what people choose. The apostle John, inspired by the Holy Spirit, explained it this way...

First John 1:5 (NASB)
...God is Light, and in Him there is no darkness at all.

Darkness is not a thing in itself. Darkness is simply the absence of light, and light, by its nature, drives darkness away. This is the reason that when a person opens a door from a well-lighted room into the night, the darkness outside in the night does not bleed back into the lighted room. Instead, the light pushes away the darkness. In the same way, since God is light, His pure, intense holiness drives back anything that is not holy.

People who hate God do so because God is not the way they want Him to be. This is human pride, and that sort of unholy pride is described in the Bible as darkness. It is called darkness because that sort of human pride obscures the truth of who God is, just as a dark cloud can obscure the brightness and beauty of the sun. Light drives away darkness because of the difference between the nature of light and dark.

To get a better idea of this difference, imagine darkness as if it were a person. If this were the case, what would darkness "feel" like when exposed to light? Clearly, from darkness' point of view, when exposed to light it would feel – burned! In a similar way, when people complain about God as He is, it is much like a person complaining about the sun when they get a sunburn. Whenever a person gets a sunburn, it is not the sun's fault. If a person complains about a sunburn, their complaint makes no difference to the sun! The sun simply is what it is. Complaining about it does not protect anyone from getting a sunburn. Instead, people should put on sunscreen!

The truth is, God hates unjust suffering, abuse, exploitation, disease, and death. These things are not God's doing because suffering, abuse, exploitation, disease, and death are not things that God created. They are only a lack of what God originally created and this lack came about because human pride chose to steer human actions away from God's way of living.

The good news of the Bible is that God loves prideful people so much He is willing to shield them from His pure, perfect light with a covering of His own perfect self. Jesus is willing to be our "Son-screen."

The coming judgements in Revelation will be God's pure light breaking unrestrained into this dark world. These judgements will not be unfair, and no one must experience them either. Anyone can call upon the name of the Lord and be saved, so God is not arbitrarily condemning anyone. Revelation 16:10 says,

> **Revelation 16:10 – 11 (NASB)**
> And the fifth angel poured out his bowl on the throne of the beast, and his kingdom became darkened; and they gnawed their tongues because of pain, [11] and they blasphemed the God of heaven because of their pain and their sores; and they did not repent of their deeds.

The fourth bowl judgement was a sudden increase in the intensity of the sun. It does not say how long this intense sunlight will last but since the first, second and third bowls will create so much environmental stress that life on earth is unlikely to survive for more than a few weeks at best, it seems likely the intensity of the sun will not last long either. However long this sun scorch lasts, it will end with an instant blackout. The darkness will be localized over the capital city of the Antichrist just as in Exodus 10:21 when the plague of darkness fell over Egypt except in the land Goshen, where the people of God were living.

People will know that God is behind this plague. It will be so dark they will feel the oppression of the darkness as if it is physical pain. They will gnaw their tongues because of it, but they will still hate God. It is irrational to wallow in a darkness so deep but not turn to God who can save. But this sort of thing happens in a spiritual way every day. Many people freely choose to live a life away from God and this can cause personal suffering so intense they will gnaw their tongues in agony. If they will not turn to the Lord today, what makes anyone think they will in the last days? Revelation 16:12 says,

Revelation 16:12 – 16 (NASB)
The sixth angel poured out his bowl on the great river, the Euphrates; and its water was dried up, so that the way would be prepared for the kings from the east. [13] And I saw coming out of the mouth of the dragon, and out of the mouth of the beast, and out of the mouth of the false prophet, three unclean spirits like frogs; [14] for they are spirits of demons, performing signs, which go out to the kings of the entire world, to gather them together for the war of the great day of God, the Almighty. [15] ("Behold, I am coming like a thief. Blessed is the one who stays awake and keeps his clothes, so that he will not walk about naked and people will not see his shame.") [16] And they gathered them together to the place which in Hebrew is called Har-Magedon.

In this example of the Revelation Refrain, the bowls are symbolic, and the resulting physical sores, blood and darkness are literal. The drying up of the Euphrates River is also literal because this geographic place will become part of the final battle called the "battle of Armageddon." The next few chapters describe how the battle of Armageddon will unfold in eight steps. First the ten kings who have supported the Antichrist will assemble their remaining forces. Second, the capital city called "Babylon" will be destroyed in two awesome steps. Third, the city of Jerusalem will fall to the forces of Antichrist and, fourth, the Antichrist will march his army from Jerusalem into the wilderness to try and destroy the final remnant of the Jewish people. Fifth, the final Jewish remnant will realize Jesus is their Messiah. From the least to the greatest, the remaining Jewish remnant hiding in the wilderness will call upon Jesus their Messiah to come and save them from the Antichrist's approaching army. Sixth, Jesus Himself will return to rescue the Jewish remnant. Since this will be the second coming of Jesus, an event no one on earth will miss, the Antichrist will know his time is finished. In the seventh step, the Antichrist will rally his troops in a vain effort to attack Jesus Himself and the Battle Armageddon will commence. The battle itself is the eighth step and it will be a very short conflict because Jesus will destroy the enemy's forces with a Word. He will capture the Antichrist and his false prophet, and they will be cast into the lake of fire.

These eight steps are described in the remaining chapters of the book of Revelation. Here in chapter sixteen, we see the preparation for these final events with the drying up of the River Euphrates. This river has been symbolic and important in ancient times. It was originally named not long after the Flood, in memory of one of the four rivers that flowed from the Garden of Eden before the Flood. In Roman times, it was the border between civilization and the barbarians. It flows from the highlands of Turkey into the Persian Gulf over a meandering course 1,800 miles long and can be up to 1,200 yards in width. [95]

The coming fall of Babylon is prophesied to happen in two stages. This is probably because in the book of Revelation, Babylon is both symbolic of a religious and an economic system and it is also the literal, physical capital city of the Antichrist. Revelation chapter seventeen describes the fall of the Babylonian inspired religious system. This system will essentially tear itself apart and the Antichrist himself will turn against it when he declares that everyone must worship him. Revelation chapter eighteen describes the fall of the Babylonian economic system which will be destroyed by an act of God. As the Antichrist rises in power, he will eventually press to totally dominate the world economic system. He will require a mark of loyalty to himself personally for anyone to do business and he will control this system from his capital city called "Babylon" in Revelation. The sudden fall of this religious and economic system and the destruction of the Antichrist's capital city will lead his followers into a final, irrational frenzy at the last battle. Revelation 16:17 says,

Revelation 16:17 - 21 (NASB)
Then the seventh angel poured out his bowl upon the air, and a loud voice came out of the temple from the throne, saying, "It is

done." **18** And there were flashes of lightning and sounds and peals of thunder; and there was a great earthquake, such as there had not been since mankind came to be upon the earth, so great an earthquake was it, and so mighty. **19** The great city was split into three parts, and the cities of the nations fell. Babylon the great was remembered in the sight of God, to give her the cup of the wine of His fierce wrath. **20** And every island fled, and no mountains were found. **21** And huge hailstones, weighing about a talent each, came down from heaven upon people; and people blasphemed God because of the plague of the hail, because the hailstone plague was extremely severe.

This earthquake will be the most powerful ever to happen on this planet. It will be, in effect, the start of the renovation process of earth because after Jesus returns, the earth will be reshaped into a paradise where the Lord will rule from Jerusalem for 1,000 years. Such a violent earthquake that splits the city of Jerusalem into three pieces and moves islands and mountains on a worldwide scale will also likely cause massive volcanic eruptions. These explosions will hurl tons of ash into the atmosphere. Ash, at extreme altitudes worldwide, will condense into hailstones. The division of the great city of Jerusalem is also described in Isaiah 24, Zechariah 14, and Haggai 2. These other prophecies describe massive geologic changes unrivaled since the days of Noah. This final earthquake coincides with the physical return of Jesus. Zechariah 14:3 says,

Zechariah 14:3 – 4 (NASB)
Then the Lord will go forth and fight against those nations, as when He fights on a day of battle. [4] On that day His feet will stand on the Mount of Olives, which is in front of Jerusalem on the east; and the Mount of Olives will be split in its middle from east to west forming a very large valley. Half of the mountain will move toward the north, and the other half toward the south.

Zechariah says this split of the Mount of Olives will literally level mountains. The prophecy in Zechariah is the same event described in Revelation 16. Such a cataclysm will reshape vast sections of the earth's surface and will be the beginning of the Messiah's healing of the earth. Zechariah goes on to describe living water flowing from Jerusalem through a brand-new valley into the Dead Sea. It will be a river of water so clean and pure that it will cause the Dead Sea to live. Isaiah prophesied that once the Messiah begins to rule, the world will be reshaped. Predators will no longer kill to eat; the earth's environment will be healed, and people will live in peace for the first time since Adam and Eve. Isaiah 11:6 describes it this way:

Isaiah 11:6 – 9 (NASB)
And the wolf will dwell with the lamb,
and the leopard will lie down with the young goat, and the calf and the young lion and the fattened steer will be together; And a little boy will lead them. [7] Also the cow and the bear will graze, their young will lie down together, and the lion will eat straw like the

ox. **8** The nursing child will play by the hole of the cobra, and the weaned child will put his hand on the viper's den. **9** They will not hurt or destroy in all My holy mountain, for the earth will be full of the knowledge of the Lord as the waters cover the sea.

End of Days:
The Book of Revelation Explained

Chapter 23: The Mother of All False Religions!
Revelation 17 explained...

Our world is filled with false religions that twist or deny truth. There is a growing popular fad to create "personal truth." Everyone wants to have their own truth even if what they believe contradicts reality or contradicts what someone else believes is truth. This trend will get increasingly popular as the last days continue.

The relentless attack on truth over the centuries is symbolized in the Bible by the city of Babylon. In Revelation 14:8 and 16:9, John describes the future fall of Babylon both in the symbolic and literal sense. Symbolically, the fall of Babylon will be the collapse of the religious system led by the Antichrist. In a literal sense, the fall of Babylon will be the physical destruction of the Antichrist's capital city. In Revelation 17 and 18, there are more details about the fall of religious and physical Babylon. In Scripture, Babylon is mentioned two hundred and eighty-seven times, more than any other city except Jerusalem.

The practical reason the Bible uses the ancient city of Babylon as a metaphor for all false religious systems comes from its long history. It is known best as the capital city of the ancient Babylonian empire. Today, it's ruins can be found fifty-five miles south of the modern city of Baghdad in Iraq, situated on the Euphrates River. In the sixth century B.C., when Daniel wrote his book while living in the city, Babylon was the largest city in the world with some two hundred thousand residents and defensive walls averaging about twenty feet thick.

Of the two hundred and eighty-seven references to Babylon in the Bible, many are literal, but some are symbolic. Some scholars believe the Antichrist will literally rebuild the actual, physical ruins of Babylon to be his capital city. Other scholars think his capital city will only be "Babylon" figuratively. Until the Antichrist is revealed, no one can say for certain, but Babylon is consistently used as a symbol of false religions. Revelation 17:1 says,

Revelation 17:1 – 7 (NASB)
Then one of the seven angels who had the seven bowls came and spoke with me, saying, "Come here, I will show you the judgement of the great prostitute who sits on many waters, [2] with whom the kings of the earth committed acts of sexual immorality, and those who live on the earth became drunk with the wine of her sexual immorality." [3] And he carried me away in the Spirit into a wilderness; and I saw a woman sitting on a scarlet beast, full of blasphemous names, having seven heads and ten horns. [4] The woman was clothed in purple and scarlet, and adorned with gold, precious stones, and pearls, holding in her hand a gold cup full of abominations and of the unclean things of her sexual immorality,

⁵ and on her forehead a name was written, a mystery: "BABYLON THE GREAT, THE MOTHER OF PROSTITUTES AND OF THE ABOMINATIONS OF THE EARTH." ⁶ And I saw the woman drunk with the blood of the saints, and with the blood of the witnesses of Jesus. When I saw her, I wondered greatly. ⁷ And the angel said to me, "Why do you wonder? I will tell you the mystery of the woman and of the beast that carries her, which has the seven heads and the ten horns.

Revelation 17:1-7 is another example of the Revelation Refrain. In this case it is clearly symbolic because John says he was carried away in the Spirit and this is what he saw. It is also clearly symbolic because the woman who is drunk with the blood of the saints is called a "mystery" and she is linked to the vision of the symbolic seven-headed beast. In fact, the angel begins to explain the vision in verse 7 because it is filled with symbols.

In Scripture, "many waters" is symbolic of Gentile (non-Jewish) people. Also, in Scripture, a prostitute in a vision or prophecy represents a seducing or adulterous religious spirit. We have already seen that the beast with seven heads is the Antichrist, and the ten horns represent ten political leaders or kings who will eventually support him. Since the context of Revelation 17:1-7 is symbolic, some scholars think the literal capital city of the Antichrist may not be built from the physical ruins of Babylon in Iraq. What is clear is that the Antichrist will lead a literal religious and economic system that will share aspects of the ancient

Babylonian religious and economic systems. In fact, Revelation 17 shows that as the Antichrist rises in power, he and his supporters will prop up a prostitute-like religious system that will be a descendent of the ancient Babylonian religion.

The religious system of the Antichrist will be blasphemous in that it will tear down the true teaching about the one true God. The colorful, expensive clothing in the vision means that this religious system will be opulent, wealthy, and full of ritual. The gold cup represents sexual immorality so this future religion will promote and accept as normal sexual behaviors that Scripture teaches are ungodly and immoral. In fact, the name on her forehead is probably a reference to the fact that ancient Roman prostitutes wore headbands or crowns bearing their names.

Revelation 17 says that Babylon is the "mother of prostitutes" which means that the original Babylonian religious and economic system has given birth to other similar systems over the centuries. In fact, Wilhelm Schmidt did a comprehensive study on ancient religions and found strong evidence that all early human cultures worshipped one invisible, all-powerful, Creator God. [96] It was only later in human history that cultures fell into polytheism, animism, and beliefs in magic, not the other way around. Scripture says that the fall of human religion into animism, polytheism and nature worship can be traced back to what happened in the ancient city of Babel (later "Babylon") just after the Flood. Genesis 10:8 says,

Genesis 10:8 - 10 (NASB)
Now Cush fathered Nimrod; he became a mighty one on the earth. ⁹ He was a mighty hunter before the Lord; therefore it is said, "Like Nimrod a mighty hunter before the Lord." ¹⁰ And the beginning of his kingdom was Babel, Erech, Accad, and Calneh, in the land of Shinar.

There is not a great deal of detail in Genesis about the origins of Babylon or the origin of its religion and economy, but the name and description of its founding king may be significant. Nimrod נִמְרֹד (nim·rōde') means "rebel" ⁹⁷ and the phrase "he was a mighty hunter before the Lord" uses the word פָּנִים (pä·nēm'), which has the deeper sense of "in the face of." ⁹⁸ A more literal translation of this phrase could be, "he was a mighty hunter up in God's face." In other words, the founder of Babel (Babylon) was a rebel and a tyrant who essentially shook his fist in the face of God. He was the leader of the building of Babel and the city was built in direct disobedience to God's command in Genesis 9:1 that people should spread out over the face of the earth rather than stay together in one large group. Nimrod was the rebel leader of those people, and under his leadership, the people said in Genesis 11:4,

Genesis 11:4 (NASB)
And they said, "Come, let's build ourselves a city, and a tower whose top will reach into heaven, and let's make a name for ourselves; otherwise we will be scattered abroad over the face of all the earth."

Genesis chapter 11 says that immediately after Noah's Flood, people were afraid of being scattered, and this fear may have been a significant factor in the development of the false religious system that Babel produced. In short, people were afraid of nature itself and this attitude eventually developed into nature worship of various kinds. It would have been easy to fear nature immediately after the flood since the competition between predators and prey was intense. Right after the flood, the only land animals on earth were those that came from the ark. Herbivores and small animals reproduced quickly and thrived since they were able to spread into unoccupied areas easily, but predators were particularly aggressive since prey animals spread out quickly and remained harder to find until larger herds developed. In addition, the after-effects of the Flood event produced an ice age within a few decades. Since the oceans were warmer for centuries because of the volcanic activity and tectonic plate movements during the Flood, there was much higher evaporation rates. This resulted in super-heavy rain or snowfall, continuing violent volcanic eruptions, earthquakes and tsunamis, sudden and catastrophic local floods that overflowed natural barriers, and atmospheric conditions that created what modern scientists call "hyper-canes." [99] A hyper-cane was a hurricane dozens of times as intense as anything seen in modern times with winds in excess of 300 miles per hour. [100] Any or all of these fearful realities probably tempted post-flood people to stick together rather than spread out into the harsh new world.

Genesis says the people following Nimrod decided to build a tower in their new city and this building may also be a clue about the Babylonian religion. The words "Tower whose top is in the heavens" are רֹאשׁ (rōshe) שָׁמַיִם (shä·mah'·yim) in Hebrew. [101] [102] These words do not exactly mean "reaches up to heaven" in the sense of a ladder, but rather "dedicated to" heaven. The Babylonian religion probably developed out of a terror of nature into an attempt to gain favor or luck by trying to placate or assuage the forces of nature. It is likely, just as people do today, that the ancients neglected to study or care about the records of God's revelation about the Creation of nature and what caused the Flood in the first place. Since the Flood had just recently destroyed the earth, and Noah had explained to his children and grandchildren that it was God who caused the Flood, how long was it after his death before people began to question his teaching? After all, it was Noah who told them it was God who caused the Flood, but God is invisible. How long after Noah's death did it take for people to question the written or oral teachings of Noah about the true God that could not be physically seen? How long was it before people began to think it was the forces of nature that caused the world to be a scary place, and maybe nature could be softened or controlled if nature itself was worshipped? In fact, since the natural world in the days of Babel was filled with storms much more violent than anything we experience today, it probably did not take long for people to imagine that God, or some concept of God, was just nature itself! This idea is the Babylonian "mother" of all false religions since that time. Scholars call this conception of God "Pantheism" which means "All is God."

Pantheism is the mother idea of all false religions because all religions, except for Judaism, Christianity, and Islam, are in some way a form of nature worship or the belief that everything we experience in nature is God. After the people of Babel spread out, it was not long before they began to worship other forces of nature such as storms, volcanos and so on. In the same way, Hindu Pantheists today worship everything from rats to rocks. Buddhist Pantheists worship an impersonal universal soul or the universe itself. Modern New Age religions teach that the individual person will eventually becoming absorbed into nature. All these concepts are various forms of Babylonian Pantheism.

Even the modern theory of evolution by natural selection is a form of pantheism. Modern macro-evolutionary theory teaches that nature created itself as it developed naturally over millions of years. This is no different than believing in "mother nature" or an "earth mother." Pantheistic ideas can turn into extreme environmentalism and even self-worship. Self-worship is rooted in the idea that since the human organism is the highest level of evolution, and after death a person becomes nothing, then life must be all about individual experience in the present. Each of these ideas is just a variation of Babylonian pantheism, which is why the Bible calls Babylon the "mother of all prostitutes."

Babylonian pantheism, as the root of false religions, also makes sense of why so many false religions tend to celebrate sexual immorality in one fashion or another. If nature is all that there is, or if nature itself is the creator in some way, then obviously the strongest drives or impulses in living things must be the most important. Cleary, sexual drives are natural and powerful. False religions founded on or based in nature worship in some way, will elevate sexual things or twist those desires in some fashion. Even religions that teach some sort of celibacy are also sexual immorality, because the Bible teaches that sexual behavior between a man and his wife was created by God. This means that teaching that sexual intimacy between a man and wife is evil is itself a form of sexual immorality.

Nature worship in any form always leads to sexual disfunction in some way, because sex is such a powerful, natural drive. The implications of pantheism also explain why the worship of the one true God (theism) is seen as a threat to non-theistic religions. This is so because if nature is supreme, and there is a great diversity in nature, then it follows that all forms of nature are equal. If all forms of nature are equal, then all forms of religion must be equal also. But, believing there is only one God means believing that all other gods and religions are false. Pantheistic religions can tolerate other forms of pantheism for the most part, but theism is a threat because if theism is true then pantheism must be false. This perceived threat has existed down through the centuries and will explode into outright persecution against Christians in the last days. Luke 17:26 says,

> **Luke 17:26 (NASB)**
> And just as it happened in the days of Noah, so will it also be in the days of the Son of Man...

During the rise of Antichrist and his followers, the false prophet who supports him will proclaim a religious philosophy founded upon the pantheistic teachings of ancient Babylon. He will teach that all religions are essentially the same since they all point back to nature as the source of life. He will offer a solution to our religious differences. He will say that everyone can continue following their chosen religion so long as they agree to accept all other religions as equally true, and the unifying religion of the Antichrist is supreme in all matters of faith and practice. The Theistic belief that there is one God, and Jesus is God in the flesh, will be seen as a supreme threat.

Babylonian-like religion has obviously been around for thousands of years. The idea that all religions are basically true, under the banner of one unifying theme, is gaining popularity in America and the world today, even at influential political levels. For example, On January 3, 2021, congressman E. Cleaver (D, Mo) ended the opening prayer for the 117th Congress of the United States by saying,

> In the name of the monotheistic god, Brahma, and god known by many names, by many different faiths. Amen and a-woman. [103]

Cleaver claimed to be a pastor. In his closing comment, however, he claims that the monotheistic god, the Brahma concept of "God" taught in Hinduism, and whatever god or faith can be found throughout the world, are all equal concepts. This is the prostitute religious philosophy spawned by ancient Babylonian pantheism. This is "Mystery

Babylon" already taking root right at the head of the U.S. Congress, but this is not out of God's control either. The book of Revelation prophesied long ago that these things would happen. Revelation 17:6 says,

> **Revelation 17:6 – 8 (NASB)**
> And I saw the woman drunk with the blood of the saints, and with the blood of the witnesses of Jesus. When I saw her, I wondered greatly. [7] And the angel said to me, "Why do you wonder? I will tell you the mystery of the woman and of the beast that carries her, which has the seven heads and the ten horns. [8] "The beast that you saw was, and is not, and is about to come up out of the abyss and go to destruction. And those who live on the earth, whose names have not been written in the book of life from the foundation of the world, will wonder when they see the beast, that he was, and is not, and will come.

In Scripture, a mystery is not usually a "who dunnit?" issue, but rather something that was once concealed and is now being revealed. In Revelation 17:7-8, the angel reveals what the symbols mean. The beast with seven heads and ten horns that will carry or support the woman is the same beast shown in Daniel chapter 7 and Revelation chapter 13. Revelation 13:3 reads,

> **Revelation 13:3 – 4 (NASB)**
> I saw one of his heads as if it had been fatally wounded, and his fatal wound was healed.

And the whole earth was amazed and followed after the beast; [4] they worshiped the dragon because he gave his authority to the beast; and they worshiped the beast, saying, "Who is like the beast, and who is able to wage war with him?"

This means the cryptic reference in Revelation 17:8 ("the beast that you saw was, is not, and is about to come up") refers to the Antichrist. He will be wounded in the head, he will die ("is not"), and he will be raised to life ("is about to come up"). This will be a false, misleading miracle ("the whole earth was amazed"). The Antichrist will be the support for the prostitute, which is the ancient Babylonian religious pantheism that will dominate the world during the Great Tribulation.

In Revelation 17:8 it says the source of the miracle which will raise the Antichrist to life comes out of the abyss. This reinforces the fact that the Antichrist, the prophet who supports him and the pantheistic religious system they use are false and evil. Yet, however amazing a man the Antichrist will appear to be, and no matter how politically or militarily successful he will be, he will go to destruction in the end. People are often misled by charismatic and successful leaders, but success does not always determine what is good or true. Revelation 17:9 says,

Revelation 17:9 – 10 (NASB)
Here is the mind which has wisdom. The seven heads are seven mountains upon which the woman sits, [10] and they are seven kings; five have fallen, one is, the other has

not yet come; and when he comes, he must remain a little while.

There has been a great deal of speculation about what the seven heads mean. Some interpreters think this is a reference to the seven hills in the city of Rome. Others think that since this could be the seven hills in Rome, it must be a reference to the Catholic church. Both these speculations are false because the interpretation of the symbols is given by the angel right in the text itself. It says the seven mountains "are" seven kings. This means the seven mountains are not hills in Rome, they represent political rulers – kings! In Scripture, mountains are often used as symbols for kings, kingdoms, and empires and that is exactly how this symbol is being used here. This means Revelation 17:9-10 is about the five major empires before John's time and that one of these "kings" was in power at the time John was writing - the Roman empire. It means that the final empire is yet to come in the future, and it will be ruled by the beast, also known as the Antichrist. As the prophecies say in other passages, this final empire will not be about the physical city of Rome, but it will be the same kind of imperialist, colonial political movement that characterized the Roman Empire.

There have been many empires in world history, more than those symbolized in Revelation 17, but the context of Revelation is about the Jews - the chosen people of God. So, this empire prophecy in Revelation 17 is only about kingdoms that rule over the Jewish people. The vision of the beasts in Daniel 2 and 7 say the same thing, except Daniel was looking forward in time from the fifth century B.C.

and John was looking backward in time from the first century A.D. John was also looking forward in time into the last days. Daniel saw four beasts in Daniel 7 and four different materials in the statue in Daniel 2. Since Israel had already been dominated by the Egyptian and Assyrian empires before Daniel's time, adding Egypt and Assyria to the first three kingdoms in Daniel's vision equals five kingdoms. The "one that is" in John's day is, therefore, the fourth beast and the fourth type of metal in Daniel's vision, but in Daniel's vision, the fourth type of metal had ten iron toes mixed with clay. The fourth beast also had seven heads and ten horns. This means the mixed-up version of the "iron" kingdom is the final kingdom John refers to in Revelation 17. In summary, the five previous kingdoms before John's time were Egypt, Assyria, Babylon, Medea-Persia and Greece. The "one that is" was the Roman Empire in John's time. The one that is to come is the future-history kingdom of the Antichrist that is a form of the Roman Empire. This explains how history and the prophecies of Daniel line up with the vision John received in the book of Revelation.

In A.D. 70, the chosen people were scattered so that for the last 2,000 years, no single empire has dominated all or even the majority of Jewish people at one time. Revelation 17 is yet another Scripture confirming that the Jewish people would become one nation again and another empire will rule over them. The Jews became a nation again on May 14, 1948, but the final empire to rule over them has not appeared yet. As of this writing, the nation of Israel is still free. As a sovereign nation, it has not been ruled over by any other nation since the Romans in

AD 70. Revelation 17 goes on to give some more details about the Antichrist when it says in verse 11,

> **Revelation 17:11 (NASB)**
> The beast which was, and is not, is himself also an eighth and is one of the seven, and he goes to destruction.

Revelation 17:11 means that the Antichrist will come out of the seven previous empires because he will have characteristics of the previous forms of government from those empires. He will also be unique because he will not be exactly like previous empires in a pure way which is the reason he is an eighth kind all together. Revelation 17:12 says,

> **Revelation 17:12 – 13 (NASB)**
> The ten horns which you saw are ten kings who have not yet received a kingdom, but they receive authority as kings with the beast for one hour. [13] These have one purpose, and they give their power and authority to the beast.

At some future point there will be an economic, military, or natural catastrophe that will force the world to reorganize into ten political districts. God will allow these ten kingdoms to develop for one purpose. They will eventually use their political, military, economic and religious power to support the Antichrist's quest for ultimate world power. The Antichrist will directly conquer three of these kingdoms or leaders, but the others will surrender. He will then appoint three loyal followers to take over as the leaders of the three he has conquered. He will then try to rule the whole earth through these ten kings as his lieutenants. Revelation 17:12 says that the ten kings did not exist in John's time. This means this prophecy cannot be about ten Roman Emperors in the past, as some scholars think, because Rome existed and was in power in the first century when John wrote these words down. Besides this, the prophecy says these ten kings will only have authority for a very limited time, which is symbolized by "one hour," and their only purpose will be to support the Antichrist. Revelation 17:14 reads,

> **Revelation 17:14 - 16 (NASB)**
> These will wage war against the Lamb, and the Lamb will overcome them because He is Lord of lords and King of kings; and those who are with Him are the called and chosen and faithful." [15] And he said to me, "The waters which you saw where the prostitute sits are peoples and multitudes, and nations and languages. [16] And the ten horns which you saw, and the beast, these will hate the prostitute and will make her desolate and naked, and will eat her flesh and will burn her up with fire.

In the end, the forces of Antichrist will try to physically attack Jesus the Messiah Himself, when He returns to rescue the Jewish people. The angel says that the waters represent many diverse people groups who will be part of the final Babylonian-style religious system that the Antichrist will lead. In Scripture, "waters" are symbolic of Gentile (non-Jewish) people, but it is interesting to note that eventually the Antichrist will turn against the pantheistic system he helped establish. In other words, at first, the Antichrist and his ten lieutenants will use the pantheistic religious idea to prop up their power, but once this religion is no longer useful, they will turn against it. Halfway through the Great Tribulation, the Antichrist will abandon the world pantheistic system when he steps into the Jewish temple, declares that he is God, and demands that everyone worship him.

A radical change in political or religious position is typical of other tyrants and dictators in history. Such leaders make wonderful promises, and they will use religion and religious language to gain a following, but as soon as they consolidate power, they discard religion or change their talking-points about it. This is what happens when power-hungry, self-absorbed people gain power. Inevitably, the power-hungry will end up eating each other. Jesus said the same thing in Mark 3:24 which reads,

> **Mark 3:24 - 26 (NASB)**
> And if a kingdom is divided against itself, that kingdom cannot stand. [25] If a house is divided against itself, that house will not be able to stand. [26] And if Satan has risen up against himself and is divided, he cannot stand, but he is finished!

In Mark 3:24, Jesus told the religious leaders at that time how stupid it was to think His miracles came from the devil since by those miracles Jesus was destroying the devil's work. The devil and his followers are self-absorbed, and any self-absorbed group will be divided since everyone in the group is only operating for their own interests. God will use the self-absorbed nature of Satanically-influenced people to bring about His ultimate plan. Revelation 17:17 says,

> **Revelation 17:17 – 18 (NASB)**
> For God has put it in their hearts to execute His purpose by having a common purpose, and by giving their kingdom to the beast, until the words of God will be fulfilled. [18] The woman whom you saw is the great city, which reigns over the kings of the earth.

Reading these step-by-step descriptions of future events may make the future seem chaotic and crazy, but it will be no more chaotic than it is today. World events in the present are unpredictable from our point of view and what seems certain one day can be gone the next. A business that has been on the stock market for a century can go under in an hour, a terrorist bombing in a little town most people have never heard of can grab the attention of the whole world. Nothing seems certain today, but the future does not frustrate God, or scare Him, or take Him by surprise. These prophecies are about complicated events that do not unfold with a nice clean plot, but they also prove that God is in control. He knows what will happen in advance.

Christians should not give in to fear but should decide, in faith, to trust in God's control and the future will unfold the way God plans.

End of Days:
The Book of Revelation Explained

Chapter 24: Beware materialism!
Revelation 18 explained...

Revelation chapter seventeen is all about the fall of the coming pantheistic religious system that the Antichrist and his followers will use to gain power. This religious system will have its ultimate origins in the pantheistic mother religion founded at the city of Babel not long after the Great Flood. But the ancient Babylonian religious system is not all that the word "Babylon" symbolizes in the book of Revelation. There is also a coming economic system the Antichrist will oversee that will be organized and operated from his capital city. The Bible also calls this economic system "Babylon." Revelation 18:1 says,

> **Revelation 18:1 – 2 (NASB)**
> After these things I saw another angel coming down from heaven, having great authority, and the earth was illuminated from his glory. ² And he cried out with a mighty voice, saying, "Fallen, fallen is Babylon the great! She has become a dwelling place of demons and a prison of every unclean spirit, and a prison of every unclean and hateful bird.

The chapter begins with the symbolic part of the Revelation Refrain because it says an angel will come down from heaven. Revelation 18:3 says,

> **Revelation 18:3 (NASB)**
> For all the nations have fallen because of the wine of the passion of her sexual immorality, and the kings of the earth have committed acts of sexual immorality with her, and the merchants of the earth have become rich from the excessive wealth of her luxury."

The Babylonian economic system is a passionate lust for wealth, luxury and power led by an elitist leadership. Genesis hints at the roots of this elitist system that has infected every kingdom on earth over the centuries. Genesis 10:10 says,

> **Genesis 10:10 – 12 (NASB)**
> And the beginning of his (Nimrod's) kingdom was Babel, Erech, Accad, and Calneh, in the land of Shinar. [11] From that land he went to Assyria, and built Nineveh, Rehoboth-Ir, Calah, [12] and Resen between Nineveh and Calah; that is the great city.

Nimrod's kingdom is a clue about elitism because his kingdom only expanded after human languages were confused in Babel. The confusion of human language caused the construction of the tower of Babel to cease and various tribes of people who could understand each other spread out over the face of the earth. The loss of cooperation and cohesion, however, did not slow Nimrod down. He somehow still managed to "build" Erech, Accad, Calneh, Nineveh, Rehoboth-Ir, Calah and Resen! Of course, when anyone says that a king "built" a city it is a figure of speech because no one imagines the king took up a hammer and built anything. Kings "build" by directing or forcing others to build what they want. Kings can do this because other people believe in their authority. Whenever a lust for wealth, luxury and power develops into an elite class that exploits everyone or enslaves or controls others by economics or force to build more luxury for the elite, it is a Babylonian-inspired economic system. Nimrod used royal elitism to manipulate people into building cities for him to rule, and that concept is exactly the opposite of the way God tells us to lead people. Jesus said in Matthew 20:25,

> **Matthew 20:25 - 28 (NASB)**
> But Jesus called them to Himself and said, "You know that the rulers of the Gentiles domineer over them, and those in high position exercise authority over them. [26] It is not this way among you, but whoever wants to become prominent among you shall be your servant, [27] and whoever desires to be first among you shall be your slave; [28] just as the Son of Man did not come to be served, but to serve, and to give His life as a ransom for many."

The Babylonian way of leadership and God's way will always be at war. God's way is to sacrifice to help others. Babylon's way is to sacrifice others to benefit the elite. The Antichrist's central control of world economics from his capital city will represent every tyrant or elitist tycoon who has built personal luxury on the backs of the poor. In the last days, God will finally cast down the economic exploitation of others that has dominated every country on earth for centuries. He will destroy this system once and for all. Revelation 18:4 reads,

> **Revelation 18: 4 – 7 (NASB)**
> I heard another voice from heaven, saying, "Come out of her, my people, so that you will not participate in her sins and receive any of her plagues; [5] for her sins have piled up as high as heaven, and God has remembered her offenses. [6] Pay her back even as she has paid, and give back to her double according to her deeds; in the cup which she has mixed, mix twice as much for her. [7] To the extent that she glorified herself and lived luxuriously, to the same extent give her torment and mourning; for she says in her heart, 'I sit as a queen and I am not a widow, and will never see mourning.'

Since the Revelation Refrain links the symbolic with the literal, it could be that this call for people to come out of Babylon will be an actual call for believers to leave the physical capital city of the Antichrist before it is destroyed. Either symbolic or literal, there is certainly a Biblical call for Christians today to stay away from greed and the exploitation of others to fulfill materialist lusts. Materialism and a lust for power and fame is an intoxicating temptation. The Bible does teach that we are to be good managers with the resources God gives us, but we are also warned against a lust for the material and luxurious things of this life. Materialism can lure people into doing what is immoral to obtain things. Many a person has sold their soul to make money or become famous. 1 Timothy 6:10 says that love of money is the root of all sorts of evil! This means that money itself is not a problem – it is the love of it, the longing for it, or the lusting after material things, that creates a problem in the heart.

> **Revelation 18:8 – 10 (NASB)**
> For this reason in one day her plagues will come, plague and mourning and famine, and she will be burned up with fire; for the Lord God who judges her is strong. **9** "And the kings of the earth, who committed acts of sexual immorality and lived luxuriously with her, will weep and mourn over her when they see the smoke of her burning, **10** standing at a distance because of the fear of her torment, saying, 'Woe, woe, the great city, Babylon, the strong city! For in one hour your judgement has come.'

While the economic and political system the Antichrist will build is symbolically called "Babylon," the Antichrist will also build a physical capital city. This city will be the center of world trade and wealth. It will be the central nerve system of the entire scheme to control everyone so that no one can buy or sell without the loyalty mark to the Antichrist. Again, this capital city could be a literal rebuilding of the ruins of Babylon, but it could also be some other city. There is Biblical evidence for both views. What is certain is that the city will be obliterated by a fire so intense that those mourning over its destruction must stand at a distance. It is possible this prophecy could be referring to a nuclear detonation since people must stand at a distance, but however God allows this destruction, the fall of Babylon will cause the collapse of the entire world system of finance, commerce, and economy. In one day, everyone on earth will know that the ultimate Great Depression has started. This is the reason Revelation 18:11 says,

Revelation 18:11 – 19 (NASB)
"And the merchants of the earth weep and mourn over her, because no one buys their cargo any more - [12] cargo of gold, silver, precious stones, and pearls; fine linen, purple, silk, and scarlet; every kind of citron wood, every article of ivory, and every article made from very valuable wood, bronze, iron, and marble; [13] cinnamon, spice, incense, perfume, frankincense, wine, olive oil, fine flour, wheat, cattle, sheep, and cargo of horses, carriages, slaves, and human lives. [14] The fruit you long for has left you, and all things that were luxurious and splendid have passed away from you and people will no longer find them. [15] The merchants of these things, who became rich from her, will stand at a distance because of the fear of her torment, weeping and mourning, [16] saying, 'Woe, woe, the great city, she who was clothed in fine linen and purple and scarlet, and adorned with gold, precious stones, and pearls; [17] for in one hour such great wealth has been laid waste!' And every shipmaster

and every passenger and sailor, and all who make their living by the sea, stood at a distance, [18] and were crying out as they saw the smoke of her burning, saying, 'What city is like the great city?' [19] And they threw dust on their heads and were crying out, weeping and mourning, saying, 'Woe, woe, the great city, in which all who had ships at sea became rich from her prosperity, for in one hour she has been laid waste!'

There are twenty-nine items listed in this prophecy. Each of these items are examples of precious materials and symbolize materialistic wealth. It is interesting to see the heart and mind behind the mourning for the fall of the city. The merchants do not mourn the loss of life. They are upset about the loss of wealth, and this shows that their hearts are self-centered and cruel.

The Bible warns Christians against materialism because on a deathbed it will not matter how much anyone has in a bank account. This is an important principle for Christians to embrace today. No matter how famous a person gets in this life, after death that person is gradually forgotten. Even those that are remembered from time to time, like the famous Pharaoh Rameses of Egypt, are still dead. Rameses left an opulent tomb that is now empty. His palace is a pile of broken stone and in hell he commands no one. For Rameses and every other elitist, famous, wealthy, powerful, or "important" person in history who dies without having a relationship with the true God, whether anyone in this life is still impressed with him, it will never change that famous person's reality in hell.

End of Days
The Book of Revelation Explained

Chapter 25: Win the crowns!
Revelation 19 explained...

Let's recap: Revelation 1:19 says that the entire prophecy of Revelation is divided into three parts. The first part (chapter 1) describes the glory and authority of Jesus, the second part (chapters 2 – 3) describes the present church age and the third part (chapters 4 – 22) describes how the future will unfold through the Great Tribulation, the Millennium kingdom and into the eternal state. The official "trigger" for the Great Tribulation is a treaty that the Antichrist will confirm with the nation of Israel. The Rapture of the church can happen at any time up to the signing of this treaty. During the rise of the Antichrist, there will be an attempt at a one-world government that will collapse almost immediately. Ten world leaders will take control of the world, but the Antichrist will conquer three of them and the other seven will simply surrender to him. The Antichrist will move to consolidate his power through a false religious system and by forcing everyone into an economic system centered on loyalty to himself.

Revelation chapters 17 and 18 describe the collapse of the Antichrist's false religion and the fall of his Babylonian-inspired, power-elite economy.

Once these power structures fall and the Antichrist is defeated by Jesus, then Jesus will take control of the earth and begin His reign as king from His capital city in Jerusalem. In Revelation chapter 19, the prophecy provides some detail about the return of Jesus the King. Revelation 19:1 says,

> **Revelation 19:1 – 6 (NASB)**
> After these things I heard something like a loud voice of a great multitude in heaven, saying, "Hallelujah! Salvation, glory, and power belong to our God, ² because His judgements are true and righteous; for He has judged the great prostitute who was corrupting the earth with her sexual immorality, and He has avenged the blood of His bond-servants on her." ³ And a second time they said, "Hallelujah! Her smoke rises forever and ever." ⁴ And the twenty-four elders and the four living creatures fell down and worshiped God who sits on the throne, saying, "Amen. Hallelujah!" ⁵ And a voice came from the throne, saying, "Give praise to our God, all you His bond-servants, you who fear Him, the small and the great." ⁶ Then I heard something like the voice of a great multitude and like the sound of many waters, and like the sound of mighty peals of thunder, saying, "Hallelujah! For the Lord our God, the Almighty, reigns.

The word "Hallelujah" means "Praise the Lord" but it is in the imperative sense. In other words, it means "do this right now – Praise the Lord!" It is an intense explosion of emotion because the true King of the earth has arrived, and He is victorious. After centuries of human conflict, thousands of years of warnings by the prophets, the Rapture of the church, the preaching of the 144,000 and the two witnesses – and after seven hard years where believers have faced the worst of persecutions while the rebels have been crushed under the greatest tribulations in the history of the earth, the King has returned! Hallelujah!

> "The term is over: the holidays have begun. The dream is ended; this is the morning…now at last. They are beginning Chapter One of the Great Story which no one on earth has read: which goes on forever: in which every chapter is better than the one before." (C.S. Lewis) [104]

This is the Christian hope. This is what the prophets have promised in the Old Testament and the New. The book of Revelation is not intended to scare anyone but to point believers to this ultimate hope. Jesus is coming again! He will make all things right and we will be part of His rulership over a healed planet. It is easy to get distracted by the worries of our present time and those worries are real issues. Our hope is not that we might elect better politicians or find better jobs in this present moment. Our hope is that Jesus will soon return for us, and the book of Revelation is intended to help us get our eyes on that hope. This is the reason it says in Revelation 19:7…

Revelation 19:7 (NASB)
Let's rejoice and be glad and give the glory to Him, because the marriage of the Lamb has come, and His bride has prepared herself.

The Revelation Refrain of the symbolic linked to the literal is not intended to confuse anyone. The Bible uses symbols so that people of all cultures and languages might understand His heart in a powerful and emotional way. Symbols can be intense, vibrant, and even thrilling. For example, saying "Jesus loves you" is a true statement. Seeing His love symbolically, like a young couple getting married, shows an intimacy, a depth, and a beauty that three little words cannot really get across. Marriage, as God originally invented it, was romantic and beautiful and full of life. When God created Adam and brought Eve to be his wife, they had a perfection in love that is hard for us to imagine today. They experienced a perfect giving of self from one being to the other. They had a one-ness that was intended by God so that each person could literally step into joy itself. This is what God intended marriage to be, so when He describes His coming back to earth to receive His followers, He describes it symbolically as a marriage between a bride and groom.

God created human beings in His image so that we would have the capacity to step into relationship with God just as God has relationship within Himself between the Father, the Son and the Holy Spirit. The relationship within the Trinity is so intense and beautiful, it is perfection itself. When believers are cleansed of their sins, resurrected, and after Jesus returns - we will be able to step into the bliss and beauty of a total completion of all that we were meant to be. In our consummated relationship with God, we will be able to enjoy Him forever in a perfect existence.

In ancient times in Israel, marriage agreements were made in advance between the parents of the bride and groom. Once the deal was made between the parents, the marriage was considered legal and binding, but the bride and groom were not immediately physically together. Once the deal was made, the groom would depart to build a house for his new wife. The bride then waited for the groom to return for her. She had absolute confidence that he was coming back to get her, but she still had to wait. The bride's wait was not an unpleasant time because no matter what was happening in her life, she was giddy just thinking that her groom would soon return. She knew that he would make her safe and take her away from whatever scared her or made her sad. This should be the picture of our own waiting for Jesus to return for us. Jesus said in John 14:1,

> **John 14:1 – 3 (NLT)**
> Don't let your hearts be troubled. Trust in God, and trust also in me. ² There is more than enough room in my Father's home. If this were not so, would I have told you that I am going to prepare a place for you? ³ When everything is ready, I will come and get you, so that you will always be with me where I am.

The book of Revelation is intended to remind us that Jesus is coming again. It is intended to promise us that no matter what happens in our lives, no matter how difficult or frightening life may become, our King is coming soon. Faith is choosing to turn away from our stress and call out to Him in praise and hope because we know the future-story of His soon return. Jesus told us not to be troubled by world events and God cannot lie, He cannot fail, nor can He ever forget us. The book of Revelation is a book of hope. Revelation 19:8 says,

> **Revelation 19:8 (NASB)**
> It was given to her to clothe herself in fine linen, bright and clean; for the fine linen is the righteous acts of the saints.

The symbol of the bride clothing herself is all about our sins being cleansed and our good deeds in this life shining through like beautiful garments. Believers are called the Bride of Christ because God wants us to understand the amazing connection He plans to have with us in the eternal realm. Christian men can picture a little of what this will be like if we think about what it feels like to see a bride come down the aisle to us. Christian women can feel a little of what this will be like if they think about what it could feel like to see a groom at the end of the aisle on a perfect wedding day. God uses the metaphor of a Bride and Groom so we can get a tiny taste of what His love for us is like.

God Himself has washed our imperfections away by the power of the blood of Messiah Jesus. Isaiah 1:18 says,

Isaiah 1:18 (NASB)
Though your sins are as scarlet, they shall become as white as snow; Though they are red like crimson, they shall be like wool.

Not only has God forgiven the sins of anyone who comes to Him in repentance, but He rewards our good deeds too. Every opportunity we get to be goodness and joy and help and a blessing in this world will be one more thing of beauty added to our hearts for that great day when He returns. Unbelievers can do and make beautiful things because of the echo of the image of God that exists within their being, but for believers, every beautiful act, every sacrifice we make to follow Him in this life will add to our eternal transformation.

Every chance we get to do good works in this life, is like getting ready for our eternal wedding day. Every good work we do with the right heart is like making our tuxedo that much nicer or like making the wedding dress that much more beautiful. God gives us this present life to get ready for eternal life. He says in Revelation 19:9,

Revelation 19:9 (NASB)
Then he said to me, "Write: 'Blessed are those who are invited to the wedding feast of the Lamb.'" And he said to me, "These are the true words of God."

Jesus told parables about servants given money to invest by a master. He told a parable about a hidden treasure someone discovers but had to sell everything they had to go and find it. He also told a parable about ten virgins waiting for a wedding party. All these teachings illustrate the same truth:

We need to be ready for the sudden, unexpected return of Jesus.

The Bible also says our opportunity to do good deeds in this life is part of earning a "crown." It is true that good deeds do not save anyone from sin, so we do not earn the crowns by sinning less. We are saved from our sins purely by God's mercy which we can only receive by faith, but He gives us the chance to do good works so we can be all the more radiant on our wedding day.

> ### Revelation 19:10 (NASB)
> Then I fell at his feet to worship him. But he said to me, "Do not do that; I am a fellow servant of yours and your brothers and sisters who hold the testimony of Jesus; worship God! For the testimony of Jesus is the spirit of prophecy."

People get fixated on John making this mistake, but it is important to remember what he sees in this moment. He is witnessing the future return of the King. He is standing near a shockingly beautiful angel, and he sees and hears a massive rock-concert-like cheer from the people of God. It is simply emotionally overwhelming. John's honesty in recording his mistake demonstrates his integrity. He tells the truth, even if he looks bad doing so, and that is proof that no matter who you are or what your background, emotional intensity can affect you. The point here is that no matter how beautiful, amazing, or emotionally intense you might find anyone or anything, only God deserves worship.

Emotional intensity can overwhelm your rational ability to make the right choices so we must learn to live by faith, not feelings.

Today there is a trend toward glitz and glitter in church, but no one should mistake emotional intensity for truth. God's Word is truth, and to guard us from error, any teaching or experience should always be weighed against what the Bible teaches. God may work through a leader in a mighty way, or bless a certain person with skills and talents, but we must be on guard not to get fixated on the leader God is using, rather than on God who is using the leader. Like John, falling into these errors can be an honest mistake. We do need help and guidance in this life that a leader can provide and that can be emotionally intense. This prophecy warns us to continually remember that no matter how skilled or wise any spiritual leader may appear, human leaders do not replace God. In fact, some people put expectations on a leader that should only be placed on Jesus. Unfortunately, people can also get disillusioned about Jesus or the Christian faith because a leader is not perfect. Worse, the world often mocks Christianity when leaders fall, but notice that the angel does not get angry at John. The angel understands that John is just being emotional, which is why he gently explains, "keep your eyes on Jesus."

Revelation 19:11 - 16 (NASB)
And I saw heaven opened, and behold, a white horse, and He who sat on it is called Faithful and True, and in righteousness He judges and wages war. [12] His eyes are a flame of fire, and on His head are many crowns; and He has a name written on Him which no one knows except Himself. [13] He is clothed with a robe dipped in blood, and His name is called The Word of God. [14] And the armies which are in heaven, clothed in fine linen, white and clean, were following Him on white horses. [15] From His mouth comes a sharp sword, so that with it He may strike down the nations, and He will rule them with a rod of iron; and He treads the wine press of the fierce wrath of God, the Almighty. [16] And on His robe and on His thigh He has a name written: "KING OF KINGS, AND LORD OF LORDS."

This is the Revelation Refrain again because it is a vision of heaven being opened, so John sees Jesus and His people symbolically. There will be a literal, physical return of the King to the earth, but symbolically in Scripture, riding in formation on horses is a sign of victory. Flames are a symbol of purification and judgement, so the eyes of the King illustrate how the Lord sees and clearly judges everyone and everything. Crowns in Scripture are symbols of authority and reward, so He will return with ultimate authority, His reward will be absolute victory, and His judgement will be certain. In Scripture, the names of people are sometimes changed by circumstances because symbolically a name is a description of the true essence of a person. Since Revelation is rooted in the Old Testament and it is a Jewish book about the fulfillment of promises God made to Jews, this description in Revelation 19 is probably a reference to a prophecy about the Messiah found in Isaiah 63:2-6 which reads,

> **Isaiah 63:2 – 6 (NASB)**
> Why is Your apparel red, and Your garments like one who treads in the wine press? [3] "I have trodden the wine trough alone, and from the peoples there was no one with Me. I also trod them in My anger and trampled them in My wrath; And their lifeblood is sprinkled on My garments, and I stained all My clothes.

Revelation 19:15 explains that Messiah Jesus, upon His return, will simply need to speak to accomplish His victory. Just as He did in the beginning when He said, "let there be light," and the sound of His voice was enough to create the universe, so His voice in the last day will be enough to destroy every rebel in an instant. When the Lord declares His authority, the war will be over. The Antichrist and his armies will be defeated, and Jesus will begin to rule.

> **Revelation 19: 17-19 (NASB)**
> Then I saw an angel standing in the sun, and he cried out with a loud voice, saying to all the birds that fly in midheaven, "Come, assemble for the great feast of God, [18] so that you may eat the flesh of kings and the flesh of commanders, the flesh of mighty men, the

flesh of horses and of those who sit on them, and the flesh of all people, both free and slaves, and small and great." **19** And I saw the beast and the kings of the earth and their armies, assembled to make war against Him who sat on the horse, and against His army.

During the Antichrist's last stand, he will try to destroy Jerusalem, going door-to-door to kill as many as he can until the Lord returns, but he and all his armies will be destroyed. This is pictured by the Old Testament prophet Zechariah. Zechariah 14:2 says,

Zechariah 14:2 – 3 (NASB)
For I will gather all the nations against Jerusalem to battle, and the city will be taken, the houses plundered, the women raped, and half of the city exiled, but the rest of the people will not be eliminated from the city. **3** Then the Lord will go forth and fight against those nations, as when He fights on a day of battle.

In that great final day, an angel will appear in the atmosphere. He will be so large that anyone looking up will see his form blocking a view of the sun. His call to the birds to assemble for the great feast of God illustrates how awful, final, and stunning will be the fall of the enemies of God. His judgements have fallen for seven years. The capital city of the Antichrist has been destroyed. The ancient pantheistic religion of Babylon that has spawned all false religions on earth is now overthrown.

For thousands of years, God in His longsuffering has allowed the freewill of human beings. He did this so that people could freely enter into a real relationship with Him, but mankind has abused freewill, choosing centuries of hatred, bigotry, cruelty, and death. In His final triumph, Messiah Jesus will pour out His indignation on the Antichrist as the armies of the enemy fall. Revelation 19:20 says,

> **Revelation 19:20 – 21 (NASB)**
> And the beast was seized, and with him the false prophet who performed the signs in his presence, by which he deceived those who had received the mark of the beast and those who worshiped his image; these two were thrown alive into the lake of fire, which burns with brimstone. [21] And the rest were killed with the sword which came from the mouth of Him who sat on the horse, and all the birds were filled with their flesh.

Those who have hated and rejected God, persecuted His people, exploited the poor, and crushed the needy to engorge themselves, will be destroyed by a single command of His voice. The Antichrist who troubled the world for seven years will be destroyed by God's Word alone. The voice of Jesus is the same voice that drew Adam up out of the dust, it is the same voice that will one day crush the enemies of God, and it is also the same voice that calls people to turn to Him today.

End of Days:
The Book of Revelation Explained

Chapter 26: No Excuse!
Revelation 20 explained...

The book of Revelation is not just a map to the future. If that were the case, then it would not be much use to us since we are going to be Raptured away from the earth before the terrible events it prophesies come to pass, but the book of Revelation also illustrates practical principles for us to use in the present. One of these principles is that we should never resist God's leading in our lives as we will see in Revelation chapter twenty.

> **Revelation 20:1 – 2 (NASB)**
> Then I saw an angel coming down from heaven, holding the key of the abyss and a great chain in his hand. ² And he took hold of the dragon, the serpent of old, who is the devil and Satan, and bound him for a thousand years...

Once again, the Revelation Refrain comes into the text. In this case, the symbolic is blended with the literal because the text says this angel is coming down from heaven. "Down" in this context means the angel comes from the spiritual realm into the physical. The chain in his hand may or may not be something physical, but it is literal in the sense that it will restrain Satan from any deception or temptation on the earth for 1,000 years. This chain will be similar to the restraints used on the fallen angels bound since the days before the Great Flood, as it says in Jude 6,

> **Jude 6 (NASB)**
> And angels who did not keep their own domain but abandoned their proper dwelling place, these He has kept in eternal restraints under darkness for the judgment of the great day.

Revelation 20:2 shows that Satan is not the opposite of God in power and essence. It is a common thought today that good and evil are opposite powers that balance. If this were the case, then evil would be just as powerful in a negative way, as good is powerful in a positive way. But this is a false teaching because evil is not a thing in itself. Evil is only the absence of good, so Satan and evil are not a power of darkness that somehow balances with God, because Satan and evil lack what God is.

The idea that good and evil, or darkness and light, form a balance in the universe is called "Dualism." Dualism fails both Biblically and logically. Biblically, for example, the Bible says that God is absolute, an infinite Being and lacks nothing. God is goodness itself and He exists in a pure state of eternal holiness. So, dualism fails because "less than" cannot balance what is whole and evil is only a lack of, or "less than," what is good. Dualism also fails logically because evil is not a thing at all. The absence of something, carried to a complete "lack," is ultimately "nothing!" How can the lack of a thing, which is nothing in the end, balance out a "thing," because a "thing" will always outweigh "no-thing!" Nothing cannot ever be the balance of any "thing." This means that God and Satan are not opposites in terms of power and essence. Satan merely lacks God's goodness; he lacks what God originally created him to be. He is not "as powerful" in darkness and evil as God is powerful in goodness and light.

This is the reason there is no real battle in Revelation 19 and 20. What resistance Satan organizes through the armies of the Antichrist is stopped in a moment by God's spoken command. Jesus throws the Antichrist and the false prophet into the Lake of Fire without any difficulty. God then sends His angel to restrain Satan and it is done immediately.

People sometimes wonder why has God not eliminated evil if He is powerful enough to do so? The answer is that He will destroy evil in the future just as it says in Revelation 19 and 20. God is powerful enough to do this without any threat or possibility He might fail - He just has not done it yet. The book of Revelation is about God finally eliminating evil. He has not destroyed evil yet in order to allow for freewill, but in the end, He will cleanse the universe of evil and sin.

Other people wonder why Satan does not just read the book of Revelation himself and do the opposite of what it teaches as a way of avoiding God's promised victory. If you had a map of the future and could see that you were going to fall into a hole, you would avoid the pit. So, if Satan knows what is going to happen at least as well as we do by reading this book, why will he fall for it?

That is a great question, but the Bible does not give a direct answer. We can only speculate, but in the first place, based on what the Bible teaches, Satan is insane. This does not mean Satan is not smart. He is very wise and by far smarter than most human beings, but just having intelligence does not guarantee anyone will be rational.

Second, while Bible scholars cannot prove it, Scripture does hint that the spiritual world is unlike our physical reality. Whatever interaction there is between the spiritual and the physical world, it is not cut and dry. In fact, based on Biblical evidence, it is unlikely that demonic forces can completely hear human thoughts. Also, demons and Satan are not omnipotent or omnipresent. They are limited in their ability to directly affect the physical world. In the book of Job, it is clear that without God's direct permission, Satanic forces cannot intervene in the physical world. There is also a hint in Scripture that the spiritual world is time-ambiguous or non-linear in terms of time. Apparently, our physical reality is murky from Satan's point of view. The flow of our history, the unfolding of prophecy and the future are unclear from the spiritual side. This is the reason there are over three hundred prophecies about the Messiah in the Old Testament, including detailed prophecies about His death and resurrection, yet Satan and his demonic hordes did not avoid fulfilling those prophecies. In fact, First Corinthians 2:7 says,

First Corinthians 2:7 – 8 (NASB)
...but we speak God's wisdom in a mystery, the hidden wisdom which God predestined before the ages to our glory; [8] the wisdom which none of the rulers of this age has understood; for if they had understood it, they would not have crucified the Lord of glory...

The "rulers of this age" probably refer to demonic powers but even if this Scripture refers to human rulers, if Satan had understood how the death of Jesus would be his ultimate undoing, he would have worked against the authorities that pushed for the Lord's death. Luke 22:3, however, says that it was Satan himself who entered into Judas to lead him to betray the Lord. If Satan had understood Old Testament prophecy, why did he not oppose Herod in Matthew 2:16 when Herod tried to kill Jesus by killing all the children in Bethlehem which was a fulfillment of the prophecy from Jeremiah 31:15? These examples show that Satan did not understand the prophecies in the Old Testament, so there is no reason to think he will understand the book of Revelation either. It is probable that the time-ambiguity of the spiritual world and the sense that the physical world is probably as veiled from the enemy as the spiritual world is to us, shows why the enemy will fall just as the prophecies describe.

This is speculation, of course, and should not be thought of as "Biblical teaching" per se. What is important is the Biblical certainty that Satan and his followers are under God's absolute control. It is important to understand that Satan and his followers are not listening into your thoughts or conversations with a secret microphone at every moment of every day. While we do not know the exact limits or specific rules that govern the spiritual world, both Revelation and the book of Job show us that we are not at the mercy of unrestrained dark forces.

> **Revelation 20:3 (NASB)**
> ...and he threw him into the abyss and shut it and sealed it over him, so that he would not deceive the nations any longer until the thousand years were completed; after these things he must be released for a short time.

Reading this may cause some confusion. If God is in control, why will God solve the world's problems and rule for a thousand years only to release the enemy? Why not confine him forever? In fact, Revelation tells us God will, at some future point, confine Satan to the Lake of Fire forever, so why not here?

The answer is that when Christians are transformed at the Rapture, we will be perfected. Our sin nature will be permanently removed since our freewill has already been tested. In this life, we freely decided to give up our pride. In repentance, we freely called out to Jesus for mercy and forgiveness, but during the 1,000 years of the Lord's rule on this earth there will be people who have not had their freewill tested. The survivors from the Tribulation who never took the mark of the beast and called upon the name of the Lord will go into the Millennial Kingdom with normal, physical bodies. They will have children and these children will grow up in a perfect environment. But freewill must be free. Freewill cannot be free if there is no possibility of failing. To allow these future children the right to a freewill choice, God will set the enemy loose so people can honestly choose if they want a relationship with God or not.

Revelation 20:4 (NASB)
Then I saw thrones, and they sat on them, and judgement was given to them.

As the book of Revelation concludes, John sees a montage of images of events. These visions are like snapshots that sum up what happens after the Great Tribulation is over, after Jesus has returned and during and after His 1,000-year rule on earth. The thrones mentioned here, and the judgement given to the people seated on those thrones is not clearly explained. In context, the timeline of Revelation chapter 20 concerns events at the start of the Millennium. The judges allowed to sit on these thrones are probably Raptured believers who have returned with the Lord Jesus to be part of His administration and rule during the Millennium. The apostle Paul revealed this in First Corinthians 6:2 which reads,

First Corinthians 6:2 – 3 (NASB)
Or do you not know that the saints will judge the world? If the world is judged by you, are you not competent to form the smallest law courts? ³ Do you not know that we will judge angels? How much more matters of this life?

We are not certain what judging angels means but the word "judge" in Greek is κρίνω (kree'-no) which means "to judge, approve, determine, rule or govern." [105] So, based on First Corinthians 6:2 and Revelation 20:4, Christians today who get Raptured and arrive with Jesus at the start of the Millennial Kingdom will have specific responsibilities given by Jesus to organize, direct, or manage what happens in the Millennial Kingdom. This is not an unfamiliar concept because most people today are used to working for a boss and yet being in charge of others as a manager or supervisor.

How we live in this life determines what reward we will experience in eternal life and at least some of that reward may be authority and responsibility in the Millennium. Jesus repeatedly warns us to focus our motivations and efforts in this life to "gain treasures in heaven." Those committed believers who pass away before the return of Jesus will also have some leadership responsibility in the Millennium kingdom. Revelation 20:4 says,

> **Revelation 20:4b – 5 (NASB)**
> ...And I saw the souls of those who had been beheaded because of their testimony of Jesus and because of the word of God, and those who had not worshiped the beast or his image, and had not received the mark on their foreheads and on their hands; and they came to life and reigned with Christ for a thousand years. [5] The rest of the dead did not come to life until the thousand years were completed. This is the first resurrection.

There is some confusion today about the "first" resurrection. This is because the Bible is an unfolding Revelation from God and not everything about God's plan is always understood in the generation it is revealed. For example, what God revealed in the Old Testament about the Messiah was not understood until after Jesus arrived. In the same way, Old Testament believers knew there would be a resurrection from the dead, but they did not know this resurrection would unfold in several distinct steps.

For example, in Matthew chapter 17, Peter, James and John saw Jesus transfigured into His glorious state in front of their eyes. They also saw Jesus in His transfigured body speaking with Moses and Elijah. They knew the ancient Old Testament prophecies saying that Messiah would rule over the earth. They saw Him speaking with Moses and Elijah, who did the greatest miracles in the Old Testament, so they naturally expected Jesus to begin ruling as King right away. They expected the Kingdom of God, what we call the Millennium Kingdom, to begin immediately. They did not understand that Jesus would be rejected or that there would be a gap in time until He began His rule.

The disciples also expected a general resurrection from the dead to be part of the beginning of the Millennial Kingdom of God. This is the reason Peter offered to build a booth for Moses and Elijah because he thought they were the first people being raised from the dead for the new kingdom. Peter, James, and John did not know that their experience on the Mount of Transfiguration was a vision and a preview of what will happen in the future. A careful examination of the Scripture, however, shows that the first resurrection of believers will unfold in six phases. After that there will be a second, general resurrection of unbelievers that will happen at the end of the Millennial Kingdom of God.

In Revelation chapter 20, John gets a peek at the first part of this resurrection. The first phase of the first resurrection was Jesus Himself (1 Cor 15:23) which is the reason His resurrection is called the "first fruits" of the resurrection. The second and third phases are the Rapture of the church because at that point the dead in Christ and then those who are living are transformed into their immortal resurrection bodies (1 Ths 4:16). The fourth phase is the raising of the two witnesses in Revelation 11:11 and in Revelation 20:4, the fifth phase takes place where God raises those who were martyred during the Great Tribulation. The sixth phase is the resurrection of the Old Testament believers (Is 26:19, Dn 12:2). As phase six is completed, God gives out rewards to those who have been raised that will include different levels of administrative, management or witness responsibilities in His Kingdom.

The second resurrection is for all those people who do not have their sins washed away. These people did not accept Jesus' free gift of salvation so they will be judged according to their deeds. Since their sins will be found to remain on their hearts, they will be found guilty and condemned to the Lake of Fire. This condemnation into the Lake of Fire is called "the second death" because the definition of "death" is "separation from life" and God is life itself. Once the immortal souls of unbelievers are fully separated from the presence of God forever, they will be separated from life itself forever, so it will truly be a second death. First Corinthians 15:20 explains it this way,

First Corinthians 15:20 – 26 (NASB)
But the fact is, Christ has been raised from the dead, the first fruits of those who are asleep. [21] For since by a man death came, by a man also came the resurrection of the dead. [22] For as in Adam all die, so also in Christ all will be made alive. [23] But each in his own order: Christ the first fruits, after that those who are Christ's at His coming, [24] then comes the end, when He hands over the kingdom to our God and Father, when He has abolished all rule and all authority and power. [25] For He must reign until He has put all His enemies under His feet. [26] The last enemy that will be abolished is death.

The resurrection of Old Testament believers is the last part of the first resurrection, after the Great Tribulation, after the Antichrist has been defeated and after Jesus has returned. First Corinthians 15:25 says that Jesus must reign until He has put all His enemies under His feet. Jesus will fully subdue the earth. The Old Testament believers will be raised into a physical, earthly kingdom with Jerusalem as the capital of the world and Israel as the central nation on earth as fulfillment of the Old Testament prophecies about the Kingdom of God. There must be a physical Millennium on earth where the Jewish people are the leaders of the world because God promised them this honor in the Old Testament and God cannot fail.

The Old Testament prophecies promised Jewish believers that God would give them the whole of the Promised Land. To this day, Israel has never possessed all the land that was promised to

Abraham and the prophets. The prophets also promised there would be world peace and the Messiah would crush all opposition, a literal promise that must also be fulfilled on earth.

The Millennial Kingdom of God is mentioned in the New Testament 318 times, but Revelation does not actually reveal much about it. The New Testament does say that Christians will be part of the Millennium, but the real details are found in the 1,845 references to the Kingdom found in the Old Testament. The Millennial Kingdom of God on earth will prove that God's promises cannot fail. Old Testament believers will be raised right into this incredible kingdom. In fact, it is so important that the Messiah's Millennial Kingdom look just right for Moses and Aaron and Elijah and all the other faithful believers from the past, that Daniel chapter 9 and chapter 12 say that once Messiah defeats the Antichrist, He will do some initial earth renovation work for 75 days before the Old Testament believers will be raised. [106] This way, those faithful believers will step right into the fulfillment of God's promises.

The 1,845 references to the Kingdom of God in the Old Testament promise that the Jewish people and the nation of Israel will be the leading nation of the world. They promise that the Jewish Messiah, Jesus, will rule the world from Jerusalem which will be raised up as the mountain of the Lord's house. For example, Isaiah 2:2 and 4 says,

> **Isaiah 2:2, 4 (NASB)**
> Now it will come about that in the last days, the mountain of the house of the Lord will be established as the chief of the mountains

and will be raised above the hills; And all the nations will stream to it...⁴ And He will judge between the nations, and will mediate for many peoples; And they will beat their swords into plowshares, and their spears into pruning knives. Nation will not lift up a sword against nation, and never again will they learn war.

The Millennial Kingdom of God will also restore the natural world to harmony as it was in the days of Adam and Eve before sin came into the world. Isaiah 11:6 says,

Isaiah 11:6 – 9 (NASB)
And the wolf will dwell with the lamb, and the leopard will lie down with the young goat, and the calf and the young lion and the fattened steer will be together; and a little boy will lead them. ⁷ Also the cow and the bear will graze, their young will lie down together, and the lion will eat straw like the ox. ⁸ The nursing child will play by the hole of the cobra, and the weaned child will put his hand on the viper's den. ⁹ They will not hurt or destroy in all My holy mountain, for the earth will be full of the knowledge of the Lord as the waters cover the sea.

The Old Testament prophets revealed that a healing river will flow from the Messiah's throne and from His house. This river will flow through a new valley that will form through the middle of what is now the Mount of Olives down to the Dead Sea. The healing waters will be so pure and healthy that the Dead Sea will live once again. Ezekiel 47: 1 and 8 says,

> **Ezekiel 47:1, 8 (NASB)**
> Then he brought me back to the door of the house; and behold, water was flowing from under the threshold of the house toward the east, for the house faced east. And the water was flowing down from under, from the right side of the house, from south of the altar... [8] Then he said to me, "These waters go out toward the eastern region and go down into the Arabah; then they go toward the sea, being made to flow into the sea, and the waters of the sea become fresh...

And the prophets said that the hero of ancient Israel, King David, will be resurrected to serve as the Lord's governor over the nation of Israel. Jeremiah 30:9 says,

> **Jeremiah 30:9 – 10 (NASB)**
> But they shall serve the Lord their God and David their king, whom I will raise up for them. [10] And do not fear, Jacob My servant,' declares the Lord, 'And do not be dismayed, Israel; For behold, I am going to save you from far away, and your descendants from the land of their captivity. And Jacob will return and be at peace, without anxiety, And no one will make him afraid.

Both the book of Revelation and other passages in Old Testament prophecy say that non-resurrected people who go into the Kingdom, or are born in the

Millennium, will live in a paradise as beautiful as the Garden of Eden. The earth will be completely renovated and those who are mortal will marry and have children. There will no infant mortality and everyone born in that kingdom will live to be at least 100 years old. Death during the Millennium will only come to those who choose rebellion against the King. There will be a time of choice when the enemy is released, but only at the end of 1,000 years of peace and prosperity, building and planting. There will be no military, no wars, no prisons, and no hospitals. Isaiah 65: 17, 20 and 25 says,

> **Isaiah 65:17, 20, 25 (NASB)**
> For behold, I create new heavens and a new earth; And the former things will not be remembered or come to mind... [20] No longer will there be in it an infant who lives only a few days, or an old person who does not live out his days; for the youth will die at the age of a hundred, and the one who does not reach the age of a hundred will be thought accursed... [25] The wolf and the lamb will graze together, and the lion will eat straw like the ox; and dust will be the serpent's food. They will do no evil or harm on all My holy mountain," says the Lord.

Of course, everyone who enters this Kingdom will be blessed. Revelation 20:6 says,

> **Revelation 20:6 (NASB)**
> Blessed and holy is the one who has a part in the first resurrection; over these the second death has no power, but they will be priests

of God and of Christ and will reign with Him for a thousand years.

In the Millennial Kingdom, the Lord Jesus will rule as King, but he will delegate authority in local jurisdictions to resurrected believers. Some will oversee entire nations; others will govern over cities and still others over smaller areas. The Lord's judgement about how much authority is given to which of His servants will be based on how a believer lives in this life. Jesus taught a parable about this in Luke 19:11. In that story, Jesus said there was a Master who gave ten minas to His servants. A mina was a specific amount of money, and each servant received the same amount. One of those servants invested what was given to him and built his mina into ten minas. The Master was impressed with his effort, so in His Kingdom that servant was put in charge of ten cities. Another servant invested and turned his mina into five minas, so the Master put him in charge of five cities - but one servant did nothing with what he was given. The Master responded to that servant in Luke 19:26 where he said,

> **Luke 19:26 (NASB)**
> I tell you that to everyone who has, more shall be given, but from the one who does not have, even what he does have shall be taken away.

Revelation 20:7 is another reference to the fact that Satan will be released at the end of the 1,000-year period. This is to allow those born during the

Millennium to have their freewill tested. Revelation 20:7 says,

> **Revelation 20:7 – 8 (NASB)**
> When the thousand years are completed, Satan will be released from his prison, [8] and will come out to deceive the nations which are at the four corners of the earth, Gog and Magog, to gather them together for the war; the number of them is like the sand of the seashore.

Revelation 20:7-8 is a powerful illustration about the potential and the peril of human freewill. Even after having lived for 1,000 years in a perfect environment, after never having lacked any good thing, a huge number of people will still rebel against God. This future disproves the common belief today that the social and physical environment around a person is what causes human behavior. It is commonly believed that things such as bad family background or poverty is the reason that people do evil things. It is commonly thought that if a great environment and opportunity are provided, people will naturally live well. But after many years of governments providing programs and initiatives, the poor are always with us, substance abuse and theft and murder are common in every social and economic group and even some children from very wealthy environments turn out badly.

Revelation chapter 20 shows that even when people live in a perfect environment where there is perfect justice, opportunity, and enjoyment in life, that environment will not guarantee good human behavior. The Bible teaches that no exterior influence or environment causes anyone to do anything. Jeremiah 17:9 says,

> **Jeremiah 17:9 – 10 (NASB)**
> The heart is more deceitful than all else and is desperately sick; who can understand it? [10] I, the Lord, search the heart, I test the mind, to give to each person according to his ways, according to the results of his deeds.

The problem of the heart that will lead millions to rebel against God, even after having lived in a perfect environment, is the same problem we experience in our less than perfect environment today. The human heart is the center of our self-awareness. It is the place within our being, in our minds, where our internal thoughts take place. In the heart we can exercise a free self-determination which is one of the most profound powers of God's image that we have been given. This power allows us to freely choose to cooperate with the Creator's plan or choose to elevate our own personal interests and agenda instead. In both a less than perfect world and in the Garden of Eden, human beings can decide they would rather be a god to themselves. Revelation 20:9 shows the end of that choice. It says,

> **Revelation 20:9 – 10 (NASB)**
> And they came up on the broad plain of the earth and surrounded the camp of the saints and the beloved city, and fire came down from heaven and devoured them. [10] And the devil who deceived them was thrown into the lake of fire and brimstone, where the

beast and the false prophet are also; and they will be tormented day and night forever and ever.

Even after 1,000 years, Satan has not changed. He will have had 1,000 years in the abyss to think about his choices, but once he is released, he will continue to be the devil. Again, it is clear, the perfect environment of the Millennial Kingdom will not insulate people from their own pride, nor does 1,000 years in a prison. This is the reason there is no delay in verse 9 - it is instant fire from heaven! People have had thousands of years of freewill in a sin-fallen world and a thousand years in a perfect world. There is more than enough proof that God is justified in judging those who rebel against Him.

Revelation 20: 11 - 15 (NASB)
Then I saw a great white throne and Him who sat upon it, from whose presence earth and heaven fled, and no place was found for them. [12] And I saw the dead, the great and the small, standing before the throne, and books were opened; and another book was opened, which is the book of life; and the dead were judged from the things which were written in the books, according to their deeds. [13] And the sea gave up the dead who were in it, and Death and Hades gave up the dead who were in them; and they were judged, each one of them according to their deeds. [14] Then Death and Hades were thrown into the lake of fire. This is the second death, the lake of fire. [15] And if anyone's name was not found written in the

book of life, he was thrown into the lake of fire.

The Great White Throne is where everyone will see what has been hidden in the heart. When the books are opened it will be clear that no one is innocent. Everyone will see how longsuffering and good God has been to warn people of the consequence of their rebellion. Everyone will see how awesome He is for having offered Himself on the cross to make a way of escape from the consequences we all deserve.

The second resurrection will happen in one swift phase. Every human being who has not turned to the living God of their own freewill during their lifetime will face this final judgement. They will all be raised from the dead, but since they did not turn in repentance to the Lord, their names will not be found written in the book of life and so they will be separated from God forever. This is the second death.

The End of the World: The Book of Revelation Explained

Chapter 27: Eternal Destiny!
Revelation 21 explained...

Eternal life! This what Jesus promised when He said in John 3:16,

> **John 3:16 – 17 (NASB)**
> "For God so loved the world, that He gave His only Son, so that everyone who believes in Him will not perish, but have eternal life. 17 For God did not send the Son into the world to judge the world, but so that the world might be saved through Him.

This is the reason Jesus came to die. This is the reason He rose again from the dead. It is to fulfill His promise to give eternal life to anyone who will, by their own freewill, cling to Him as their Lord and King. After 1,000 years of the Lord's perfect rule on earth, those people born during the Millennial Kingdom of God will have a moment when their freewill will be put to the test. Unfortunately, many will rebel when Satan is released from his thousand-year prison sentence and so God will pour out His judgement immediately. In that final moment, God will end human mortality. The freewill choice of believers from this mortal existence will be locked in forever and a new existence will begin. Revelation 21:1 says,

> **Revelation 21:1 (NASB)**
> Then I saw a new heaven and a new earth; for the first heaven and the first earth passed away, and there is no longer any sea.

Revelation 21 only gives a tiny glimpse of what may be called "the eternal state." As finite human beings we can only get a hint of eternity because our existence in that realm is too wonderful to describe. It will be something completely different from anything we have experienced in this life. It will not be a renovation of the universe like the Millennial Kingdom but instead, it will be a new heaven and a new earth. The eternal state, what Jesus calls "eternal life," will be an existence by far better than the Garden of Eden. It will be a place with no sorrow, no curse, no darkness, no sickness, and no death. We will exist forever with perfect bodies that never age or decay.

Jesus said that this eternal destiny is a place of many mansions. It will be a place of eternal intimacy with God where we will each find perfect occupation and absolute joy. In that eternal home there will be the greatest of reunions with our loved ones who came before and introductions to the heroes of old. It will be a place of perfect knowledge, and we will be amazed at every person, because each person's story will be yet another amazing triumph of God's grace. Every personal story we hear will be a new wonder of God's amazing grace.

Here on this earth today, as mortal, imperfect beings recovering from our sins, we cannot intimately experience the essence of God's Being and survive the experience. His holiness is so pure that in our finite state we would be consumed, but in our resurrection bodies we will be made perfect, sinless, and able to connect with God directly. And since God is infinite, our connection with Him will be an eternal discovery of His awesome Being. Every discovery we make about Him will only lead to another discovery that is deeper still. It will be "world within world" without end. [107]

Jesus said in Matthew 22:37, that the greatest of God's commandments is that we should...

> **Matthew 22:37 (NASB)**
> ...love the Lord your God with all your heart, and with all your soul, and with all your mind.' This is the great and foremost commandment.

But this is more than a commandment. This is the goal of our existence in the first place. In fact, Jesus said in John 17:3,

> **John 17:3 (NASB)**
> And this is eternal life, that they may know You, the only true God, and Jesus Christ whom You have sent.

God created us to know Him and to enjoy Him forever and since God is the ultimate, infinite source of all that exists, to know Him means to experience Him as He is in His essence. Sin and evil are not things, but only a lack of what God is in His pure

Being. God is love itself. God is goodness itself. Anything that we think of as love or goodness is only a fraction of who God is. When the day comes that we can truly love God will all our heart, it will be to experience love where there can never be a lack of love ever again. It will be to experience goodness where there can never be a lack of goodness again. In that knowing, our freewill choice to connect in this relationship with God will be forever seared into our being. This means that sin will be impossible after having known Him in this way. In knowing God, we will find a perfect fulfillment of our freewill. We will experience the promise and the hope of never making a mistake again. In that holy, eternal state there will be no failures, there will be no weakness, or danger or fear ever again. We will simply dive further into knowing God and each other in perfect love - forever and ever. Revelation 21:2 says,

Revelation 21:2 – 5 (NASB)
And I saw the holy city, new Jerusalem, coming down out of heaven from God, prepared as a bride adorned for her husband. [3] And I heard a loud voice from the throne, saying, "Behold, the tabernacle of God is among the people, and He will dwell among them, and they shall be His people, and God Himself will be among them, [4] and He will wipe away every tear from their eyes; and there will no longer be any death; there will no longer be any mourning, or crying, or pain; the first things have passed away." [5] And He who sits on the throne said, "Behold, I am making all things new." And

He said, "Write, for these words are faithful and true."

In Revelation 21:1-5, John is so overwhelmed by what is being revealed to him that he forgets to write, so an angel must say, "Write, for these words are faithful and true." In John 14:2, Jesus said He was going to prepare this place and here in Revelation 21, John gets a moment to see the New Jerusalem Jesus promised to build. The sight of it nearly takes over John's soul. The prophet Isaiah said the new creation will be so stunning that everything in this life will fade into forgetfulness. Isaiah 65:17 says,

> **<u>Isaiah 65:17 (NASB)</u>**
> For behold, I create new heavens and a new earth; and the former things will not be remembered or come to mind.

In that future glory, we will finally understand why God invented eyes and ears and nerves in the first place. The most beautiful sight we can imagine in this life will pale in comparison to the least part of the beauty that is to come. In this new earth there will be no sea because about 70% of our planet today is under water. This means that most of the earth is unusable to us, just a scary, black, abysmal depth, but on the new earth there is no fear and no inaccessible black depths. The new earth will be a place of staggering beauty, full of light and love and joy.

In context, Revelation 21 echoes John 14:2, Second Peter 3:13 and so many other verses. This means that the New Jerusalem is not a vision or a symbol. It is a real city that God has promised as a place of joy and rest for believers. It is the place your soul has longed for all your life, though you never really knew it. Hebrews 11:10 says Abraham...

> **Hebrew 11:10 (NASB)**
> ...was looking for the city which has foundations, whose architect and builder is God.

This is the hope of the Christian faith, a hope too many people today may miss. We need to keep our eyes fixed on this hope, just as the prophets of old did long ago.

> **Revelation 21:6 - 7 (NASB)**
> Then He said to me, "It is done. I am the Alpha and the Omega, the beginning, and the end. I will give water to the one who thirsts from the spring of the water of life, without cost. [7] The one who overcomes will inherit these things, and I will be his God and he will be My son...

The word "done" in Revelation 21:6 in Greek means "this is already a done deal and there is no possibility it will not happen." This is so because God is eternal. God is not subject to time because He is the Creator of time. In fact, God describes Himself using the first and last letters of the Greek alphabet to make this point. He has laid out history in front of Himself like a map, so He sees the end from the beginning in one eternal moment. There is nothing to fear because God has our eternal destiny in His mind. Anyone who hears about this, anyone who longs to see these things and thirsts to know God this way can come to Him freely. God holds out this wonderful hope because He is willing to freely give it to anyone who will receive it. It comes without a cost to us, because no one can earn this hope by good deeds or pay for it at any price. It can only be inherited, so God offers to adopt anyone who will surrender to Him.

The cost spoken of here means any attempt to earn eternal life. Jesus did say to "count the cost" of what it means to surrender to Him, but when a person counts the cost, is there any "cost" in giving up a dead existence on a path to hell to follow Jesus? Is there any loss or "cost" in losing a job or friends or even a life in comparison to the eternal state of absolute perfection that He promises to give us? The truth is eternal life is offered at no real cost at all because our Lord and Savior Jesus paid it all. Revelation 12:11 says,

> **Revelation 12:11 (NASB)**
> And they overcame him because of the blood of the Lamb and because of the word of their testimony, and they did not love their life even when faced with death.

Revelation 21 is a visual peek into the promise of eternal life, but there is a difference between people who just say they are Christians and those who overcome the world through Jesus. Only those who overcome will inherit these things. We are reminded and warned about this once again in Revelation 21:7,

Revelation 21:7 – 8 (NASB)
The one who overcomes will inherit these things, and I will be his God and he will be My son. **⁸** But for the cowardly, and unbelieving, and abominable, and murderers, and sexually immoral persons, and sorcerers, and idolaters, and all liars, their part will be in the lake that burns with fire and brimstone, which is the second death."

The word "cowardly" is δειλός (di-los') in Greek. [108] It means "timid," and the word "unbelieving" is ἄπιστος (ápistos) which means "incredulous." [109] In other words, there are people who claim to be Christians but remain afraid to really believe. They read about this hope of eternal life, and they scoff at it. They claim to be Christians but refuse to believe God created the heavens and the earth as it says in Genesis. They have cheapened the Christian faith into a spiritual tradition, a moral code, or a way of life. They are timid and afraid of "taking the Bible literally." In this unbelief they build charity organizations they call churches but openly promote what God says is horrific or abominable. They believe that taking a human life before a child is born is perfectly acceptable and think that any sort of sexual preference is acceptable to "God." They mix modern, New Age spirituality into their "Christian" traditions and pretend that all religions are equally acceptable ways to get to "God."

There are plenty of religious movements that claim to be Christian but work hard to appear "reasonable" and "tolerant" at the expense of teaching the Bible as it is. They so idolize an acceptable reputation that they twist or ignore the Scriptures to avoid anything they do not like or anything that might potentially offend. They ignore or try to explain away any Biblical teaching that might appear "unscientific" and in doing so they lie about what the Bible really teaches. They twist the word "Christian" into something so far from Biblical honesty that they become "Christian" in name only. They will not overcome the lure of being accepted by the world, so they will not inherit eternal life.

These verses do not say that only perfect people get to heaven. Revelation 21:7-8 show the difference between true believers and those who are Christian in name only. True believers are those who overcome, and the word "overcome" in Greek is νικάω (nik-ah'-o) which means "to conquer or come off victorious." [110] This word is in the continuous sense in Greek meaning that an overcomer is a person who continues in the process of turning to Jesus (repentance) until the very end of life. The true believer overcomes failures and sin by continually turning back to Jesus so that being repentant becomes a way of life. We are, in short, continually recovering sinners who cling to Jesus, putting all our hope in Him.

Revelation 21:9 - 14 (NASB)
Then one of the seven angels who had the seven bowls, full of the seven last plagues, came and spoke with me, saying, "Come here, I will show you the bride, the wife of the Lamb." [10] And he carried me away in the Spirit to a great and high mountain, and showed me the holy city, Jerusalem, coming

down out of heaven from God, [11] having the glory of God. Her brilliance was like a very valuable stone, like a stone of crystal-clear jasper. [12] It had a great and high wall, with twelve gates, and at the gates twelve angels; and names were written on the gates, which are the names of the twelve tribes of the sons of Israel. [13] There were three gates on the east, three gates on the north, three gates on the south, and three gates on the west. [14] And the wall of the city had twelve foundation stones, and on them were the twelve names of the twelve apostles of the Lamb.

Jesus promised in John chapter 14 that He was going away to build this eternal place of reward. The New Jerusalem is called "His bride" just like New York is called the "Big Apple." In the New Jerusalem, our eternal relationship with God will be as close as the connection between a man and his wife. Even though John is taken away in the spirit to see this real city that is called "the wife of the Lamb," John must use the words "it was like" over and over because the colors, the beauty and the size of the city is so staggering John can barely breathe. This will be the center of our eternal existence. The New Jerusalem has magnificent walls made of stunning precious gems, but the walls are not for protection since the gates are always open. Sin and evil and death are forever cast away from this place, so the walls are there for definition, a sense of solidity and for grandeur and beauty.

Revelation 21:15 - 17 (NASB)
The one who spoke with me had a gold measuring rod to measure the city, its gates, and its wall. **16** The city is laid out as a square, and its length is as great as the width; and he measured the city with the rod, twelve thousand stadia; its length, width, and height are equal. **17** And he measured its wall, 144 cubits, by human measurements, which are also angelic measurements.

Whenever measuring is used in a symbolic or visionary way in Scripture it is a sign of ownership. This city belongs to God and to His servants forever. The dimensions translate roughly to a cubic shaped city with walls 1,500 miles on each side. Each wall is roughly 216 feet high with an internal area of 3,375 million cubic miles. Dr. Henry Morris estimates that about 100 billion human beings have been conceived since Adam was created, so if 20% of the human population has been saved over the centuries then everyone will fit into this city in only 25% of the available space. [111]

The Scriptures imply that gravity within the city will be relative to a surface, so people will occupy every square foot on the top, bottom, and sides. John sees this city descending to the earth, but since the size of the city is about the same as our current moon, the new earth must be significantly larger than our planet today.

The gates of our eternal home are always open since this is the capital city of the universe. There will be constant activity as we go further up and further into His new creation. It seems that we will go out to explore the mysteries of His new universe with ever increasing wonder at the creative genius of our King. We will probably return through the gates to proclaim to everyone the glories of our God and His amazing genius. Forever and ever, we will go further into His creation and there will be no end to our amazement! We will tell everyone in the capital what magnificent things we have seen that He has made. Over and over again, we will find new ways to give Him glory and worship because of something else we discover. And the capital city itself will be a wonder that no one could get to the end of in a thousand lifetimes. Revelation 21:18 says,

> **Revelation 21:18 – 21 (NASB)**
> The material of the wall was jasper; and the city was pure gold, like clear glass. [19] The foundation stones of the city wall were decorated with every kind of precious stone. The first foundation stone was jasper; the second, sapphire; the third, chalcedony; the fourth, emerald; [20] the fifth, sardonyx; the sixth, sardius; the seventh, chrysolite; the eighth, beryl; the ninth, topaz; the tenth, chrysoprase; the eleventh, jacinth; the twelfth, amethyst. [21] And the twelve gates were twelve pearls; each one of the gates was a single pearl. And the street of the city was pure gold, like transparent glass.

Each gate in the wall will be one massive, carved pearl. The whole of it will be illuminated by the glory of God. It will shine forever through the prism of trillions of perfect gems, so blinding and beautiful that our human words cringe in embarrassment trying to describe it. Each wall is made of three 500-mile sections of living jewels.

The gems John describes to us are difficult to picture because what we know today is imperfect and impure. The jasper will be diamond-like, the gold so pure that light will be able to shine through it turning everything in its wake into the purest of yellow. The sapphire will be as blue as the deepest sea, the chalcedony as blue as the evening sky with yellow streaks to make it shimmer. The emerald will be as green as the purest of forest meadows, the sardonyx deep and red with white in its depths. The sardius will nearly bleed as red as a ruby. The chrysolite will shine the brightest blue and green, the beryl and topaz will be a cascade of golden shades. The chrysoprase will amaze the eyes with blue and green, the jacinth will be riot of violet while the amethyst will smother the senses in the deepest purple.

But every color we have ever seen in this life can only be a muddy reflection of these colors. Today, in this life, the bluest of blues is really dead, gold is just a dull yellow and purple is only a shadow. In that place, it will be a living blue, a gold that is alive, and a purple so rich it could burn your living eyes today. [112] We will need resurrection eyes just to be able to endure this kind of beauty.

Revelation 21:22 - 27 (NASB)
> I saw no temple in it, for the Lord God the Almighty and the Lamb are its temple. [23] And the city has no need of the sun or of the moon to shine on it, for the glory of God has illuminated it, and its lamp is the Lamb. [24] The nations will walk by its light, and the

kings of the earth will bring their glory into it. **²⁵** In the daytime (for there will be no night there) its gates will never be closed; **²⁶** and they will bring the glory and the honor of the nations into it; **²⁷** and nothing unclean, and no one who practices abomination and lying, shall ever come into it, but only those whose names are written in the Lamb's book of life.

There will be no temple in the New Jerusalem because the entire city is the habitation of God. Every street, every gem, every mansion will be aflame with the Being and the beauty and the brightness of the Glory of God. The new heavens and the new earth will quiver with possibility and discovery. Everything we discover about God and what He has made will be greater and bigger and more beautiful on the inside than it was on the outside. [113] This is the reason the apostle Paul, who like John, was allowed to see this city, could only shout, "How can anyone fear death when this is our destiny?" This is the reason Paul said in First Corinthians 15:53,

> **First Corinthians 15:53 - 55 (NASB)**
> For this perishable must put on the imperishable, and this mortal must put on immortality. **⁵⁴** But when this perishable puts on the imperishable, and this mortal puts on immortality, then will come about the saying that is written: "Death has been swallowed up in victory. **⁵⁵** Where, O Death, is your victory? Where, O Death, is your sting?"

End of Days:
The Book of Revelation Explained

Chapter 28: Now what?
Revelation 22 explained...

The greatest miracle that could possibly take place has already happened. The evidence from physics and astronomy shows that once upon a time, there was nothing in existence, but then suddenly, in a mighty explosion, everything came into being. No one can explain how nothing can do anything because nothing is nothing. In fact, if ever there was a time when there had been nothing, there should still be nothing right now so there must be something that is eternal. [114] The Bible teaches that God is the eternal Being, an infinite Spirit who is not composed of matter. God is greater than time, space, and matter and since the evidence shows that at some point in the distant past the universe did not exist, it makes perfect sense that the God of the Bible created it. Since making something out of nothing is the greatest miracle of all, and God has already done this, then it is no stretch to believe that God can know and control the future.

God has revealed Himself to human beings through the Jewish prophets. God used mighty miracles though the prophets to authenticate their message. The greatest of these was Jesus Himself. In fact, Jesus claimed to be God incarnated in human form, and He proved that He was telling the truth by doing the second greatest miracle in history - Jesus rose from the dead! The God who can make everything out of nothing, including life itself, can enter into His own physical creation to live a human life, and die a human death and rise from the dead to authenticate His message. It is Jesus who revealed the book of Revelation to John and by His authority, demonstrated by His power to raise Himself from the dead, we can be certain that His revelation is true future-history.

In the first century, in the first few weeks after the followers of Jesus began to proclaim that they had seen Jesus alive, even His enemies agreed the tomb Jesus had been buried in was empty. The guards at His tomb had abandoned their post, a crime punishable by death. Some of them took bribes to say His followers had come and stolen the body of Jesus, but everyone in town knew that was ridiculous. The Romans were fearless warriors with a fierce reputation after having conquered the world and no one was fooled into thinking a group of local fishermen had scared them off. And the local fisherman who claimed they had seen Jesus alive were willing to suffer torture and death for their testimony. People do not normally die a horrific death if they can avoid it and, normally, no one dies for something if they know it is not true.

The Bible is the most historically accurate book ever written. There are more ancient documents of the Bible or portions and quotes from the Bible to study, than there are for any other ancient document ever written. The Bible was written over a 1,500-year time span on three continents in three languages and yet there are no contradictions in its message. There are over 800 Scriptures where critics think they have found a contradiction, but in each and every case a reasonable explanation can be seen. [115]

The creation of everything from nothing, the resurrection of Jesus from the dead and the miracle of the preservation of the Bible through the centuries, all show that God, through His Bible, is trustworthy to tell us what will happen after death. The good news from God is that Jesus has promised eternal life to everyone who trusts in Him. He is the Creator of time itself, so He is Master of the future also. When the days of human rebellion are ended, the eternal reward God has promised to His servants will begin. Revelation 22:1 says,

Revelation 22:1 – 7 (NASB)
And he showed me a river of the water of life, clear as crystal, coming from the throne of God and of the Lamb, [2] in the middle of its street. On either side of the river was the tree of life, bearing twelve kinds of fruit, yielding its fruit every month; and the leaves of the tree were for the healing of the nations. [3] There will no longer be any curse; and the throne of God and of the Lamb will be in it, and His bond-servants will serve Him; [4] they will see His face, and His name will be on their foreheads. [5] And there will no longer be any night; and they will not have need of the light of a lamp nor the light of the sun, because the Lord God will illuminate them; and they will reign forever and ever. [6] And he said to me, "These words are faithful and true"; and the Lord, the God

of the spirits of the prophets, sent His angel to show His bond-servants the things which must soon take place. ⁷ "And behold, I am coming quickly. Blessed is the one who keeps the words of the prophecy of this book."

Revelation chapters 21 and 22 describe the new heaven where eternal life will flower into the mists of the infinite future. But these rewards are for those who have turned to Jesus as their Lord and King. Anyone reading this book should understand how to be certain that heaven is their eternal destiny.

The book of Revelation is all about how God will judge evil in this world. Unfortunately, everyone on earth has been contaminated by evil to one degree or another. Romans 3:23 says,

> **Romans 3:23 (NLT)**
> For everyone has sinned; we all fall short of God's glorious standard.

God's perfection is so pure that His essence will literally consume anything that is imperfect, just like the power of the sun would consume anything unlike the sun - such as a paper airplane. Paper airplanes lack "sun-ness" so they can never get near the sun. In the same way, God is perfect so the consequence of anyone imperfect getting too near His perfection would be destruction. The Bible says this is like earning a wage for having done something evil. Romans 6:23 says,

Romans 6:23 (NLT)
For the wages of sin is death, but the free gift of God is eternal life through Christ Jesus our Lord.

Death is a separation from life and God is life itself. A person can exist and be conscious of existing and yet still be separated from God. That is what the Lake of Fire will be like – a place where people are forever aware of their own existence, but forever tormented at being separated from God by their own freewill choice. But God offers Himself, since He took on a human form in the person of Jesus, as a substitute life for anyone who will accept Him. Romans 10:9 says,

Romans 10:9 – 13 (NLT)
If you openly declare that Jesus is Lord and believe in your heart that God raised him from the dead, you will be saved. [10] For it is by believing in your heart that you are made right with God, and it is by openly declaring your faith that you are saved. [11] As the Scriptures tell us, "Anyone who trusts in him will never be disgraced." [12] Jew and Gentile are the same in this respect. They have the same Lord, who gives generously to all who call on him. [13] For "Everyone who calls on the name of the Lord will be saved."

In the first century, to openly declare Jesus as your Lord was to put your life on the line. The Emperors of Rome wanted everyone to say that the emperor was their highest loyalty over every other god or political leader. What the Bible reveals here is that a person must decide from the heart and openly declare that their highest loyalty is to Jesus over any other god or leader. They must believe that Jesus died to pay for their sins and rose from the dead. This is a decision of the heart, not anything that can be earned by good deeds or religious actions. It is free, so anyone who calls out to God with this attitude of the heart will be saved from the Lake of Fire. Jesus said that anyone who trusted in Him would drink from the water of life (John 4:14). Revelation 22:1 says,

> **Revelation 22:1 – 2 (NASB)**
> And he showed me a river of the water of life, clear as crystal, coming from the throne of God and of the Lamb, ² in the middle of its street.

Since the Revelation Refrain of something symbolic linked to something literal has been the pattern in Revelation from the start, it is possible this view of the River of Life may be symbolic also. It is unclear since everything in the eternal state will be so unlike anything we have experienced in this life. In fact, this word "life" in Greek is ζωή (dzo-ay') which means "life in its fullness." [116] This river of the water of life is a picture of the essence of life itself. It is a picture of pure existence in a state of ultimate fulfillment. It is life that completes the soul and satisfies the needs of existence itself.

The Bible teaches that human beings were created to be physical beings. In the beginning, Adam and Eve were flawless, perfect, immortal, physical beings. But human life was also created to allow human beings a free opportunity to accept relationship with God or reject that relationship. The perfect physical life of man was contaminated when Adam and Eve rebelled against God so that all the sons and daughters of Adam and Eve now suffer aging and sickness and death. This was allowed so that we could have freewill which gives us the capacity to have a real relationship with God, but someday God will restore our physical bodies to the same perfect existence that Adam and Eve once enjoyed. Revelation 22:2 says,

> **Revelation 22:2 (NASB)**
> On either side of the river was the tree of life, bearing twelve kinds of fruit, yielding its fruit every month; and the leaves of the tree were for the healing of the nations.

We do not know how "time" will be measured in heaven. There will not be time as we understand it, but there will be some point of reference or else there could be no "fruit every month." We can only get a hint of the eternal, but it says the fruit of this eternally flowing life will be the "healing" of the nations. The word "healing" in Greek is θεραπεία (ther-ap-i'-ah), which means "service rendered by one to another." [117] It is from this Greek word that we get our word "therapy." In Greek, this word is also related to the Greek word for "household," so this is a picture of that awesome feeling you get when you get home, drop into the most comfortable couch in the room and let out a huge sigh. After a lifetime of feeling the distance of God, since He has pulled back to allow for human freewill, and after having had to endure evil in this life, God promises an eternity of refreshment and therapy for the soul - and it will continue forever. Revelation 22:3 says,

> **Revelation 22:3 – 4 (NASB)**
> There will no longer be any curse; and the throne of God and of the Lamb will be in it, and His bond-servants will serve Him; [4] they will see His face, and His name will be on their foreheads.

In ancient times, the words "see His face" are a figure of speech for "intimate knowledge." In other words, in this eternal place, there will be no emotional or social distance between you and God. And this intimate knowledge will go both ways, because His "Name on their foreheads" is symbolic of acceptance. This is something like traditional marriage where a woman takes her husband's last name. By taking the last name of her husband, a new wife identifies herself with her husband's family. In the ideal, Godly marriage, there is no separation between a husband and wife and complete acceptance by the husband of his wife. She becomes a part of his family for life. In the same way, God offers eternal life so that we will be completely accepted by Him. We will experience a connection so deep, we will be part of God's family. There will be no curse there so all our mistakes, all our failure and weakness, any darkness or foolishness or regret, will all be washed away.

> **Revelation 22:5 - 7 (NASB)**
> And there will no longer be any night; and they will not have need of the light of a lamp nor the light of the sun, because the Lord

God will illuminate them; and they will reign forever and ever. ⁶ And he said to me, "These words are faithful and true"; and the Lord, the God of the spirits of the prophets, sent His angel to show His bond-servants the things which must soon take place. ⁷ "And behold, I am coming quickly. Blessed is the one who keeps the words of the prophecy of this book."

Revelation 21 and 22 show the eternal destiny of anyone who puts their trust in Jesus for the forgiveness of sins. Jesus also promises blessing here and now for anyone who "keeps" the words of the prophecy of the book of Revelation. The word "keep" is τηρέω (tay-reh'-o) which means "to attend to carefully, to respond." [118] Unfortunately, many people do not "attend carefully" to what the Bible teaches. Jesus said in John 3:19,

John 3:19 (NASB)
And this is the judgement, that the Light has come into the world, and people loved the darkness rather than the Light; for their deeds were evil.

Remember that evil is merely a "lack" of something. In this case, people love a "lack of God" because they want to keep their self-centered decisions covered up in the dark. People resent God's right to rule in their lives. Many people do not want God to call the shots in life but there is a real irony with that choice. The same people who reject God and complain that following Jesus would amount to God "killing the fun in life," are the same people who risk the dreadful consequences of immoral behavior. Where is the fun in getting a sexually transmitted disease? Where is the fun in risking cirrhosis of the liver or drunk driving accidents from drunkenness? Where is the excitement in addiction and emptiness and unfulfillment in life?

Jesus offers living water that will bubble up from within the heart so anyone can thrive even in this broken world. Jesus offers the crystal-clear waters of eternal life in a future so golden the prophets could barely breathe just seeing it in a vision. In fact, when John saw the glimpse of the New Jerusalem and the waters of eternal life, he was once again emotionally compromised. Revelation 22:8 says,

Revelation 22:8 – 9 (NASB)
I, John, am the one who heard and saw these things. And when I heard and saw them, I fell down to worship at the feet of the angel who showed me these things. ⁹ And he said to me, "Do not do that; I am a fellow servant of yours and of your brothers the prophets, and of those who keep the words of this book. Worship God!"

John was well known to Christians in the first century. Everyone knew his reputation as an eyewitness of the risen Jesus. He had great credibility. He also had true humility. He told the truth, even though it made him look bad. He knew that falling down to worship an angel was wrong, but John wanted everyone to know exactly what he saw, even when doing so would tarnish his own reputation. John did not change the vision in any way, even to protect his own reputation.

John was a witness to Jesus doing incredible miracles. He was there when Jesus turned water into wine. He saw Jesus give the blind sight and he heard the praises men and women cried out when Jesus gave them back their hearing. John saw Jesus walk on water and John saw the emotionally overwhelming things written in the book of Revelation. Here at the end, writing as an old man, he risks his reputation and credibility to tell the truth about his own mistakes, but he wrote this so we would know he has told us everything he was supposed to reveal.

Christians today need to "attend carefully" to John's example, particularly when it comes to emotions. Christians today are easily swayed from one teaching to another by emotions rather than carefully considering their actions based on what the Bible teaches is true. Twice in the book of Revelation, John makes the mistake of letting his emotions overcome him. Falling down to worship an angel is an emotional response. We do not know how long it took for John to receive this vision. It seems unlikely it all happened in one night and even more unlikely that he wrote it all down in one day. It is not clear from the text but is seems reasonable to think seeing this vision and writing down what he saw must have been an exhausting experience. The vision of dragons and demons breathing fire are vivid, powerful, and chilling. Today, we have the experience of computer-generated effects in our movies and media, but John had never seen anything like this in all his life. There is no way he could have endured this without some effect on his feelings.

There is one way we might be able to get a glimpse of what John went through. Remember a long night when you went through the worst of nightmares. No matter how modern or scientific-minded you might be, even the most sophisticated person will probably have a whole day ruined from one bad dream.

And John did not just see symbolic things in heaven. He also saw the future events those symbols linked to a future-history far removed from the first century. How could John make sense of the modern weapons and warfare he must have seen? John had never seen an airplane or a gun or a bomb, but he saw the destruction of the Antichrist's capital city in one blinding flash.

John had little frame of reference to understand the distant future and yet more, he was given a glimpse of eternity. He saw the New Jerusalem, a city roughly the size of our moon, with walls 216 feet high and 1,500 miles long on a side made of perfect, pure gems radiating the glory of God. Then he saw the river of life. He heard the voice of God. How could anyone see that and not experience spiritual shock? No wonder he falls down to worship the glorious being standing at his side. It was the wrong choice, since we are commanded to worship only God Himself, but it shows that no matter how well trained anyone is in theology or the Bible, our emotions can lead us astray. Remember that John had the best seminary education in history because he had lived with Jesus and learned directly from Him for years. It does not matter how long anyone has been a follower of Jesus either, since John was probably in his nineties when he wrote this book and had been serving God since he was a teenager. The point is clear, human emotions can still trip us up, so it is imperative that Christians compare what they think and feel with what God's Word teaches.

> **Revelation 22:9 (NASB)**
> And he said to me, "Do not do that; I am a fellow servant of yours and of your brothers the prophets, and of those who keep the words of this book. Worship God!"

The angel points John back to God's Word – the Bible – and tells him he is part of the group that keeps the words of this book. Remember, the word "keep" in Greek is τηρέω (tay-reh'-o) and it means "attend to carefully." In other words, if you "attend carefully" to God's word, you will know you are expected to worship God alone. Your emotions may draw you into error, but it is the revealed Word of God that will guard you against being led astray by your feelings.

> **Revelation 22:10 - 11 (NASB)**
> And he said to me, "Do not seal up the words of the prophecy of this book, for the time is near. [11] Let the one who does wrong still do wrong, and the one who is filthy still be filthy; and let the one who is righteous still practice righteousness, and the one who is holy still keep himself holy."

From the start, God did not want the prophecy of the book of Revelation to be hidden. This book is intended to be understood. It requires seeing the difference in the Revelation Refrain between what is symbolic and what is literal, and it requires seeing how the symbols link back to the Old Testament, but with a little discernment - it can be understood. Nevertheless, verse eleven means that Jesus is not holding John or anyone else responsible for the results of the teaching of this book in any person's life. People who choose wickedness are likely to keep doing wrong regardless of whether they understand this book. Believers, however, can see the principles illustrated in this, apply those principles and practice righteousness all the more.

The world will continue to mock the Christian lifestyle and beliefs. People will pick and choose Scriptures out of the book of Revelation to make fun of Christian belief. Others will laugh at the Christian belief in the coming Rapture. Unbelievers may think anyone trying to find anything literal in this book about dragons and demons with tails like scorpions is crazy. We should not let their attitude seal up the words of this book. Christians should not be afraid of Revelation or afraid to explain it. The reason we should not is found in Revelation 22:12. It says,

> **Revelation 22:12 – 13 (NASB)**
> "Behold, I am coming quickly, and My reward is with Me, to reward each one as his work deserves. [13] I am the Alpha and the Omega, the first and the last, the beginning and the end."

It is true that people have speculated for two thousand years about what exactly "I am coming quickly" may mean since two thousand years does not seem exactly "quick." But the Greek word for "quick" in this verse is ταχύ (takh-oo') and that means "soon, without delay, by surprise and suddenly." [119] In other words, this verse did not mean Jesus was going to return within a few months or years of the day that John wrote the book of Revelation. In context, He means that when the events prophesied in Revelation begin, they will unfold rapidly, "without delay, by surprise and suddenly."

In Matthew 24:6-8, Jesus said there would be "wars and rumors" of wars for a long time but "when you see nation rise against nation and kingdom against kingdom," that would be the start of the end of the age. Remember that "nation against nation and kingdom against kingdom" is a figure of speech meaning "the whole world at war." The First World War was the start of end of the age. In 1914, for the first time in human history, the entire globe was at war at the same time and that is a fulfillment of what Jesus said in Matthew 24:6. Jesus also said that the beginning of the end of the age would be like the birth pains a woman will experience before she gives birth. Each of these birth pains will be more intense and the pains will come closer together before the birth. The birth itself, however, only happens after the most intense and final part of the birth process that some doctors call "transition to final labor."

Since World War I we have seen other "birth pains" which have been either world-wide events or events that affected all Jewish people. There have been plenty of local economic problems, but the Great Depression affected the entire planet. There have been many local wars, but World War II affected everyone on earth, even the most remote tribes in the jungles of New Guinea and South

America. There have been many persecutions of the Jewish people since they were forced out of Israel in A.D. 70, but the horrific genocide of the Holocaust during World War II affected the heart and soul of every Jewish person on earth. On May 14, 1948, in one day, Israel was declared a recognized nation once again, an event that shook the civilized world and affected every Jewish person in every country. This was also a fulfillment of a prophecy that needed fulfillment before any of the events in Revelation could take place - and it has now happened.

In June 1967, the city of Jerusalem came back under Israeli control for the first time since Titus the Roman destroyed the city in the first century A.D. This was another prophecy fulfilled in modern times and it was, again, an event that affected the whole world as well as every Jewish person. From the establishment of the nation of Israel in 1948 until the Israeli army took control of Jerusalem, there was only a nineteen-year gap. Truly, these events are unfolding quickly.

In January 2020, hardly anyone had ever heard of Covid-19, but by March of 2020 the world was shut down. Tens of thousands of people died from Covid-19 or were sickened by it, but the fear of the disease changed politics, medicine, and economics worldwide in just a few weeks.

"Behold, I come quickly..."

These events in the book of Revelation are beginning to unfold. The Ezekiel war could begin before this book goes to press. The Rapture may happen before it lands on a single bookstore shelf.

Based on the birth pains that have shaken the world in the last century, it is not inconceivable that either the opening of the seals have already started or else they could begin at any moment.

Some Christians avoid reading Revelation because it seems confusing, but it was meant to be understood. Other Christians avoid Revelation because there have been too many examples of false teachers foolishly setting dates for the Rapture that have turned out to be false. But as we have seen, those false teachers gave into the emotion of the moment and fell into error. John teaches us by his example not to be led by emotions such as fear or excitement but to compare what we feel with what God has revealed to us - and Jesus warned us not to set dates. But we are equally warned to be prepared. Remember, Jesus did say that when these things begin to unfold, they will unroll very quickly. The point of knowing this is that we should live our lives intentionally. In fact, Revelation 22:14 says,

> **<u>Revelation 22:14 – 15 (NASB)</u>**
> Blessed are those who wash their robes, so that they will have the right to the tree of life, and may enter the city by the gates. [15] Outside are the dogs, the sorcerers, the sexually immoral persons, the murderers, the idolaters, and everyone who loves and practices lying.

This is another example of the Revelation Refrain. A robe, for example, is an external covering symbolic of how a person lives in this life, but the context of this Scripture links to the literal Tree of Life that is in heaven. Also, the word "wash" in verse 14 is in the present tense, so it has a sense of "they are washing their robes right now and continuing to wash them." So, since this part of the book of Revelation is written for believers, He is saying that what believers are doing in the present should be a sign to everyone. People who examine our Christian lives should be able to see that we are the people who have the right to the Tree of Life and the right to enter the New Jerusalem someday. John explains this in another letter...

> **First John 3:2 (NASB)**
> Beloved, now we are children of God, and it has not appeared as yet what we will be. We know that when He appears, we will be like Him, because we will see Him just as He is. ³ And everyone who has this hope set on Him purifies himself, just as He is pure.

Just as in Revelation 22:14, John says that the evidence a person is committed to Jesus from the heart is a "purifying" lifestyle. This is also the reason John says in First John 1:8-9 which says,

> **First John 1:8 – 9 (NLT)**
> If we claim we have no sin, we are only fooling ourselves and not living in the truth. ⁹ But if we confess our sins to him, he is faithful and just to forgive us our sins and to cleanse us from all wickedness.

This means a believer does not earn the right to the Tree of Life by living a good life or being perfect. A true believer is in a constant, present state of purifying his or her life or "washing" his or her robes. Christians are not perfect, but they should live as "recovering sinners." When we fall into error, we should confess this, thank God for His forgiveness and strive to live better for Him. This is what "washing their robes" is all about. Jesus goes on to say,

> **Revelation 22:16 - 17 (NASB)**
> "I, Jesus, have sent My angel to testify to you of these things for the churches. I am the root and the descendant of David, the bright morning star." [17] The Spirit and the bride say, "Come." And let the one who hears say, "Come." And let the one who is thirsty come; let the one who desires, take the water of life without cost.

Since Jesus says the prophecy in Revelation is for the churches, He means the book of Revelation is for the believer today. This book does not need to be a mystery and the principles it illustrates can and should bless the believer's life in the present. Jesus is the Root, which means He is the Creator, but He is also the descendant of David, which means He entered into His own creation as a real man. He is both God and the rightful King of your life and He is also a true man so He is completely aware of what it is like to be in your shoes. Jesus truly knows what you are going through in this life so there is no temptation, no worry and no struggle that Jesus has not already faced. He has conquered both life and death and He is absolutely trustworthy to lead us. It is tempting to watch the evening news and feel fear or despair, but Jesus tells us in this book that there is nothing to fear because He holds the future. Revelation 22:18 reads,

> **Revelation 22:18 – 21 (NASB)**
> I testify to everyone who hears the words of the prophecy of this book: if anyone adds to them, God will add to him the plagues that are written in this book; [19] and if anyone takes away from the words of the book of this prophecy, God will take away his part from the tree of life and from the holy city, which are written in this book. [20] He who testifies to these things says, "Yes, I am coming quickly." Amen. Come, Lord Jesus. [21] The grace of the Lord Jesus be with all. Amen.

The book of Revelation is "the prophecy," but it is the prophecy of "a book." In short, Jesus is saying that the book of Revelation is the prophecy of the book which He has revealed, and that book is the whole revealed Word of God from Genesis to Revelation. This is a clear warning not to add to or take away from the words of God.

The Bible has been transmitted through history with greater accuracy than any other book in human history. By comparing the oldest ancient copies of the Bible, it is estimated the Bible we have today is over 99% accurate to the original text. [120] It is also clear that the tiny fraction of unknown or uncertain words have absolutely no effect on any of the teachings in the Bible. There is no place in the Scripture where anyone can find a teaching or truth that is unknown because of an uncertain word.

God's truth has come down to us better preserved than any other book ever written.

This warning and the witness of the history of the Bible gives us great confidence that the future events the book of Revelation describes will happen exactly as Jesus says they will happen. It is vital that we "attend carefully" to learning what the Bible teaches. We must be intentional to apply the principles it teaches into our actions day-by-day. We must do this because the greatest witness in the history of the human race shouts down through the centuries that "Jesus is coming again, awfully soon!"

NOTES

Chapter 1
[1] Strong's G601, accessed May 9, 2021, https://www.blueletterbible.org/lexicon/g601/kjv/tr/0-1/.

[2] "From the first century to the present, orthodox Christians have almost unanimously agreed that he is the Apostle John…The evidence, however, shows that orthodox theologians readily accepted the book as genuinely inspired. Early fathers who recognized the book as Scripture include Irenaeus, Justin Martyr, Eusebius, Apollonius, and Theophilus, the bishop of Antioch." John Walvoord, *"Revelation,"* The Bible Knowledge Commentary: An Exposition of the Scriptures by Dallas Seminary Faculty, New Testament Edition (Colorado Springs, CO: Cook Communications Ministries, 1983, 2000), 925.

[3] "The ancients tell us that John lived longest of all the twelve apostles, and was the only one of them that died a natural death, all the rest suffering martyrdom; and some of them say that he wrote this gospel (of John) at Ephesus…" Matthew Henry, *Matthew Henry's Commentary on the Whole Bible, Vol. V, Matthew to John* (McLean, VA: MacDonald Publishing Company), 847.

[4] "The Book of Revelation has no direct quotations from the Old Testament, but it has about 550 references back to the Old Testament." Arnold Fruchtenbaum, *The Footsteps of the Messiah: A Study of the Sequence of Prophetic Events*, revised edition (San Antonio, TX: Ariel Ministries, 2018), 10.

[5] "One scholar claimed that 278 of the 404 verses in Revelation contain references to the Old Testament. William Barclay claimed that John quoted or alluded to the Old Testament 245 times, citing about 20 Old Testament books—his favorites being: Isaiah, Daniel, Ezekiel, Psalms, Exodus, Jeremiah, and Zechariah. The United Bible Society's Greek New Testament lists over 500 Old Testament passages. Despite all these allusions, however, there are no formal quotations from the Old Testament." Thomas Constable, *Constable's Bible Notes*, 2021 Edition, accessed May 9, 2021, https://www.planobiblechapel.org/tcon/notes/html/nt/revelation/revelation.htm.

[6] Dictionary.com, accessed May 18, 2021, https://www.dictionary.com/browse/allegory.

[7] "Most evangelical scholars affirm that Revelation was written in A.D. 95 or 96. This based on accounts of the early church fathers that the Apostle John had been exiled on Patmos Island during the reign of Domitian who died in A.D. 96. John was then allowed to return to Ephesus." Walvoord, "Revelation," *The Bible Knowledge Commentary*, 925.

[8] "The unconditional land-promise God made to Abraham and his descendants (e.g. Gen. 13: 1-17) has never been fulfilled; it must have a future fulfillment for national Israel." Norman Geisler, *Systematic Theology* (Minneapolis, MN: Bethany House, 2011), 1404.

Chapter 2
[9] Strong's G5083, accessed May 25, 2021, https://www.blueletterbible.org/lexicon/g5083/kjv/tr/0-1/.

[10] Strong's G1451, accessed May 25, 2021, https://www.blueletterbible.org/lexicon/g1451/kjv/tr/0-1/.

[11] "Verse 4a states to whom this book is being written, especially chapters two and three of the book: the seven churches that are in Asia. John uses the Greek definite article the, indicating totality…The number seven throughout Scripture signifies completeness. The point here, then is that this is a message to the whole church…All believers are to learn from what will be written to the seven churches of Asia." Fruchtenbaum, *Footsteps*, 14.

[12] Strong's G32, accessed May 25, 2021, https://www.blueletterbible.org/lexicon/g32/kjv/tr/0-1/.

[13] Strong's G1577, accessed May 25, 2021, https://www.blueletterbible.org/lexicon/g1577/kjv/tr/0-1/.

Chapter 3
[14] Fruchtenbaum, *Footsteps*, 626-627.

[15] Strong's G4413, accessed May 27, 2021, https://www.blueletterbible.org/lexicon/g4413/kjv/tr/0-1/.

[16] Strong's G26, accessed May 27, 2021, https://www.blueletterbible.org/lexicon/g26/kjv/tr/0-1/.
[17] Strong's G3421, accessed May 27, 2021, https://www.blueletterbible.org/lexicon/g26/kjv/tr/0-1/.

Chapter 4

[18] "The political unity wrought by the Roman Empire allowed the early Christians to travel without having to fear bandits or local wars. When reading about Paul's journeys, we see that the great threat to shipping at that time was bad weather. A few decades earlier, an encounter with pirates was much more to be feared than any storm. In the first century, well-paved and well-guarded roads ran to the most distant provinces. Since trade flourished, travel was constant; thus Christianity often reached a new region, not through the work of missionaries or preachers, but rather through traveling traders, slaves, and others." Justo Gonzalez, *The Story of Christianity, Vol. 1*. (San Francisco, CA: Harper Collins Publishers, 1984), 14.
[19] Alliance Defending Freedom, "Elane Photography v. Willock," last modified May 29, 2020, accessed May 26, 2021, https://adflegal.org/case/elane-photography-v-willock; Find Law for Legal Professionals, accessed May 26, 2021, https://caselaw.findlaw.com/nm-supreme-court/1642684.html.
[20] *The Archaeological Study Bible*. (Grand Rapids, MI: Zondervan, 2005, 2:12 – 17n), 2049.
[21] Walvoord, *The Bible Knowledge Commentary*, 935-936.
[22] Pew Research Center, *Many Americans Mix Multiple Faiths*, December 9, 2009, accessed May 27, 2021, https://www.pewforum.org/2009/12/09/many-americans-mix-multiple-faiths/.
[23] Strong's G2902, accessed May 27, 2021, https://www.blueletterbible.org/lexicon/g2902/kjv/tr/0-1/.
[24] David J. Ayers, *Sex and the Single Evangelical*, August 14, 2019, accessed June 9, 2021, https://ifstudies.org/blog/sex-and-the-single-evangelical#.
[25] Strong's G3531, accessed May 27, 2021, https://www.blueletterbible.org/lexicon/g3531/kjv/tr/0-1/.
[26] Strong's G3340, accessed May 27, 2021, https://www.blueletterbible.org/lexicon/g3340/kjv/tr/0-1/.
[27] https://www.britannica.com/animal/dye-murex, accessed June 8, 2021.
[28] Strong's G4202, accessed May 27, 2021, https://www.blueletterbible.org/lexicon/g4202/kjv/tr/0-1/.

Chapter 5

[29] "Sardis," accessed June 2, 2021, https://sardisexpedition.org/en/essays/about-sardis.
[30] Strong's G1577, accessed June 1, 2021, https://www.blueletterbible.org/lexicon/g1577/kjv/tr/0-1/.
[31] Strong's G3498, accessed June 2, 2021, https://www.blueletterbible.org/lexicon/g3498/kjv/tr/0-1/.
[32] Strong's G4459, accessed June 2, 2021, https://www.blueletterbible.org/lexicon/g4459/kjv/tr/0-1/.
[33] Strong's G3398, accessed June 4, 2021, https://www.blueletterbible.org/lexicon/g3398/kjv/tr/0-1/.
[34] Strong's G2902, accessed June 4, 2021, https://www.blueletterbible.org/lexicon/g2902/kjv/tr/0-1/.

Chapter 6

[35] Strong's G746, accessed June 8, 2021, https://www.blueletterbible.org/lexicon/g746/kjv/tr/0-1/.
[36] Strong's G281, accessed June 8, 2021, https://www.blueletterbible.org/lexicon/g281/kjv/tr/0-1/.
[37] Strong's G1692, accessed June 8, 2021, https://www.blueletterbible.org/lexicon/g1692/kjv/tr/0-1/.
[38] Strong's G3568, accessed June 9, 2021, https://www.blueletterbible.org/lexicon/g3568/kjv/tr/0-1/.

Chapter 7

[39] Fruchtenbaum, *Footsteps*, 22.
[40] Strong's H8133, accessed June 9, 2021, https://www.blueletterbible.org/lexicon/h8133/kjv/wlc/0-1/.

Chapter 8
[41] Strong's G726, https://www.blueletterbible.org/lexicon/g726/kjv/tr/0-1/.
[42] Strong's G2752, https://www.blueletterbible.org/lexicon/g2752/kjv/tr/0-1/.

Chapter 9
[43] Fruchtenbaum, *Footsteps,* 626.
[44] Fruchtenbaum, *Footsteps,* 96.
[45] Fruchtenbaum, *Footsteps,* 95.
[46] Strong's H8314, accessed June 27, 2021, https://www.blueletterbible.org/lexicon/h8314/kjv/wlc/0-1/.
[47] Strong's H3742, accessed June 27, 2021, https://www.blueletterbible.org/lexicon/h3742/kjv/wlc/0-1/.

Chapter 10
[48] "Mount Tambora and the Year Without A Summer," UCAR Center For Science Education, accessed June 24, 2021, https://scied.ucar.edu/learning-zone/how-climate-works/mount-tambora-and-year-without-summer.

Chapter 11
[49] Strong's G4735, accessed June 8, 2021, https://www.blueletterbible.org/lexicon/g4735/kjv/tr/0-1/.

Chapter 12
[50] National Archives Museum, "Featured Document Display: The Atomic Bombing of Hiroshima and Nagasaki," accessed June 19, 2021, https://museum.archives.gov/featured-document-display-atomic-bombing-hiroshima-and-nagasaki.
[51] Dr. Philip Webber and Dr. Stuart Parkinson. "UK nuclear weapons: a catastrophe in the making?", accessed August 6, 2015, https://www.sgr.org.uk/resources/uk-nuclear-weapons-catastrophe-making.
[52] "World military spending rises to almost $2 trillion in 2020," Stockholm International Peace Research Institute, accessed June 9, 2021, https://www.sipri.org/media/press-release/2021/world-military-spending-rises-almost-2-trillion-2020.
[53] Henry Morris, *The Revelation Record, A Scientific and Devotional Commentary on the Book of Revelation*, (Wheaton, IL: Tyndale House Publishers, 1985), 109.
[54] Fruchtenbaum. *Footsteps*, 106-107.
[55] Amy MacKinnon, "With Base in Sudan, Russia Expands Its Military Reach in Africa," Foreign Policy News, December 20, 2020, accessed June 21, 2021, https://foreignpolicy.com/2020/12/14/russia-expands-military-reach-africa-navy-base-sudan/.
[56] Lahav Harkov, Eytan Halon, "Israel enters pipeline agreement with Greek, Cyprus leaders," The Jerusalem Post, June 22 2020, accessed June 21 2021, https://www.jpost.com/israel-news/israel-enters-pipeline-agreement-with-greek-cyprus-leaders-612950.
[57] "Persian Gulf War," The Encyclopedia Britannica, accessed November 11, 2021, https://www.britannica.com/event/Persian-Gulf-War.
[58] Seki, A.; Tobo, I.; Omori, Y.; Muto, J.; Nagahama, H., "Luminous phenomena and electromagnetic VHF wave emission originated from earthquake-related radon exhalation, NASA Astrophysics Data System (ADS)," December 1, 2013, accessed June 23, 2021, https://www.science.gov/topicpages/e/earthquake+related+phenomena.

Chapter 13
[59] Robert Peels, "The Great Depression," Encyclopedia Britannica, accessed June 22, 2021, https://www.britannica.com/event/Great-Depression.
[60] David Morens, Jeffery Taubenberger, "The mother of all pandemics is 100 years old (and going strong)," US National Library of Medicine, National Institutes of Health, November, 2018, accessed July 6, 2021, https://www.ncbi.nlm.nih.gov/pmc/articles/PMC6187799/.
[61] Max Roser, "The Spanish flu (1918-20): The global impact of the largest influenza pandemic in history," April 20, 2020, accessed July 6, 2021, https://ourworldindata.org/spanish-flu-largest-influenza-pandemic-in-history.
[62] Strong's G792, accessed July 6, 2021, https://www.blueletterbible.org/lexicon/g792/kjv/tr/0-1/.
[63] History.com Editors, "Krakatoa Explodes," History.com, November 24, 2009, accessed July 7, 2021, https://www.history.com/this-day-in-history/krakatau-explodes.

Chapter 14
[64] Walvoord, *The Bible Knowledge Commentary*, 949.

Chapter 15
[65] National Geographic Society: Resource Library, Encyclopedic Entry "Pyroclastic Flow," accessed December 14, 2021, https://www.nationalgeographic.org/encyclopedia/pyroclastic-flow/#.
[66] Pidwirny, Michael, "Surface area of our planet covered by oceans and continents. (Table 8o-1)," Encyclopedia of Earth, last updated June 5, 2008, accessed November 1, 2021, https://odysseyexpeditions.com/curriculum/Ocean.pdf.
[67] Bast F, et al. Phylogenetics & Evolutionary Biology, "European Species of Subaerial Green Alga Trentepohlia annulate (Trentepohliales, Ulvophyceae) Caused Blood Rain in Kerala, India", accessed December 14, 2021, https://www.hilarispublisher.com/open-access/european-species-of-subaerial-green-alga-trentepohlia-annulata-trentepohliales-ulvophyceae-caused-blood-rain-in-kerala-india-2329-9002-15-144.pdf
[68] Chris Trayner, "The Tunguska event," Journal of the British Astronomical Association, vol. 107, no. 3, (1997): 117-130, accessed December 13, 2021, https://adsabs.harvard.edu/full/1997JBAA..107..117T.
[69] Steven Collins, Latayne Scott, *Discovering the City of Sodom*, (New York, NY: Howard Books, 2013), 200-230.
[70] Strong's G32, accessed November 9, 2021, https://www.blueletterbible.org/lexicon/g32/kjv/tr/0-1/.
[71] Strong's G105, accessed November 9, 2021 https://www.blueletterbible.org/lexicon/g105/kjv/tr/0-1/.

Chapter 16
[72] "The key is the perfect tense of the verb, which should be translated "fallen" (instead of "fall," as in the King James). It refers to action completed in the past. John beheld, not a falling star, but a fallen star…it does seem most probable that Satan is indeed this fallen star," Morris, *The Revelation Record*, 156.
[73] Strong's G623, accessed October 11, 2021, https://www.blueletterbible.org/lexicon/g623/kjv/tr/0-1/.
[74] Fruchtenbaum, *Footsteps*, 22
[75] Strong's G3461, accessed August 11, 2021, https://www.blueletterbible.org/lexicon/g3461/kjv/tr/0-1/.
[76] C.S. Lewis, *Mere Christianity* (New York, NY: Harper One, 2001, edition), 92.

Chapter 17
[77] Strong's G243, https://www.blueletterbible.org/lexicon/g243/kjv/tr/0-1/.
[78] Strong's G2896, https://www.blueletterbible.org/lexicon/g2896/kjv/tr/0-1/.

Chapter 18
[79] The Temple Institute of Jerusalem – Learn About the Temple, accessed June 29, 2021, https://templeinstitute.org/.

Chapter 19
[80] Fruchtenbaum, *Footsteps*, 292-293.

Chapter 20
[81] Fruchtenbaum, *Footsteps*, 21-46.
[82] Ibid, 22.
[83] Ibid, 251.
[84] Ian Boxall, "Gematria" Bible Odyssey, accessed December 14, 2021, https://www.bibleodyssey.org/en/passages/related-articles/gematria.
[85] Morris, *The Revelation Record*, p. 255.

Chapter 21
[86] Strong's G3435, accessed July 15, 2021, https://www.blueletterbible.org/lexicon/g3435/kjv/tr/0-1/.
[87] Strong's G3321, accessed July 15, 2021, https://www.blueletterbible.org/lexicon/g3321/kjv/tr/0-1/.

[88] Mike Gianfagna, "What is Moore's Law?", Synopsys.com, June 30, 2021, accessed December 14, 2021. https://www.synopsys.com/glossary/what-is-moores-law.html.
[89] C.S. Lewis, *"The Great Divorce,"* The Best of C.S. Lewis, (Grand Rapids, MI: Baker Book House, 1969), 156.
[90] Strong's G3438, accessed July 15, 2021, https://www.blueletterbible.org/lexicon/g3438/kjv/tr/0-1/.
[91] C.S. Lewis, *The Last Battle,* (New York, NY: Harper Collins, 1984), 225.
[92] Randy Alcorn, "Heaven," accessed July 19, 2021, https://www.goodreads.com/work/quotes/86257-heaven#:~:text=As%20a%20Christian%2C%20the%20day,giant%20leap%20for%20God's%20glory.
[93] Strong's G3583, accessed July 15, 2021, https://www.blueletterbible.org/lexicon/g3583/kjv/tr/0-1/.

Chapter 22
[94] "How Much Oxygen Comes for the Ocean?", NOAA, accessed December 14, 2021, https://oceanservice.noaa.gov/facts/ocean-oxygen.html#:~:text=Scientists%20estimate%20that%2050%2D80,smallest%20photosynthetic%20organism%20on%20Earth.
[95] New World Encyclopedia contributors, "Euphrates River," New World Encyclopedia, accessed December 15, 2021, https://www.newworldencyclopedia.org/p/index.php?title=Euphrates_River&oldid=1006274.

Chapter 23
[96] Winfried Corduan, *Neighboring Faiths*, (Downers Grove, IL: IVP Academic, 2012), 44-46.
[97] Strong's H5248, accessed July 27, 2021, https://www.blueletterbible.org/lexicon/h5248/kjv/wlc/0-1/.
[98] Strong's H6440, accessed July 27, 2021, https://www.blueletterbible.org/lexicon/h6440/kjv/wlc/0-1/.
[99] Timothy Clarey, *Carved in Stone: Geologic Evidence of the Worldwide Flood*, ICR: (Dallas, TX: ICR, 2020), 482-484.
[100] Larry Vardiman, *"Hypercanes following the Genesis Flood,"* Proceedings of the Fifth International Conference on Creationism, R.L. Ivey, Jr. (Ed.), pp. 17 – 28, 2003, accessed July 28, 2021, https://www.icr.org/article/hypercanes-genesis-flood.
[101] Strong's H7218, accessed July 27, 2021, https://www.blueletterbible.org/lexicon/h7218/kjv/wlc/0-1/.
[102] Strong's H8064, accessed July 27, 2021, https://www.blueletterbible.org/lexicon/h8064/kjv/wlc/0-1/.
[103] Emanuel Cleaver II, "Opening Prayer of the 117th Congress," 1-3-21, Office of the Chaplain: United States House of Representatives, accessed December 12, 2021, https://chaplain.house.gov/archive/index.html?id=3203.

Chapter 25
[104] C.S. Lewis, *The Last Battle*, 228.

Chapter 26
[105] Strong's G2919, accessed August 11, 2021, https://www.blueletterbible.org/lexicon/g2919/kjv/tr/0-1/.
[106] Fruchtenbaum, *Footsteps*, 361-367.

Chapter 27
[107] C.S. Lewis, *The Last Battle*, 225.
[108] Strong's G1169, accessed August 12, 2021, https://www.blueletterbible.org/lexicon/g1169/kjv/tr/0-1/.
[109] Strong's G571, accessed August 12, 2021, https://www.blueletterbible.org/lexicon/g571/kjv/tr/0-1/.
[110] Strong's G3528, accessed August 12, 2021, https://www.blueletterbible.org/lexicon/g3528/kjv/tr/0-1/.
[111] Morris, *The Revelation Record*, 450-451.
[112] "I have heard of those little scratches in the crust that you Topdwellers call mines. But that's where you get dead gold, dead silver, dead gems. Down in Bism we have them alive and growing. There I'll pick you bunches of rubies that you can eat and squeeze you a cupful of

diamond juice. You won't care much about fingering the cold, dead treasures of your shallow mines after you have tasted the live ones in Bism," C.S. Lewis, *The Silver Chair*, (New York, NY: Harper Collins Publishers, 1981), 218.

[113] "Of course, Daughter of Eve," said the Faun. "The further up and the further in you go, the bigger everything gets. The inside is larger than the outside," C.S. Lewis, *The Last Battle*, 224.

Chapter 28

[114] "Therefore, if everything is possible not to be, then at one time there could have been nothing in existence. Now if this were true, even now there would be nothing in existence, because that which does not exist only begins to exist by something already existing. Therefore, if at one time nothing was in existence, it would have been impossible for anything to have begun to exist; and thus even now nothing would be in existence – which is absurd. Therefore, not all beings are merely possible, but there must exist something the existence of which is necessary." Thomas Aquinas, *Summa Theologica, Vol. 1*, Third Article, Question 2, (Notre Dame, IN: Christian Classics, 1948), 13.

[115] "The truth is there is not even one demonstrated error in the original text of the Bible…Why? Because the Bible is the Word of God, and God cannot err." Norman Geisler, Thomas Howe, *The Big Book of Bible Difficulties*, Baker Books, (Grand Rapids, MI: Baker Books, 1992), 11.

[116] Strong's G2222, accessed August 13, 2021, https://www.blueletterbible.org/lexicon/g2222/kjv/tr/0-1/.

[117] Strong's G2322, accessed August 13, 2021, https://www.blueletterbible.org/lexicon/g2322/kjv/tr/0-1/.

[118] Strong's G5083, accessed August 13, 2021, https://www.blueletterbible.org/lexicon/g5083/kjv/tr/0-1/.

[119] Strong's G5035, accessed August 14, 2021, https://www.blueletterbible.org/lexicon/g5035/kjv/tr/0-1/.

[120] "God in his providence preserved the copies from substantial error. In fact, the degree of accuracy is greater than that of any other book from the ancient world, exceeding 99 percent." Norman Geisler, *The Big Book of Christian Apologetics: An A to Z Guide*, (Grand Rapids, MI: Baker Books, 2012), 52-53.

Made in the USA
Las Vegas, NV
26 July 2023

75289217R00246